PRAISE FOR LEADERSHIP PROGRAMMES

MW01148659

'This book is extremely well written, accessible and easy to understand, whilst being very well researched. Nigel Paine has a unique perspective on what makes leadership development effective and it will help anyone interested or involved in this field.' **Dr Annie McKee, Senior Fellow, University of Pennsylvania, and Director of the PennCLO Executive Doctoral Program**

'Learning in organizations is changing rapidly because the world is changing even faster. Anyone in learning has to fight to stay on top of those changes and deliver brilliant learning which meets business and organizational needs. I am delighted to see that same tough, no-nonsense approach applied to leadership development. Someone has to cut through the leadership BS (in Jeffrey Pfeffer's words) and explain what works and why it works in terms that everyone can understand and with practical examples that can be taken on board. This book is well researched, covers the right ground, gives some fascinating examples of great programmes from all over the world and extracts the learning from all of this. For me, it is the right book at the right time.' **Elliott Masie, CEO and President, The Masie Center**

'This book should be required reading for everyone in leadership development. It covers the ground thoroughly and makes the vital point that what justifies investment in leadership is not programmes or content, but impact: consistent behaviour change across the whole organization. Anyone paying attention to its messages will deliver better and more effective leadership programmes. Highly recommended.' **Donald H Taylor, Chair, Learning and Performance Institute**

Building Leadership Development Programmes

Zero-cost to high-investment programmes that work

Nigel Paine

Kogan Page

First published in Great Britain and the United States in 2017 by Kogan Page Limited

2nd Floor, 45 Gee Street
London
EC1V 3RS
United Kingdom

122 W 27th St
10th Floor
New York NY 10001
USA

4737/23 Ansari Road
Daryaganj
New Delhi 110002
India

www.koganpage.com

ISBN   978 0 7494 7693 9
E-ISBN 978 0 7494 7694 6

British Library Cataloguing-in-Publication Data

A CIP record for this book is available from the British Library.

Library of Congress Cataloging-in-Publication Data

Names: Paine, Nigel, 1952- author.
Title: Building leadership development programmes : zero-cost to
   high-investment programmes that work / Nigel Paine.
Description: London ; New York : Kogan Page, 2016. | Includes
   bibliographical references and index.
Identifiers: LCCN 2016035517 (print) | LCCN 2016044076 (ebook) | ISBN
   9780749476939 (pbk.) | ISBN 9780749476946 (ebook)
Subjects: LCSH: Leadership. | Executive coaching. | Executive ability. |
   Organizational behavior.
Classification: LCC HD57.7 .P3455 2016 (print) | LCC HD57.7 (ebook) | DDC
   658.4/092–dc23
LC record available at https://lccn.loc.gov/2016035517

Typeset by SPi Global
Print production managed by Jellyfish
Printed and bound by CPI Group (UK) Ltd, Croydon CR0 4YY

References to websites (URLs) were accurate at the time of writing. Some URLs may have changed since the manuscript was prepared.

CONTENTS

Acknowledgements x

Introduction: Why this book? 1

PART ONE The Leadership Challenge 7

01 The leadership context 9
The changing climate **11**
What skills are required? **12**
The importance of context **15**
Keith Grint's Four-Fold Typology of Leadership **17**
Moving away from individual to organization and
    culture **19**
Work is changing **23**
The social age **26**
Conclusions **29**
References **30**

PART TWO Improving the Paradigm 33

02 Beyond the corporate university: GE's Crotonville 35
Introduction **35**
The background **37**
Reimagining Crotonville **43**
Start with the experience you want to create **47**
What can we learn from Crotonville? **50**
Conclusion **54**
References **55**

03   Leadership on the edge: Discomfort as a learning experience 57

What is Foundation 2041? 59
Leadership and the Antarctic 61
The journey 63
A chronology of the expedition 65
What does a day look like in the Antarctic? 68
The elements of the leadership programme 70
More detailed examination of some of the
    participants 71
Did the initial promise of change last? 76
Follow-up and conclusions 78
References 81

04   Rethinking executive leadership development: DeakinPrime 83

The context 83
What is different? 85
The core principles 88
Structure and critical success factors 89
Outcomes 95
Core lessons to take away 96
References 99

05   Leadership as a catalyst for change: The example of the NHS 101

The context 101
NHS Leadership Academy programmes 104
The NHS leadership suite of programmes 108
The special contribution of blended learning 121
Core lessons 122
References 124

PART THREE   Changing the Paradigm 127

06   **Any time, any place leadership: BP's digital leadership development** 129

Digital age learning at BP 129
Capgemini: from virtualization to digitization 130
Leadership online at BP 132
The seven principles 133
How were the programmes organized? 135
What did the programmes look like? 136
How does it work? 138
The design principle 139
The digital offer 141
The app 142
Measurement of outcomes 144
Individual or community 145
Mentoring and expert input 146
The senior leaders programme 146
Points you should take away 147
References 149

07   **Leadership development as storytelling: Social leadership in a large company** 151

Introduction and context 151
What is the structure? 153
What is the programme like? 155
Who runs the programme? 158
The lessons learned 161
Key issues to consider 162
References 165

08   **Making online learning an immersive experience** 167

The context 167
The development process 171

The virtual campus 171
What else? 174
Building a sense of reality 175
What is the impact? 179
Issues to note 181
Lessons for others 182
Conclusions 184
References 185

PART FOUR   Elements for Transformation 187

09   Action learning: The community develops itself 189
Introduction 189
What is a typical action learning set? 200
The three stages of an action learning set 202
Facilitation 204
Conclusions and next steps 207
References 208

10   DIY leadership development: Ensuring leadership development when you have a very low budget 209
Google's focus on fast internal solutions 209
Other strategies 215
Conclusion 232
References 232

11   The shape of the future: The increasingly powerful role of technology 235
Virtual reality 238
Artificial intelligence 240
Personal digital assistant 244
The rise of social networking software 246
What you should take from this chapter 248
References 249

PART FIVE   Lessons Learned 251

12   **How to move forward** 253

Conclusions 254
How to build better leadership programmes 262
Ten top tips to finish 265
References 266

Index 267

ACKNOWLEDGEMENTS

This book has had a long genus. I have been interested, maybe even obsessed, with the impact leaders make on organizations, for good and for ill, ever since I started my own journey to leadership a few decades ago. Having been the CEO of three organizations, led a start-up and run a huge L&D operation at the BBC with over 500 staff, I know what it is like at the sharp end, and I realize how much I learned by doing, when a bit more formal development may have made a huge difference at the right time. I got better at it, but I could always have improved. Now I have the audacity to teach others a little bit of what it takes to lead, and how you have, ultimately, to be responsible for your own development.

The list of people who helped me on the way is far too long to include here. Some of the great leaders I have worked with deserve a mention; as do some of the absolute worst, but I will pass over them in silence. So thank you Bob Lochrie, Alistair Fleming, Stephen Dando, Greg Dyke and above all David Puttnam. I learned a lot from you all, and everything I did would have been even less impressive but for your patience, mentoring and good example.

This book was based, as was so much of what I learned throughout my career, on conversations with fascinating people. Those that directly helped me with this book include: Peter Cavanaugh, Rob Swan, Simon Hann, Louise Scott-Worrall, Nick Shackleton-Jones, Julian Stodd, Piers Lea, Mike Pedlar, Celine Mullins and Camille Donegan. Steffan Landauer helped me get to Antarctica and his daughter Sasha worked with me whilst on the ship. And 2014 expeditionaries James Veness, Emma Davie, Ghazala Mear, Dev Amratia, Morgan Bell-Smith, Othman Al Serri, Payton Marie Sierra, Persis Buffum, Ben Williams, Chris Lambert, Malek Al-Chalabi, Quang Nu Tuong Nhan (Nhan), Pratul Narayan and Shaivya Rathore all inspired me by their commitment and dedication to making a difference. Additional thanks go to a few inspirational friends who kept me going when I needed a push – notably Annie McKee and many of her doctoral students at the University of Pennsylvania. Also, Mike Gibbs and Arnie Longboy from Chicago Booth's London campus, together with the terrific support staff for helping me share some leadership ideas with students in Kuwait, Qatar and London. In addition, Sharon Kaliouby, Shanshan Ge, Steven Smith, Stuart Martin, Marie-Louise Angoujard, Wolfgang Reichelt, Colin Steed, Martin Couzins, Mauricio Wendling Lopes and Doug Lynch. All helped me more than they realize. Plus colleagues in Australia, New Zealand, Brazil, Spain, Belgium, the Netherlands, Canada and, of course, the UK. I am also grateful to Don Taylor, Beryl Oldham and Rustica Lamb for letting me try out my ideas on unsuspecting audiences around the world. Those building the next generation of leadership programmes, like Hanneke Swart and Rob Robertson, deserve my respect as well as thanks. My continuing contact with many Penn faculty is always stimulating, particularly Matthew Bidwell, Peter Cappelli, Yasmin Kafai and Stanton Wortham. Penn doctoral students, whose excellent dissertations challenged and fascinated me, include Peppe Aurichio, Kandi Weins, Candice Reimers, Christopher McLaverty and Matt Lippincott. What a fantastic institution, doing outstanding work, and the best students I have ever engaged with and who are completing important, ground-breaking research in the L&D field. Special thanks to Elliott Masie for years of friendship and challenging conversations.

The development of our leaders is of critical importance. We can all make it better and deliver more impact. Although there is much criticism of the state of leadership development generally, I have seen some brilliant and effective examples that really inspired me to share their insights, and work out what they were doing that was right that others seemed to ignore. I hope some of those ideas which found their way into this book can inspire readers too.

This is, above all, a practical book. I wanted to help those charged with delivering or commissioning leadership programmes to make what they do better and more effective. It is easy to criticize but harder to say what might work better. I have done that and I did it in the full knowledge that I may have missed some great examples and some powerful motivators for others. But although many people helped me, all the errors and omissions are mine alone.

Much of the drudge that is referencing and checking and proofing and sense making is all down to one amazing person. Thank you

Erina Rayner for, yet again, stepping up to the mark and making my life easier in every way. I never take what you do for granted. I promise. I also want to thank the staff from Kogan Page, who were tolerant of my weaknesses, never failed to believe in this project, and gave unerringly good advice. This book is better thanks to Amy Minshull, Lucy Carter, Katy Hamilton and Arthur Thompson.

Finally, I want to dedicate this book to the next generation of leaders: my three grandchildren, Phoebe Ioana and Delilah Samphrey, together with Amy Rose Cotter in New Zealand, who was born prematurely, weighing just 3 lb. I hope that she thrives. It may take another 30 years for their talents to change the world, but this book will be their unerring guide!

Introduction

Why this book?

Do we need another book about leadership?

I became very confused about what was being said about the nature of leadership. Firstly it was about being this kind of leader or that kind of leader, and secondly there was some dubiety around the role itself. How did you know you were any good at being a leader and how did you know that what you were doing made any difference? Were you part of the problem or part of the solution? Anyone in a leadership position has domain competence. They have specific expertise, which is what got them promoted into leadership positions in the first place, but leadership competence is not so simple. It is always about people. The simplest definition of a leader is someone who has followers. It is also about systems and strategy and guiding the organization to success. Some things are obvious: whether the strategy is working is pretty clear, but what else should be important? How do you present yourself to the rest of the organization and, above all, how do you get better at what you do? If the world is moving in your direction, then running an organization and motivating your team is relatively easy. But when circumstances change and the environment becomes much more difficult, nothing seems to work. You cannot argue that all successful outcomes herald brilliant leadership, and less successful outcomes the opposite. What is down to you, to the environment in which you are working, and to plain and simple luck?

Then there are the models of leadership. Each one is compelling in itself. But I never felt that any one of them unlocked the keys to the mystery of leadership and the confusing messages that abounded around the concept. Was being an authentic leader the key? Or perhaps the appropriate model for the age was to become a servant leader. On the other hand being resonant and emotionally intelligent made a lot of sense, but so did the concept of leaders as teachers. Finding the most important elements for success became more and more difficult, not easier. Perhaps we had to be all of these, and the important thread that joined them all was to be a conscious and deliberate leader. Everything else was icing.

I pondered over what all this actually meant for the day-to-day process of working in an organization and dealing with its issues and helping shape its future. Did investing in leadership development mean anyone did anything differently? I was also frustrated by witnessing the steep fall-off in commitment post-course. I saw people complete a leadership programme full of enthusiasm, and fired up to change everything as soon as they got back into the workplace, yet within two weeks they returned to doing exactly what they had been doing before attending the programme. Did that make it a huge waste of money and effort? Or was the chance to think and step outside the day-to-day inherently beneficial? Maybe the changes were not radical and far-reaching, but small and evolutionary. Over time good things would happen. Maybe just discussing issues around being a leader was beneficial in itself. Airing the difficulties, even if they were hard to resolve, perhaps had some merit.

That was not my only experience, however. I also met people who had been transformed by a specific leadership programme. I witnessed organizations changing before my eyes under that influence, and people changing because now they got it! They saw what they had to change in themselves and in the organization with a new clarity. And there was something powerful about a leadership cadre who worked together, tackled problems as a team, and presented a united and consistent front to the world. Things could change but not often enough and with no consistency.

I also witnessed the ruinous waste of human talent by leadership incompetence, and the unhappiness and frustration of staff who felt marginalized and brutalized by the regime that they worked under. I hated self-seeking leaders who nakedly demonstrated to the world that it was all about them and their compensation and who took a really short-term narrow view of their role and then moved on, leaving the chaos for someone else to sort out. But I did witness people, on the other hand, who simply blossomed and grew in the rich soil of great leadership development. Clearly leaders made a difference, and some leadership development worked well. So I had to try to work out what made the difference. Were there any common factors that made some programmes work whilst many failed to deliver?

There were a few things that I was sure of. What we certainly did not need was another book with a new magic formula that claimed that this particular model of leadership was the 'right' one. It also seemed clear that defining a specific leadership curriculum that everyone could follow did not hold out any great hope of success. Essentially the same curriculum delivered in different ways would be a success or a miserable failure. The key that drove this book was to try to work out what could be done to help leaders in their increasingly difficult and demanding roles, that would change them and their behaviour forever and not just for the fortnight when they were bathed in the warm, fading afterglow of a programme. That was the quest and it led me to follow leaders in action and leadership programmes that seemed to have some of the answers.

I quickly realized that the answers I needed required a different approach to many leadership books. It became clear that it was not about models or content, but about the way leadership programmes were implemented and the commitment shown to generating outcomes from the top of the organization. There were elements that seemed to define and differentiate the good from the rest in terms of process and application that could help define the degree to which any programme made a lasting impact. If there were no magic bullets, or simple 'answers', then there were ideas and suggestions gleaned from others that might help other programmes.

I was keen to make a unique contribution, based on what people actually did in leadership programmes, to create a new way of thinking about leadership development that would enable those responsible for leadership programmes to think it all through more clearly. I was aware that so much investment in leadership development did not yield an adequate return. But I did not want to become cynical and angry about the cost of leadership programmes, because I know that leaders needed help and support. Most programmes were put together with the best of intentions and with clear aims in mind. Leadership development was not a cynical and corrupt industry that took money knowing that the results were going to be insignificant. All of the hundreds of people I met who were designing or implementing leadership programmes were doing their best, and there was evidence of good practice all around. Leadership development and supporting leaders was an honourable idea, but it was being trashed by quite compelling evidence of failure.

No one can read the first chapter of Stanford Business School professor Jeffrey Pfeffer's 2015 book *Leadership BS* to be in any doubt about the catastrophic failures of leadership. He lists the headline disasters and the leaders who were instrumental in causing them, one by one: Rick Wagoner of General Motors, Richard Fuld of Lehman Brothers, Ed Lamprey of Sears. 'Workplaces are mostly horrible' (Pfeffer, 2015: 31) he claims, and everyone reading this knows what he is talking about. He waxes lyrically about the dire state of the workplace and the appalling leadership that engenders this. 'There are too few good leaders and too many bad ones' (Pfeffer, 2015: 46) he fumes, and the vast leadership development industry does not seem to help. Pfeffer's three recommendations are straightforward:

- Measure and hold people accountable for workplace outcomes.
- Acknowledge the different interests of leaders and their companies.
- Use more scientific methods and worry about credentials.

But this medicine is disproportionately weak compared to the disease it is purporting to cure. These conclusions cover familiar ground and have not changed much about leaders or leadership.

This book tells its story through examples that are never models, but show elements of excellence or different ways of thinking about leadership development that could be shared and reproduced in a different context. My book does not offer any one guaranteed solution, but suggests direction and commitment that emerge from great practice.

It does not seem to matter, ultimately, whether you have a big budget or no budget, whether you are in the private sector or the public sector – the core principles remain consistent, and they can be summed up in a few words.

Leadership development is a process, not an event. Implementation goals need time. Think months and years, not days and weeks. That process is multifaceted and potentially never-ending. One set of needs elides into another, and the need to keep leadership to the forefront of people's minds and to improve it year on year never goes away.

Context is critical. If you apply generic leadership development, divorced from the context in which leaders operate, you are almost guaranteed to fail. There are generic lessons, but these have to be honed and shaped to reflect what actually goes on at a particular time and place. If there is a gap between what should happen in theory and what is done in day-to-day practice, then there is no hope for serious change. If, for example, you buy in someone's off-the-shelf leadership programme, then the organization has to work hard to supply the context and explain in some detail what an individual actually has to do and what has to change in order to empower that individual to do it.

Face the truth. What is the state of leadership that you are starting from? What is it really like to work in your organization, and what difference would it make if leadership were better? You need to gather the worst elements and surface the frustrations of people actually working in the place, not just concentrate on what are the best elements. Gather the great stories too. There may be some practices that you must preserve or need to extend across the whole organization, but the simple truth is that if you fail to confront the reality of what it is like to work in your organization, then you are building the foundations of leadership on sand. A veneer of leadership on top of a rotten carcass of bad practice embodies everything that is bad about leadership programmes.

Always start with the end in mind. What changes do you want to see around here that build a hopeful and optimistic vision for the future? What would you notice if you walked around the place? How would the behaviours of executives change? What could the organization do that it cannot do now? How important is it to make those changes? How committed are you to making this work and seeing it through with ruthless commitment?

Poor leadership has to have consequences if leaders flagrantly break the rules. If leaders ignore the agreed way of working and go back to old ways, there have to be sanctions. The one thing that the workplace craves is consistency, from one leader and from all leaders working together. If you forgive breaches, you undermine the entire operation.

Ultimately leaders have to be able to help themselves and solve their own problems. Part of any programme has to be focused on developing long-term skills to enthuse and create mechanisms for self-development and to ensure that leaders as a cohort have processes in place to get better at what they do month on month and year on year.

The focus should be on leadership, not on leaders. The organization should have strong views on the nature of leadership, and leaders need to accept that and work with it. It is a consistent approach that looks holistically at what is needed and is not driven by the egos of individuals. It is important to establish a leadership ethos that everyone can be part of and to recognize that it is about leaders working together that makes the greatest impact. Being a leader at an organization should mean something that you can define. It also determines a raft of behaviours that are consistently implemented across the organization, so that everyone has clear expectations of what leadership and followership actually mean in practice.

The case studies in this book show what can be achieved when conviction, commitment and determination are applied to leadership development. Each takes a radically different approach to the subject in a way that illustrates that you do not need models to follow. Each approach has been carefully tailored to the needs of the organization and reflects the budget available and the task in hand. The important point to note is that none of them is perfect, but that each one is making a substantial difference to their organization.

Reference

Pfeffer, J (2015) *Leadership BS: Fixing workplaces and careers one truth at a time*, HarperCollins, New York

PART ONE
The Leadership Challenge

The leadership context   01

When asking what is leadership, the answer depends on what one is looking for, and from where one is looking. Leadership is many things to many people.
WESTERN, 2008: CHAPTER 2

How much do we know about leadership?

Leadership is a bewildering field. It is so complex and multifaceted that it is daunting to explore. And after thousands of years' debate, according to Grint (2010: chapter 1), we can hardly even agree what it means, let alone agree how to make better leaders in organizations. There is so much contradiction and loud shouting that 'my way' is the only way, that finding direction and making good decisions is hard. For example, in a random dip into Twitter in May 2016 I came across the following statements related to leadership, in rapid succession:

Most important thing for a manager? Provide clarity.

Always be curious.
Be happy for no reason.
Fight tirelessly for what we want.

Actions not words are the ultimate results of leadership.

Too many leaders disappear when times are tough.

Be optimistic
Enthusiastic
Focus forward
Joyful
Faithful
Determined
Aggressive
Energetic
Purposeful
and Loving

Leaders are visionaries with a poorly developed sense of fear and no concept of the odds against them.

When you manage focus on execution. When you lead focus on purpose and direction.

The function of leadership is to produce more leaders, not more followers. – Ralph Nader

Any day, at any time, would reveal similar complementary or contradictory sentiments. We all have strong opinions about what makes good leaders. We all have strong images in our mind of poor leadership, and fewer usually of great leadership. We have all been led, and many of us are leaders too. This means we think we know what works and what does not. We have felt the pain and frustration of terrible leadership, and admired good leadership. Many claim to know the component parts of what effective leadership comprises, and there are competence frameworks in profusion to codify those views. If you ask Google for examples of leadership competency frameworks, you get 268,000 hits. There are hundreds of diagrams of models for leadership.

This whole area buzzes with life and debate and, of course, contradiction. We need authentic leaders, leaders as teachers, humble leaders, leaders as followers, resonant leaders etc. And these frameworks and models sustain tens of thousands of courses, run internally and externally by huge corporations, as well as small boutique companies, business schools and consultants. It is a huge industry that 'could be worth US$50 billion a year' (Corporate Research Forum Report (Pillans), 2015). But the CRF Report asks a very interesting question. Is that industry, in spite of its obvious size and power, fit for purpose in the 21st century?

There is something strange in the way that most leadership programmes are delivered and the curriculum around which they are built. That something is the fact that they look now, for the most part, pretty much as they did 20 years ago, and yet our world and organizations have been transformed over that same period. There is a clear dislocation between 'what is taught and what is experienced' (CRF Report (Pillans), 2015: 11) in the world of work.

The changing climate

The major research report of the Corporate Research Forum, *Leadership Development – is it fit for purpose?* (2015), graphically describes the changes in the world that leaders inhabit:

> Increasing complexity and ambiguity, fiercer global competition and the accelerating pace of change mean leaders need to be strong adaptive- and systems-thinkers, agile learners, self-aware and comfortable with leading through uncertainty. (CRF Report (Pillans), 2015: 11)

What is being stated is that where the environment becomes more volatile, uncertain, complex and ambiguous (the term VUCA was coined by the US military to capture the idea of that environment), how we run organizations has to change and the skills needed to run organizations in that climate has to change too. The obvious response is to focus on equipping leaders in organizations with the right skills to do a good job in a new context. And that context will not get any easier. In fact, if we believe Mervyn King, the former Governor of the Bank of England – 'it is getting more complex and therefore leadership is getting more challenging' (King, 2016: chapter 4). In his recent book, *The End of Alchemy*, King (the man who held sway at the Bank during the global financial crisis of 2008) devotes an entire chapter of his book to the concept of 'radical uncertainty' (King, 2016: chapter 4).

It is, for him, one of the defining forces of the age. He defines radical uncertainty as: 'Uncertainty... so profound that it is impossible to represent the future in terms of a knowable and exhaustive list of outcomes to which we can attach probabilities.'

This means that everyone, including the most well informed leader, is unable 'to conceive of what the future may hold' (King, 2016: 19). This not only changes the world of finance, but the demands on any leader seeking some form of certainty. In King's view that VUCA world of volatility, uncertainty, complexity and ambiguity becomes the VrUCA world where intelligence, agility, the ability to work with contradiction and fast reaction hold sway.

The CRF Report is based on research and an online survey of over 1,000 UK member companies of the Forum. It is this report that estimates – from collating data from a number of sources – that the global spend on leadership development is now around US$50 billion per year out of a total learning and development spend – estimated by Bersin by Deloitte – of US$130 billion (CRF Report (Pillans), 2015: 12). Leadership is the single biggest ticket item. Yet both the CRF survey, Deloitte's *Human Capital Trends* (2015), and the Marshall School of Business's ePulse survey (CRF Report (Pillans), 2015:13), show a widening gap between leadership needs and capability, satisfaction with the quality of leadership development, and overall confidence of CEOs in the leadership quality in their organizations (CRF Report (Pillans), 2015: 13).

What skills are required?

In January 2015, the *McKinsey Quarterly* (Feser, Mayol and Srinivasan, 2015) published some extensive research on what leadership skills really matter. This was based on the survey results of 189,000 people in

81 diverse organizations around the world. The research indicated that four types of behaviour stand out as critical in terms of leadership effectiveness. They are:

- Be supportive.
- Operate with strong results orientation.
- Seek different perspectives.
- Solve problems effectively.

The problem is, that stating these behaviours is one thing – developing them, and building them into a consistent leadership culture is a very different challenge, even if you accept that the McKinsey analysis is accurate. The article is set in the context of the opening line: 'Telling CEOs these days that leadership drives performance is a bit like saying that oxygen is necessary to breathe' (McKinsey Quarterly, 2015). It is axiomatic that all CEOs would want their leaders to be supportive and operate with a strong results orientation, etc. That is why so much money is invested in leadership: the impact that leaders make on an organization – good and bad – is amplified to the point where, ultimately, the success or failure of the organization is at stake. Everybody knows that good leadership makes a difference. Quoting a joint Conference Board/McKinsey report from October 2012 on the state of human capital in organizations, the authors claim that over 90 per cent of CEOs are planning to increase their investment in leadership development because 'they see it as the single most important human-capital issue their organizations face' (The Conference Board/McKinsey & Company, 2012).

In spite of this impressive statistic, only 43 per cent of CEOs have any confidence that the investment they make in developing their leaders will bear any fruit, and there is no consensus from academia or the leadership field about what core issues leadership development programmes should address and how to make the development stick and deliver lasting impact. And even if we can all agree that the McKinsey research puts its finger on the four key, critical leadership behaviours, there is still no consensus on how you should develop leaders to manifest those behaviours consistently or sustain that behaviour change over time.

You could conclude that leadership development is a mess, as there is no agreement on what constitutes a suitable curriculum for leaders, or how best to make any kind of development stick that actually leads to permanent and consistent changed behaviour in the workplace. As investment in leadership shoots up, confidence in its impact goes down. This is borne out by the research from the Corporate Research Forum (CRF Report (Pillans), 2015: 8). In some way the CRF Report paints a bleaker picture than even McKinsey's analysis:

> ... levels of satisfaction with the quality of leaders and the effectiveness of leadership development are low. Less than one-third (31 per cent) of respondents to the CRF leadership survey rated their overall ability to develop leaders as 'Good' or 'Excellent'. There is also little evidence that investments in leadership development lead to improved business performance. (CRF Report (Pillans), 2015: 8)

If this were the whole story, we could all learn its lesson, save our money, dump our leadership development programmes, and move on! There are, however, many success stories in the leadership development field, as well as many corporate transformations based around the implementation of successful leadership programmes. The investment by GE and their consistent belief over decades in performance unleashed by good leadership is undiminished. GE would argue that its consistent approach to leadership across the many different industries in which it operates is a huge strength and one of the main components of the glue that holds the company together and makes the whole more impressive than the sum of its parts (conversation with Peter Cavanaugh, head of Crotonville Centre). In fact, the company's commitment to Crotonville (and subsequent investment in it) is stronger than ever and the brand has been expanded into local sites around the world where the Crotonville message is delivered (see Chapter 2).

The answer to what makes some leadership development so successful and much of the rest fairly ineffective is not as straightforward as simply picking the right model or focusing on the most useful areas of competence to develop. It is not about delivering appropriate content, or finding the correct delivery mode or buying in charismatic faculty, but a more complex intermeshing of need, insight, process and learning community development that leads to sustained behaviour change. This book will tease out the strands of what makes leadership development successful and suggest ways that will help those charged with making leadership more effective to gain more focus, context and direction as they work out the way forward for their organizations.

The two reports mentioned above were published in 2015. That is not the first time anyone noticed that something was wrong with how leaders behaved in organizations, or the fact that investment in leadership development appears to be a bottomless pit in terms of the resources it consumes, but a shallow trench if you look at impact. However, no one appears to assert that leadership is easy or unimportant – quite the opposite. The problem is not whether leadership development is worth doing, but how to get it right and begin to support leaders as they grapple with an increasingly difficult environment, with increasingly higher expectations imposed upon this corporate elite. This is because, to a great extent, they are the ones who, in turn, support and motivate the core staff who will, increasingly, make or break an organization by their engagement or indifference.

The importance of context

I was flying to Australia a couple of years ago and fell asleep. Not unusual when you are flying for 26 hours! I awoke in a darkened cabin with all the blinds down. I had no idea where we were, and equally no idea how long I had been asleep. Planes take away that sense of time completely. I could have been asleep for hours or minutes and I wanted to know which, hoping for the former and dreading the latter.

I did not want to switch on the light and wake myself up completely and I could not read my watch in the dark, so I switched on the TV screen in front of me to check the flight path. If I knew where the plane was, I would know how long I had been asleep. Simple really, but when I touched the screen, all I could see was the small image of the plane in the centre of an entirely featureless blue and yellow landscape. The information provided was, although accurate, completely useless because it was context-free. I took a picture of it for posterity. It was a perfect image of something being correct but useless in terms of interpretation. Where was the data to make sense of that information? I needed some idea of scale, coupled with a few reference points that I could recognize. With scale and reference points I would have been able to work out where I was and therefore how long I had been asleep. I would argue that much leadership development is like that. In itself, accurate and perfectly competent, but lacking the context to turn it into the real issues: 'So what do I do now? Who can help me? And what happens if it goes wrong?' And above all: 'How can I make this work in my situation?'

Barbara Kellerman, a professor of public leadership at the John F Kennedy School of Government at Harvard University, would appear to agree with me. She believes that the current leadership industry is no longer fit for purpose, and that leadership development has not yet grown into the 21st century (Kellerman, 2012: 18). This means that it peddles inappropriate models that no longer work, based around a number of incorrect assumptions: that leadership is static; leadership can be learned easily and quickly; that it can be taught in a context-free environment; and finally that being a leader is somehow innately superior to being a follower. The failure of leadership development has been on Kellerman's mind for quite a while: her 1999 book was called *Reinventing Leadership* and her 2004 book *Bad Leadership*. There is a theme running here! Her latest book is even more stark in its perspective: it is called *The End of Leadership* (2012).

The research reports cited above, my own investigations and Kellerman's books appear to be in alignment. There seems to be a growing gap between the teaching of leadership (the leadership industry) and what leaders actually have to do to be successful: the practice of leadership. Pouring money into that industry to improve the practice of leadership may, therefore, be wrong-headed. No one is challenging the quality of the teaching or the brilliance of the models or approach – it is more fundamental. The issue concerns the fundamental philosophy and approach based on incorrect underlying assumptions about what leadership development actually is and what leaders actually do in the context of their role and their organization.

Keith Grint's Four-Fold Typology of Leadership

Some perspective may help here. That is provided by Keith Grint, who developed his four-fold typology in a 2005 book, *Leadership: Limits and possibilities* (I am grateful to Barton Friesland for suggesting the Grint typology), and reframes this in the later volume *Leadership:A very short introduction* (2010). The typology describes four distinct models, approaches and philosophies of leadership. Each one has its own context and meaning. He also shows that each has a specific development approach linked to it. These models of leadership evolved over time. So, to some degree, how we define leadership has an element of social context linked to a specific era.

The first model assumes that leadership is about the position you win, inherit or take over. This is the WHY of leadership. It is based on the idea of hierarchy and the belief that the individual subsumes his or her personality into the new role. It is the belief that the individual actually morphs into the role they have been given. Therefore, the person who is given the attributes and the symbols of power, immediately assumes that role and over time becomes that leader. No better illustration of this is afforded than by Shakespeare's *Henry IV, Part 2* and *Henry V*, when the misbehaving, wild prince takes on the mantel of kingship on his father's death:

The Archbishop of Canterbury captures this in the opening scene of *Henry V* (Shakespeare, 1623):

> The courses of his youth promised it not.
> The breath no sooner left his father's body
> But that his wildness, mortified him,
> Seem'd to die too; yea at that very moment,
> Consideration like an angel came
> And whipp'd th' offending Adam out of him.

The second is about the person. The WHO of leadership. This is essentially 'great man' theory. It is all about the person and their intrinsic leadership qualities. 'Cometh the hour, cometh the man' is the apposite quote, which stretches back in origin to the Bible (John

4:23) and various permutations since. But it was largely in the 19th century that it became popularized in both the UK and the United States. It found most articulate resonance in the work of Thomas Carlyle (1795–1881) who wrote about the need for heroes to take control when chaos threatens. Heroic human action would and should triumph over dogma. Many biographies of Carlyle allude to this fundamental keystone of his beliefs.

The third is about getting results. The WHAT of leadership, or the output of leadership. A leader is judged on what that person achieves, not what they talk about achieving. The fourth is about the process of leadership – in other words HOW they operate in practice and what kind of a difference this makes.

There is also a quiet fifth assumption lurking in the background, and it is the obvious conclusion that all four of those models have some merit, and no single model can possibly provide all the answers. In reality, leadership is a combination of the why, who, what and how to a greater or lesser extent, depending on the circumstances.

Position-based leadership relies on the idea of being appointed into a position of authority and only then taking on those attributes as you 'become' a leader. In a sense the individual takes on an appropriate stance that fits the role to which the person is appointed. The hierarchy maintains its integrity by appointees subsuming their individuality into their new role.

Person-based leadership is about the individual and their characteristics as a human being that makes them leadership material. It is a traditional view of leadership. We can list the 'great men' of history, in British terms, from Oliver Cromwell to Nelson to Churchill. This model focuses not so much on leadership development but *leader* development. Nurture the right leaders and everything else falls into place. Single individuals with courage and vision are able by force of personality to make the difference between success and failure.

Results-based leadership focuses more on the outcomes produced by leaders. Churchill would not have been considered a leader of the same stature, for example, if Britain had lost the Second World War, Cromwell the Civil War, and Nelson the Battle of Trafalgar. These defining moments confer a mythical status to that achievement. So if leadership is not so much the person, but what that person achieves, then the focus should be on how someone gets results. This too suggests a different focus from an approach that concentrates only on the development of leaders.

Process-based leadership is built around how leaders act. The assumption is that leaders are special, and act in special ways, and if we tap into those behaviours, we have the key to successful leadership. Whether that is taught skills or skills that emerge naturally in the gifted leader is a moot point. But this model too defines a different kind of leader development. And it implies context too. You cannot succeed if others do not choose to follow you. Your leadership is not innate – it emerges in the doing.

Grint likens the development of these models of leadership to an increasing rationality over time from the 'great men theory' of the 1900s, through scientific management, time and motion studies of the 1920s, through to the quality circles of the 1980s, and finally distributed leadership of the 2000s (Grint, 2010: 48). This encompasses the why, who, what and how of leadership over a century of thinking about this topic. It can also mirror the fundamental shift in the philosophical approach towards organizational structure, from the decentralized notion of great man, via the centralized scientific approach, through to the decentralized model of distributed leadership. Leadership theory is normative; it reflects the wider social and political philosophies of the day. These have to evolve as the nature of work and social values have evolved. Essentially this moves from 'Who can we find to lead us?' towards 'What kind of an organization can we build that allows us to excel, and who can help us do that?'

Moving away from individual to organization and culture

It is far too simplistic to concentrate all our energies on leadership, onto the role of the individual, however capable. This is why we made a critical shift from the idea of developing leaders to that of developing better leadership. One is narrow and the other focuses on other factors apart from the individual. In the 25th anniversary issue of *The Leadership Quarterly* journal, David Day reviewed advances in leaders and leadership development as seen through the pages of that journal (Day *et al*, 2014: 63–82). He notes the important distinction between developing leaders and developing leadership.

> Leader development focuses on developing individual leaders whereas leadership development focuses on a process of development that inherently involves multiple individuals (eg leaders and followers or among peers in a self-managed work team). (Day *et al*, 2014: 64)

Day also notes the gap between theories of leadership and modes of leadership development. There is a far more complex interaction between how leaders work in a real situation and a theory of leadership; he calls for more work on development to try to understand this.

Barbara Kellerman addresses the same issue by proposing a model of leadership development that is more like an equilateral triangle. This form has one side ascribed as 'leader', the second side as 'follower' and the third side as 'context'. The three occupy equal sides of the triangle and depend on and support each other. No leaders without followers, no followers without leaders, and no leadership without context. And linked to that triangle is the author's distinction between power (to compel) vested in the authority of the role, this is based on status and rank, and something more important but less obvious: influence (persuasion). The distinction is the same as the distinction that is used to understand political processes between hard power, given by virtue of rank and status, and soft power based on connections, likes and acknowledged expertise. So 'effectiveness' is context driven and a combination of hard and soft power. As context changes, so does what constitutes effective leadership. In effect:

> Leading is, as we know by now, different from what it was before, even a decade or two ago. And as it changes, so must the leadership industry, lest it be relegated to the dustbin of history. (Kellerman, 2012: 18)

We are all in alignment. Grint and his historical perspective, Day and his analysis of research and theory, and Kellerman with her emphasis on context.

No context, no meaning.

If you are going to run a leadership business you would probably need to make it as general a programme as you can to appeal to as many as possible. That is why so much development is context free and turnkey in nature. Yet, as I work with company after company, the key element to understand is the situation in which leadership is taking place. Offering generic decontextualized leadership development – unless someone else supplies the context – is as meaningless and ineffective as my aeroplane screen was in telling me where I was and hence for how long I had been sleeping. In other words we need to move from abstract and general to concrete and particular, from theory to practice in context, from pure to applied.

The leadership industry is now global and is responding to the growing need to better equip leaders to cope in a world of increasing volatility and real uncertainty. *The End of Alchemy* distinguishes between 'known unknowns and unknown unknowns' (King, 2016), the latter growing more prevalent and complex as uncertainty prevails. Increasingly, focusing on the leader in isolation is not a viable model. If the focus is always on the 'star' Boris Groysberg (2012) proved just how fragile a foundation this is.

The truth of 'star' performance is intimately connected with the connections, support and knowledge sharing in a particular organization as much as it is to do with the performer acting solo. That is our context again. Teaching the individual how to lead in isolation, and out of context, is too simplistic to succeed. Although that generic model of leadership development still abounds and in every bookshop, the shelves are stocked with books that purport to provide the reader with tips on personal (and context-free) transformation. Just a cursory glance is indicative: *The Three Levels of Leadership* (Scouller, 2011), *True North: Discover your authentic leadership* (George, 2007), *Act Like a Leader, Think Like a Leader* (Ibarra, 2015). The list goes on and on.

The leadership industry, on the other hand, has scant metrics on sustained performance, instead relying on instant feedback by the participant about the quality of the experience rather than its enduring benefit. It is more about liking the content rather than applying its logic, or finding the programme interesting rather than useful. Rarely is follow-up adjudged necessary. Very little research is conducted about the long-term benefits and the sustained change that has been engendered.

This is quite disappointing and not a reflection of any value-for-money perspective. It smacks of smugness and complacency. This paradigm has remained largely unaltered despite the enormous changes in the external environment. If it is possible to disrupt huge, stable industries with the deployment of a single app on a smartphone, we are in new territory in terms of vulnerability. How do leaders respond? What new skills do they need? There is not much on the basic leadership curriculum about this and the climate it invokes.

Bad leadership is the news. The global financial crisis drew attention to it and it still constitutes a plague running right across corporate and public sector organizations (Kellerman, 2012: 229). And there is much evidence to back this up (CRF Report (Pillans), 2015). The collapse of the finance industry brought no glory on either leaders or those that developed them. This revealed unethical and dishonourable leadership coupled with naivety and appalling judgement. You could argue that the collapse of the sub-prime mortgage market and then the wider financial industry was an acute failure of leadership, but also a failure of the leadership industry (Kellerman, 2012: 411).

The naivety of putting our entire emphasis on the ability of the single leader, in isolation, to make a unique difference, has proved disastrous! However, many types of leadership model are still promoted: from John Kotter's work that promoted leadership over management; Bill George's 'authentic leadership', Robert Greenleaf's 'servant leader' and James MacGregor Burns' 'transformational leader'.

What they have in common is an explicit model that is based on variations of a leader-centric view of the organization. Is that viable in our VrUCA world? This approach is also predicated on the assumption that good leadership can be taught quickly and in isolation. Most of these approaches offer courses that describe the model; they offer a few exercises to practise the ideas and then send the individual back out into the world without a second glance or anything much in the way of follow-up. If we look for empirical evidence to justify the grandiose claims concerning one or other particular model, it is not there in abundance. This applies to leadership programmes led by business schools and universities, as well as dedicated providers. Large companies also have significant high-cost development programmes such as those in Goldman Sachs, GE and IBM. What makes some work and some not?

If the presupposition is that an ineffective and uninformed individual can enter a programme, be tumbled around, and emerge as a strong visionary and capable leader several days or weeks later, it is at best naive. Human beings, unfortunately, do not transform that easily from caterpillar to butterfly.

The evidence points toward taking a more holistic view and look at how the organization itself works, and therefore how the leader's role slots in. If there is no magic bullet for leadership, then the leadership industry has to think bigger and more analytically about its role and contribution. In other words, 'It must end the leader-centrism that constricts the conversation. It must transcend situational specifics that make it so myopic. It must subject itself to critical analysis. And it must reflect the object of its affection – change with the changing times' (Kellerman, 2012: 474). We have to ask, if these approaches do not work, what specifically does? And what are the elements that you can take from this vast multibillion dollar leadership industry that can be usefully incorporated into a new kind of development process? It seems inconceivable that something that has developed for over 100 years and is so massive in scope and ambition, something that has captivated some of the brightest minds in business schools and companies, that has been rolled out to millions of people, is now completely redundant! Do we have to pull out a blank sheet of paper and start again? Perhaps the answer lies elsewhere. Has anyone else got a better answer?

Work is changing

There is a strong link between quality leadership, care for staff and customers, and high performing organizations. This was demonstrated in Alex Edmans' seminal article of 2011 in which he demonstrated that investment in people and quality leadership pays off in terms of profitability year on year (Edmans, 2011). In spite of the cynics, leadership investment that works is an excellent investment and will help a company sustain and evolve in our VUCA world. This causality is important to Harvard academic Gary Hamel who, in his 2007 book *The Future of Management*, put forward a compelling case for reinventing management for the 21st century:

> For the first time since the dawning of the industrial age, the only way to build a company that's fit for the future is to build one that's fit for human beings as well. *This* is your opportunity – to build a 21st century management model that truly elicits, honors, and cherishes human initiative, creativity and passion – these tender, essential ingredients of business success in this new millennium. Do that, and you will have built an organization that is fully human and fully prepared for the extraordinary opportunities that lie ahead. (Hamel, 2007: 255)

Clearly the quality of leadership can be part of the problem, or a significant element of the solution. Only good leadership can sustain companies and make them – in Hamel's words – 'capable of spontaneous renewal, where the drama of change is unaccompanied by the wrenching trauma of a turnaround' (Hamel, 2007: xi). To thrive requires new approaches and inspired management able to generate a leadership culture that can generate innovation and build tomorrow's companies. If old models do not work and a new ethos is required to sustain those organizations, then old models of leadership development cannot possibly work either.

Only by changing leadership can you change organizations fundamentally. And one key area of focus is to create empowered and engaged staff. Leadership is more about facilitation and enablement than it is about control. Leaders need to clear the way to allow their employees to function effectively. So leadership is more about resonating and aggregating effort and creating a framework of trust. It involves building commitment, passion, creativity, initiative, intellect, diligence, and proactivity in the entire workforce and not just in a handful of leaders.

The essence of Hamel's vision is to build organizations that reflect a new social reality of complex connectivity, information surplus and continuous networking. And he looks to tech-based start-ups to point the way forward. Their different ways of working, and their different models of organizing work can be extrapolated from Silicon Valley into the wider business world. But that still does not fully give us the answers we need.

If we accept Harvard Business School professor John Kotter's 1990 distinction between management and leadership, whereby management is essentially a process role: 'planning and budgeting, organizing and staffing, controlling and problem-solving; whereas leadership is more about developing a vision and sense of direction, aligning people behind that vision, and motivating and inspiring those people to keep moving in the right direction' (Kotter, 1990), then we should keep those roles separate in our minds.

In his latest book, *Accelerate*, Kotter asserts that 'The world is now changing at a rate at which the basic systems, structures, and cultures built over the past centuries cannot keep up with the demands being placed on them' (2014: viii). He takes this idea further by attempting to adapt his thinking. On the one hand we should not throw out the past, which delivers reliability and efficiency, but he wants us to build a second system of organization in parallel (taken from start-ups) to add agility and speed. He calls this the dual operating system. This incorporates new ideas into the old model, in order to be able to cope with uncertainty, disruption and tumult, whilst retaining the solid efficiency and delivery capabilities of the old model.

The hierarchy serves us well, but is not sufficient. The management hierarchy and structures in many organizations 'are still absolutely necessary to make organizations work' (Kotter, 2014: 18). But if you add to this a more flexible network structure you can galvanize talent from across the organization, encouraging more democratic and less hierarchical teams to work on big problems and issues quickly and efficiently. An employee therefore works in the hierarchy and joins network teams when required. The silos, which are an inherent part of the hierarchy, can be dismantled in the network model, and the development of a whole company has the added benefit of making the hierarchy itself function more successfully.

The new model requires new leadership competences that reflect that new world. These are first talked about in Kotter's book *Leading*

Change (1996), but he returns to them in subsequent books including *Accelerate* (2014). He lists his top five as: risk taking, humble self-reflection; solicitation of opinions; careful listening; and openness to new ideas. There is still a focus on the power of the leader, but good leadership requires a degree of humility and respect for both staff and customers and is predicated on working with others and seeking answers rather than having all the answers. It is accepting that having a particular position or status does not yield all the answers, and this indeed can insulate the leader from facing up to reality.

The social age

If the world is changing then how can we begin to define what this new world looks like? Are we entering a new age? Just as agrarian Britain was transformed by the Industrial Revolution into a manufacturing economy, this new age transplants the knowledge age by reflecting a world of instant global communications and constant linking of individual-to-individual and customer-to-customer and business. This is the age of ubiquitous computing, not driven by laptops or desktop machines but by the 'super computer in your pocket' (*The Economist*, 2015). *The Economist* predicts that by 2020 80 per cent of the world's adult population will own some kind of smartphone, and it calls the smartphone 'ubiquitous, addictive and transformative' (2015). That is not 80 per cent of the developed world but 80 per cent of the entire world! To emphasize the power of this networked world, it is often referred to as the social age.

A vociferous exponent of the demands of the Social Age is Julian Stodd (2016), who has written and blogged widely on this phenomenon. This world is capable of enormous and rapid disruption and is defined not by its stability but by its impermanence. Here 'finding stuff out is easy. Making sense of it is what counts' (Stodd, 2014: 15). The key shifts are: social authority taking over from formal control, authenticity emerging as more important than marketing, and broadcast communication giving way to co-creation of stories. Even brand status can be controlled by the community. In addition, power changes its locus facilitated by technology. There is a new transparency of information (Stodd, 2014: 15) that can switch power around. A well-aimed tweet, for instance, can carry more weight than a CEO's address.

Obviously in the face of this reality the social age demands a different kind of leadership that is 'anchored in the principles and ethics of value-led behaviour: it is about authenticity and support' (Stodd, 2014: 5). And it requires agility and a capability for dynamic change on the part of the leader (Stodd, 2014: 5).

Stodd defines social leadership in terms of nine components in three dimensions. The first dimension is around narrative: this comprises 'curation', 'storytelling' and 'sharing'. Social leaders attempt to make sense of the huge amount of data that confronts them and then refine this, share it, and try to make meaning. It is what the Canadian blogger and author Harold Jarche (2015) refers to as: seek, sense and share.

For Stodd and Jarche, this acute need to make sense from the information that bombards us, is a necessary reaction to complexity and the only way to understand what on earth is going on! We need networks that are digitally connected, that can help us to see the patterns of emergent practice (Jarche, 2016) and therefore begin to make sense, which allows us to then make choices and decisions. By its very nature, this cannot be a solo occupation; it can only be accomplished in cooperation with others. So to survive you have to be connected and networked and a diligent searcher for meaning through others. We are not far from Kotter's humble self-reflection, solicitation of opinions and careful listening.

Stodd sums this up by talking about 'curating knowledge, and finding the meaning within it, forming stories and understanding how to share and amplify these' (Stodd, 2014: 7).

The second dimension is called engagement and is built from three elements: community, reputation and authority. Community is essentially the many spaces occupied by leaders, and where their stories resonate. It is about forming or sustaining those communities, be they physical or virtual or both.

Reputation is about power that is given by acclaim rather than power that is meted out by virtue of a position or by hierarchy. And it develops out of our stories and our ability to make and share meaning in our communities. Communities can be purely social or formal or both. If we track our role in organizations, then we join, facilitate, grow and sustain many communities that operate in parallel to our position in the hierarchy. For example, when I was a senior executive in the BBC, the Director of News (on the Executive Board) spent part of his time blogging internally and joining communities outside the News division. His reputation as a community builder and someone who helped the rest of the organization make sense of the tumultuous issues impacting the BBC, transcended his reputation as the Head of News and leader of that powerful division in the BBC. He had authority born from reputation and based on the stories he shared with the wider organization. Reputation and authority are closely aligned in social leadership – both are fragile and offered, and cannot be imposed.

The third dimension should inevitably be technology. It is hard to go anywhere in the contemporary world without bumping into the transformations wrought by technology. This dimension is made up of three elements: co-creation, social capital and collaboration.

Co-creation is the way that meaning is built and shared in communities by individuals working together. It is the sense making in Jarche's model, the critical second element before sharing. We develop social capital when we join, share and listen in these communities. It is about humility and generosity rather than imposed authority. Social capital revolves around fairness and equity and is built on reputation and acclaim that are awarded by and within the network. Finally, collaboration is the coming together and sharing of ideas and outcomes and building meaning. It is the product of humble reflection and active listening. How a social leader collaborates 'is what makes them effective and respected' (Stodd, 2014: 10). All of these elements are facilitated and enabled by technology.

What does this tell us about leadership?

Dr Nigel Wilson, the CEO of Legal & General in the UK, reflects the increased pressure of the social age on an insurance company. Not the traditional image of a radical new work environment. He says:

> I think our social purpose and the associated emotional engagement
> from our colleagues is one of the keys to developing a winning

successful strategy for Legal & General. Why that is important is it creates tremendous trust amongst our customers and the other politicians who are helping shape the future... they want to engage with trustworthy companies. (PwC, 2016: 14)

Trust, social purpose and emotional engagement rise to the fore in an age where a customer disappointment, shared on social media, can almost destroy a company. Customer experience, good and bad is shared instantly and requires an immediate and authentic response.

Grint sums this up and in so doing sums up the message from this entire chapter: 'Leaders are important. But there are whole rafts of other elements that are also important, and it is often these that make the difference between success and failure' (Grint, 2010: 110). And we cannot decouple those other elements from the way we develop leaders.

Conclusions

There are a number of different components which will be explored throughout the book. There is a real, context-rich world that leaders inhabit. Leadership development that does not recognize what that actually means in practice will struggle to have impact.

This means that context is critical and generic leadership development programmes without any context will always struggle to succeed. This does not mean that all generic leadership programmes must inevitably fail; instead what it implies is that the context and the anchoring have to be inserted at some point by someone who deeply understands the environment that a specific group of leaders work inside.

A whole raft of new and sometimes bewildering skills and competences are needed by leaders to cope with the increase in volatility, complexity, radical uncertainty and ambiguity. These have to be at the heart of any development programme. But we need to develop the capacity to learn. Nothing lasts forever and relearning and adapting to that environment are important elements of leadership. And, critically, as soon as new competences have been learned, there has to be sufficient space to practise those skills.

In a world of new approaches and new skills and new thinking, the leader who does not take time out to reflect is not going to be effective. And neither is thinking that we know it all. In the social age learning from colleagues will not be a one-off experience, but a continuous process. And the more diverse those colleagues are in terms of age, experience, and job role, the more successful that learning and sharing of insight will be.

There has to be a close relationship between any leadership programme and the day-to-day work ethic of the participants. Perhaps that has to be reinforced almost to the point where learning and work become indistinguishable.

Leadership programmes that only last a few days with little or no follow-up will never be effective unless the context is supplied and any new skills and competences can be practised again and again until the behaviours become habitual.

It is clear that a singular focus on the leader, rather than the processes of work and the importance of work teams, is ultimately going to fail.

Leadership has to be inclusive and reach deeply into the workforce. It is clearer than ever now that what leaders do is seen by everyone. This means that good leaders can build great organizations. And good leaders emerge from great organizations, and what they do is share insight and attempt to make sense of the world.

In other chapters we will look at precisely what that means in different organizations and in different ways of developing leaders.

References

The Conference Board/McKinsey & Company (October 2012) *The State of Human Capital 2012 – False Summit: Why the human capital function still has far to go*, New York

Corporate Research Forum Report (Pillans, G) (2015) *Leadership Development – is it fit for purpose?*, Corporate Research Forum, London

Day, D V, Fleenor, J W, Atwater, L E, Sturm, R E and McKee, R A (2014) Advances in leader and leadership development: a review of 25 years of research and theory, *The Leadership Quarterly*, 25 (1), pp 63–82

Deloitte (2015) *Human Capital Trends*, Deloitte University Press

The Economist (28 February 2015) The Planet of the Phones, *The Economist*

Edmans, A (2011) Does the stock market fully value intangibles? Employee satisfaction and equity prices, *Journal of Financial Economics*, **101** (3), pp 612–40

Feser, C, Mayol, F and Srinivasan, R (January 2015) Decoding leadership: what really matters, *McKinsey Quarterly*

George, B (2007) *True North: Discover your authentic leadership*, Wiley, San Francisco, CA

Grint, K (2005) *Leadership: Limits and possibilities*, Palgrave Macmillan, Basingstoke

Grint, K (2010) *Leadership: A very short introduction*, Oxford University Press, Oxford

Groysberg, B (2012) *Chasing Stars: The myth of talent and the portability of performance*, Princeton University Press, Princeton, NJ

Hamel, G (2007) *The Future of Management*, Harvard Business School Publishing, Boston, MA

Ibarra, H (2015) *Act Like a Leader, Think Like a Leader*, Harvard Business School Publishing, Boston, MA

Jarche, H (2015) Adapting to Perpetual Beta, Blog, http://jarche.com/2015/02/adapting-to-perpetual-beta/

Jarche, H (2016) Complexity and Social Learning, Blog, http://jarche.com/2016/04/complexity-and-social-learning/

Kellerman, B (1999) *Reinventing Leadership: Making the connection between politics and business*, State University of New York Press, Albany, NY

Kellerman, B (2004) *Bad Leadership: What it is, how it happens, why it matters*, Harvard Business School Publishing, Boston, MA

Kellerman, B (2012) *The End of Leadership*, HarperCollins Publishers, New York, NY

King, M (2016) *The End of Alchemy: Money, banking and the future of the global economy*, Little, Brown Book Group, London

Kotter, J (1990) *A Force for Change: How leadership differs from management*, Harvard Business Review Press, Boston, MA

Kotter, J (1996) *Leading Change*, Harvard Business Review Press, Boston, MA

Kotter, J (2014) *Accelerate*, Harvard Business Review Press, Boston, MA

PwC (2016) *19th Annual Global CEO Survey*, PricewaterhouseCoopers

Scouller, J (2011) *The Three Levels of Leadership: How to develop your leadership presence, knowhow and skill*, Scouller Management Books, Cirencester

Shakespeare, W (1623) *Henry V*, Allen Lane, The Penguin Press, London

Stodd, J (2014) *The Social Leadership Handbook*, Sea Salt Learning and Smashwords, Bournemouth

Stodd, J (2016) A Guide to the Social Age 2016, Learning Blog, https://julianstodd.wordpress.com/2016/01/06/a-guide-to-the-social-age-2016/

Western, S (2008) *Leadership: A critical text*, SAGE Publications, London

PART TWO
Improving the Paradigm

Beyond the corporate university

02

GE's Crotonville

Introduction

This chapter looks in some detail at GE's leadership centre in New York State, called by repute and by reputation simply as Crotonville. It was established in 1956 and currently is going through something of a rebirth under the auspices of GE's Chief Learning Officer Raghu Krishnamoorthy and the Head of Crotonville Peter Cavanaugh.

It examines the logistics of running such a huge operation at the centre and speculates on what that adds to GE's leadership capabilities and how it unites in no small measure the culture and aspirations of a very diversified conglomerate that builds anything from aero engines to MRI scanners. It is one of the oldest and most successful manufacturing companies in the world having been founded by Thomas Edison in 1892, and is unique, as it has stayed in the Fortune 500 Company listing since the listing began. It currently has 305,000 employees and a turnover of around US$118 billion.

The small community of Crotonville is located in New York State some 50 or 60 miles from New York City. It is a pleasant, middle-class, semi-rural community that is a world away from the frenetic bustle of New York City. This town is known throughout the world, not because of what it is, but because of its location as the home of the GE leadership centre. Consequently the word 'Crotonville' has now become synonymous with leadership development the world over and has been for decades.

This is ironic for two reasons. The first is that the Crotonville centre is not actually located in the town of Crotonville but is located in an unincorporated part of its neighbouring town, Ossining. The second reason is that officially the Centre began as the GE Management Development and Research Institute, and was renamed in 2001 the 'John F Welch Leadership Development Center'. In reality it has always simply been known as Crotonville.

There are literally hundreds of articles written about Crotonville and it has almost mythic status. Indeed, when I was planning the BBC leadership development programme in 2005, we constantly referred back to Jack Welch's book *Jack: Straight from the gut* (2001), in particular Chapter 12 which describes Crotonville. We had in our minds the need to build an iconic centre for leadership; this would never be a physical location but an identity and strong image that would stand for, and represent, everything we did around that programme – our own Crotonville.

The iconic and symbolic role of Crotonville was summed up by Jack Welch:

> I wanted (Crotonville) focused on leadership development, not specific functional training. I wanted it to be the place to reach the hearts and minds of the company's best people – the inspirational glue that held things together as we changed. (Welch, 2001: 135)

That role as a core element of the company's vision and values continues in the next generation of leaders. Raghu Krishnamoorthy, in a recent interview, described Crotonville as 'the Why of our company' and as 'The incubator for the company's future, since we discuss and develop our guiding principles there and thus shape our values' (Von Butler, 2015: 74–80).

The core delivery is the three fundamental leadership programmes which reached over 40,000 employees from 40 countries along with 4,200 customers in 2015. The insights from these programmes radiate out from this one location to all the major parts of the GE universe. The big ideas are hatched in Crotonville and then become part of the evolution process of GE. Formerly, the biggest and most powerful embodiment of that was a programme called 'Work-Out'. This was started at Crotonville and involved structured discussions on product and process improvement. Eventually it incorporated all the businesses throughout the world. By the end of that programme, 200,000 employees had participated in workouts. Again, Jack Welch:

> Work-Out helped us to create a culture where everyone began playing a part, where everyone's ideas began to count, and where leaders led rather than controlled. They coached – rather than preached – and they got better results. (Welch, 2001: 269)

More recently the current CEO Jeff Immelt is trying to simplify GE and is using a tool called 'Fast Works' to do that. Like Work-Out it emerged *from* Crotonville and has set tens of thousands of staff to focus on changing the way GE works and letting that radiate into all 175 countries in which GE has a presence.

The background

Crotonville's background is remarkably straightforward. GE purchased the estate of Harry A. Hopf. This estate had housed the Hopf Institute of Management located in Croton-on-Hudson in 1954. That was the vision of GE's chairman Ralph Cordiner who wanted a location where a sustained focus on professional management could be built that would transform the efficiency and effectiveness of GE. This was not a decision in isolation but the continuation of a company-wide focus on developing leadership that actually began way back in 1892 with the appointment of Charles Coffin as GE's second CEO, succeeding Thomas Edison (Bartlett and McLean, 2006: 1).

As GE had expanded massively during and immediately after the Second World War, Cordiner realized its centralized planning model and structure was becoming increasingly unmanageable. GE would need radical surgery to continue to grow. He took on the task of decentralizing GE and creating more manageable business units that had budget and forecasting responsibility. He set up nearly 100 business units that were known as departments. With this higher level of delegation, came higher management responsibilities and hence the need for increased levels of development, and logically this led to Crotonville. Its role was to develop a new generation of managers who would run the restructured and decentralized organization. The industrial conglomerate was born. This new model required a huge number of additional managers who were capable of running these separate organizations, from CEOs to heads of finance, operations, strategy etc. These key staff had to be trained to do their job and take much greater responsibility than hitherto.

Management practice had to be defined, refined and delivered consistently to the new breed of devolved manager. Crotonville was the perfect place to do this. So Crotonville was set up with a very important role. Therefore, from the very beginning, it was integral to the future shape and direction of the company.

The 'rules' for GE management practice were enshrined in what became known as the 'Blue Books'. The blue books espoused the science of management and detailed domain agnostic management practices. Much of the content still stands, but the notion of 'domain agnostic' rules has been overtaken by leadership in context. The books comprised 'nearly 3,500 pages of management dos and don'ts' according to Jack Welch (2001: 135).

They defined what were known as the Plan-Organize-Integrate-Measure (POIM) principles. They closely defined the generic operating procedures for GE and they were taught in Crotonville and followed to the letter. This was a detailed and complex process, and the first courses there were 13 weeks long, delivered as a residential programme. The idea that you can take an executive out of the work-flow for 13 weeks has long disappeared, along with the Blue Books. But if you wanted a senior role in GE you had to pass through Crotonville. A member of the first cohort to go through was Reg Jones. He later became the CEO before Jack Welch. So an enduring myth developed early in its history: Crotonville was a rite of passage for anyone wanting to move up the corporate ladder.

In many ways, Crotonville was the world's first corporate university (Bartlett and McLean, 2006: 2), and the investment in it was huge. The Harvard case study tells us that the investment in Crotonville during its early years, was almost 10 per cent of its pre-tax earnings of US$424 million (Bartlett and McLean, 2006: 2). Crotonville did not operate in isolation; its programmes were integrated into a state of the art career management scheme that involved self-assessment and line manager assessment and the agreement of career development plans for all executives. This process coincided with the rise of the General Manager and role rotation from department to department in GE and other companies to gain increasingly broad experience and skills. These career reviews were known as 'Session C' reviews and were managed centrally by HR. They continue to this day (Bartlett and McLean, 2006: 3) but are being revised to take account of contemporary needs. The Wharton Academic, Peter Cappelli charts this GE process in his book *Talent on Demand* (2008). He shows that, although GE was following a trend, it was taking a pioneering role in this area, and many of its processes were imitated by other companies attempting to emulate GE's success (Cappelli, 2008: 55ff).

Crotonville quickly established itself as the place to go if you wanted to be promoted, and there was significant status attached to being added to the delegates' list. It quickly developed its own rules and rituals. These had little to do with the management content that was being delivered, and much to do with fitting into GE culture. In some ways it was as much a gentlemen's club as a training centre. For example, at the heart of Crotonville sat the White House. This was the original wooden farmhouse. It was retained, and converted into a post-course recreation building and set up as a bar. It gave middle managers the opportunity to speak informally to top company leadership – conversations that could last far into the night. This was where the informal contacts were established, and networks were built. It therefore had a unique role, and it all added to the legend (conversation with Peter Cavanaugh, Manager of Crotonville). That humble wood frame building was deeply symbolic, and that is why in the reimagining of Crotonville it was retained as a building, but converted into a centre for informal meetings and a coffee bar which opened during the day.

Jack Welch took over GE in 1982. He shifted Crotonville from a management training centre (this is what you have to do) to a place for leadership development (this is where you think). He restructured and refreshed Crotonville and threw out the Blue Books in order to be able to focus on his new style of empowered leadership rather than rule-based management. He showed his commitment to the place by attending almost every programme. This enabled him to get to know and challenge all of the emerging executive talent. He wrote copiously about the importance of Crotonville.

His key, big idea was to be *boundaryless*. 'A boundaryless company would knock down external walls, making suppliers and customers part of a single process. It would eliminate the less visible walls of race and gender. It would put the team ahead of individual ego' (Welch, 2001: 273). Executives had to be able to negotiate the whole of GE and be prepared to work in any of its divisions. Welch wanted Crotonville to be the crucible for a new, single GE culture that would be carved out of the old GE. For that, he needed all his key executive staff to share the same values and appreciate the primacy and unique culture of GE, rather than focus narrowly on the business unit they belonged to. So ideas flowed and informed the whole company, percolating deep inside every Division. What was required was an integrated approach so that a problem in Plastics could be solved by teams from Health or Power Generation. There were no boundaries, and loyalties were built to GE as an entity. Crotonville was a kind of glue that ensured the whole was always greater than the sum of its parts.

According to Bartlett and McLean:

> Participation in a Crotonville course changed from being a seniority-driven rite of passage (and sometimes a consolation prize for a missed promotion) to a sought-after reward, and signal of future potential. Readiness for attendance on a course was closely monitored by Welch and his HR leaders during Session C wrap-ups, and Crotonville's Management Development Course, Business Management Course, and Executive Development Course [the three core executive development programmes] were soon recognized as preparation for next band promotions. (Bartlett and McLean, 2006: 3)

Welch made fundamental changes that helped adapt Crotonville to serve GE for a completely new industrial landscape and business reality. He did not do this on his own. He hired a Harvard Business School professor, Jim Baughman, to lead the charge. He was succeeded by a University of Michigan management professor Noel Tichy. Tichy was largely responsible for redesigning the Crotonville curricula (Welch, 2001: 138) and is best known for his work on 'teachable moments' and his philosophy of 'leaders as teachers' (Cohen and Tichy, 1997: 16). Tichy influenced GE executives to act as coaches to their staff. A teachable moment was a process where a manager used an incident, or a failure of some sort, not as an excuse to blame the member of staff, but as an opportunity for that person to learn. This encouraged more openness and dialogue, and encouraged staff to admit difficulties or failures rather than try to hide them. These were ideas he developed at Crotonville and were integral parts of the learning experience and became, by extension, part of the executive toolbox once graduates from the programmes returned to their substantive positions.

In 1994 the third of Jack Welch's appointments to lead Crotonville was made. His name was Steve Kerr. He, too, was a management professor, this time Dean of the Management School at USC. He originally came into GE as a consultant, recruited from Marshall School of Business at the University of Southern California, to facilitate 'Work-Out' sessions in the nuclear business, and then in many other of GE's businesses in the United States. Kerr's transition into GE was gradual. He was brought in as a consultant working in some GE businesses from 1989. He relocated from USC to the University of Michigan in 1992 to give himself more flexibility in terms of the GE work, and his consultancy commitment moved from 25 to 210 days a year. He finally agreed to move into GE in March 1994. Kerr took leave of absence from Michigan in order to go to GE. He always thought he would return to academia afterwards, but he never did, as his career took him from GE, after 11 years, to Goldman Sachs as their CLO. As he became more and more embedded in GE, running Crotonville became a logical extension of his role.

He brought customers into Crotonville to share leadership best practices, and further refined the curricula. He was given the title Vice President of Leadership Development and CLO (Chief Learning Officer). His responsibilities included Crotonville but extended beyond it (Greiner, 2003: 2). The title of CLO that Jack Welch came up with made Steve Kerr the world's first CLO. The CLO title came when Welch refused to agree a title of Chief Education Officer as there was room for only one CEO at GE! (Greiner, 2003: 4) The title was designed to register to the company and the outside world just how important learning was to the company. CLO implied C-suite membership and high status.

Kerr informally reported to Welch as he always had done as an external consultant, although the formal reporting structure was through to the Global Head of HR. The current CLO reports to the Global Head of HR still. So the centre grew in status and stature in GE, and beyond. Welch remade Crotonville for the third time. According to Greiner 'Kerr contributed significantly to GE's transformation, although he does not take much credit' (Greiner, 2003: 3). So learning and leadership were at the heart of the business transformation process and Crotonville was at the heart of learning and leadership. And it was Kerr who began to run Crotonville programmes around the world, aimed at staff who were unlikely or unable to make the trip to New York State.

Kerr had a role on a par with the Chief Information Officer. He defined the difference in what each did:

> What is it about the way we organize work and build rewards? What is it that keeps people from wanting to communicate, what adjustments in rewards and norms, and so on, would create more motivation? That was the division of labour... The CIO worked on ability to communicate, and the CLO worked on desire to communicate.
> (Greiner, 2003: 4)

There appeared to be a simple formula going on in GE which Kerr encouraged but did not control. As GE's products became more technically complex, and as the business environment evolved, it was imperative that strong trust developed amongst the people closest to the technologies and the customer. To be confident that those high trust relationships were built and sustained, you needed excellent leaders throughout the company and cadres of younger leaders ready to step into their shoes. The emphasis on leadership was always business-driven and remains a specific 'selling point' for the company to this day. On the GE careers website, Crotonville is highlighted:

> Crotonville established GE as a pioneer and global standard-setter for leadership development and learning. Today, we continue to advance an

evoluti[...]ulture where learning shapes strategy, and
leaders a[...]d inspired to succeed. (GE, 2016)

Crotonville [...]ed enormously since 2007. It has continued to
grow, investm[...]it has increased, and at the same time it has been
completely rei[...]ned under the watchful eye of Jeff Immelt, the current CEO, and [...]e then CLO, now SVP, of Human Resources, Susan
Peters.

Jeff Immelt had been CEO since the day before 9/11. He has had
to deal with the colossal fall-out from that event. So when he
appointed Susan Peters as his Executive Vice President for Human
Resources in 2007, he needed to realign GE for a new economic
reality. Crotonville was the place to do this. One of the first tasks he
set her was to reimagine Crotonville and rebuild it for a 21st-century
GE. In order to facilitate this she appointed Raghu Krishnamoorthy
as her new CLO, and Peter Cavanaugh as her Head of Operations.
Eight years later, Cavanaugh is still there and he now runs Crotonville.
Raghu Krishnamoorthy has been promoted to Senior HR Leader for
GE Healthcare, and leadership learning now reports directly to Susan
Peters. What they both achieved is unassailable. It is nothing short of
a Crotonville renaissance.

Reimagining Crotonville

A small board of directors was established to oversee this redesign
task, largely drawn from across the GE businesses, and they met
every quarter from 2010 to 2013 to shape the direction and hear progress reports. This was a powerful catalytic group who challenged
every aspect of what went on in Crotonville and became a forum for
ideas. Meanwhile, every other week on a Wednesday afternoon there
was a 'Reimagine Crotonville' seminar that involved staff and faculty
at Crotonville as well as external guests. So the process of remaking
Crotonville was extensive, ideas-focused and systematic. The idea
was to ensure not only that it was fit for purpose in the world that GE
found itself, but also capable of remaining aligned and integrated as
both GE and the external world evolved. Crotonville still builds the
kind of leaders GE requires for both the changing external and

internal culture. It is able to develop leaders capable of adapting to changed external environments. It helps evolve business culture in order to maintain GE's economic position. Crotonville, therefore, is still at the heart of the company, and the place GE comes to change itself and inspire its next generation of leaders.

During the Reimagine process, the entire curriculum was re-crafted, the site redesigned with increased residential capacity, and new more flexible teaching spaces were built. That is why the iconic White House was radically redesigned and repurposed as a clear visual symbol of that evolution. The now community coffee shop is used as a drop-in space for small meetings, or simply a place to quietly reflect, and is mostly used during the day rather than at night. Former plaques that adorned the walls were removed in order to focus on the relevance of the present and the current journey, rather than celebrate the past.

In many ways Crotonville shifted from tight to loose: from the Ralph Cordiner scientific management centre, where rules could be applied systematically, to a place where flexibility, agility, and curiosity were encouraged and developed and leaders were taught to think for them-selves. There are no Blue Books now, just guidelines and techniques for learning to respond to the current economic climate and steer GE to success by navigating it.

This new era of leadership has five precepts. They are known as the GE beliefs.

1 Customers determine our success.

2 Stay lean to go fast.

3 Learn and adapt to win.

4 Empower and inspire each other.

5 Deliver results in an uncertain world.

The dominant philosophy for Crotonville is: 'We all rise'. This simple three-word phrase embodies the trajectory of this transformation of approach and philosophy for leadership. The 'we' is not an elite group of Crotonville senior executive delegates, but the entire com-pany. The Programmes ensure that the vast majority of participants get much better at what they do. That is the nature of the intense programmes which run at Crotonville, but the participants' responsibility is far wider: it is to ensure that the entire company gets better at what it does, and it rises as well.

Elements of the new curriculum include a huge global programme to deliver the Crotonville experience all around the world, going further than Steve Kerr's initial attempts to globalize. Its impact has been extended into all of the geographical areas where GE is active.

Participants are encouraged to think about their whole career not just the next move, and to discuss their role, not in the context of their narrow job description, but in the wider GE context. It is career navigation, not career planning, and this distinction embodies the changes in the purpose of the Centre as a whole. One of the key strengths at Crotonville is the continuing focus on bringing people together from across the world, and from the various GE divisions such as healthcare, power transmission, aeronautics, etc to work on common business problems, so that the contribution of GE leaders spreads out beyond their individual business units.

There is time for reflection on the learning process and there are stretch extension classes called 'lunch and learns' which are voluntary and outside the formal curriculum. The idea is to challenge the leaders' assumptions and broaden their imagination. Reflection is seen as an integral part of the leader's tool kit and a critical element for any adaptable leader. A lot of time is also spent working on those five GE beliefs (Customers determine our success; Stay lean to go fast; Learn and adapt to win; Empower and inspire each other; Deliver results in an uncertain world) so that everyone can work out the implications for each individual, their teams and business unit.

There is now a much larger focus on the bigger picture. Global trends that impact GE as well as the current economic climate are thoroughly debated. The aim is to build a strong context so that strategy remains aligned and GE remains relevant.

All participants are encouraged to keep a Leadership Journal in order to retain insights, develop a record of their learning journey, and spot key changes that need to be made on a personal, team or business unit level. The journal models the idea of reflection and the process begun at Crotonville is designed to become a career-long habit. The learning is designed to be conscious and practical so that each leader evolves into a conscious learner.

This is expensive. GE spends around two and a half times what the average company spends on learning (ATD Research, 2015). The company sees this as an investment in the future, as much as an investment in individuals. Crotonville shapes the culture of the company across geographies and across business units. Staff in Crotonville would argue that it is the shaper of the culture across the entire corporation, as well as a place to ignite ideas, build connections and develop people. It is also a place where specific skills are developed and embedded that will enable executives to be more successful in their roles.

The task of rebuilding Crotonville was both an internal and inward-looking process as well as an acute look at the company and its place in the world. The curriculum that was developed reattached itself at every point to the wider business, but did so through the lens of what would make excellent learning in terms of content, and excellent learning in terms of process. The development involved business leaders working with learning leaders and external experts to develop what was necessary, but did it in context, sharing the best ideas possible in order to deliver the most memorable holistic experience. Doing everything in context was one of the big ideas that emerged from the reimagining Crotonville process.

No one gets to Crotonville without their line manager's recommendation, and the list of participants for the top programmes are still reviewed by the CEO and the senior executives. And the participant's manager has a critical role in ensuring that the learning is embedded once the participant returns to base. It is a team effort throughout. Each course has a significant time for reflection built into the programme to allow quiet thought as well as intense learning. The onus, however, is on the individual to make a difference once he or she returns from the Centre. Going to Crotonville is only the first part of the story. Making a difference once you return is equally important. That is where the return on investment comes into its own. Once you are there, the pressure is on to plan precisely what you will do when you return. The focus always extends beyond the place, so that Crotonville is merely one step on a much longer journey.

Start with the experience you want to create

(Much of what follows is taken from a long descriptive mural on the wall at Crotonville and from discussion with Peter Cavanaugh.)

Every aspect of Crotonville was put under the microscope during the reimagining process. The idea was to create not just a complete experience but also a consistent narrative that was authentic and aligned. No one, for example, is notified by e-mail of a place on a programme. The notification is delivered one-to-one by a senior manager. This is a profoundly personal opportunity and the excitement and inspiration builds from that very moment of engagement. This is defined as the point the Programme Manager, for that specific course, contacts the delegate and welcomes him or her. Registration takes place online and the delegate is then taken to the Global Learning Website which curates key content. This is drawn widely from TED talks and other sources, so that the initial intellectual engagement and challenge takes the individual, deliberately, beyond the world of GE. There are pre-read materials, and a pre-course conference call designed to prepare, excite and engage the individual.

The cars used to ferry delegates into Crotonville are mostly hybrids or electric. There are wind turbines on the hill – a quiet, implicit 'what if' message to everyone from a company heavily into power generators. GE will embrace a green, lower carbon future, and to make a subtle message first paves the way for more substantial discussion later. Even the way that the individual is greeted at the Gatehouse is defined. It is a friendly, informal welcome, not a security check. And registration at Crotonville is not organized from behind a table. Everything is done to make the delegate feel special and to make the week a unique experience that is different from day-to-day work. The detailed programme for the week is on a phone app, and each element of the physical space – classroom, breakout space, restaurant or casual meeting area – is carefully designed to encourage sharing and debate, as well as quiet reflection.

And the outside environment has been redesigned to include a running track around the campus, a walking trail through the woods, and deliberate, quiet spaces sheltered from the elements that allow individuals to think quietly away from the crowd. The steep terrain continues the metaphor of a journey, and even the contoured design of the internal teaching space subtly suggests the same.

There is a fitness centre and a yoga studio which couples as a painting/craft studio. There are kitchens where delegates cook for each other, and the accommodation blocks are new and state of the art. This means that the vast majority of delegates sleep on campus in quality, connected, five-star accommodation. If delegates are put into off site accommodation (a specific hotel in downtown Croton–Harmon) a bit of Crotonville goes with them as the information kiosks around campus are also installed in the hotel lobby. Even the dining room is a carefully crafted experience where attention is paid even to the choice and style of cutlery.

The programme content is a mixture of personal leadership insight, global trends and their impact on GE, and skill development to enhance competence and build commitment to the five GE beliefs. It is about collaboration, insight and inspiration. It is about personal journeys as well as the journey that GE itself is on. Insight comes from internal Crotonville faculty, senior GE executives and outside experts. Each week one senior executive takes leave of absence from his or her job to be on campus and have informal meetings with the group of delegates.

At the end of the programme, the post-session tasks are activated. Teams stay in touch wherever they happen to be based, using telepresence or webinar technology so that the bonds forged in the two weeks on campus can be sustained and deepened as the individual's career moves forward. And a digital yearbook is created to remind everyone of both the experience and the individuals with whom they worked.

In many ways the reimagined Crotonville is completely different from the one developed in the Jack Welch era, and as different as Welch's one from the previous iterations. But at a profound level the heart and soul of Crotonville remain intact, simply inhabiting a different body. That alignment between a place and a company is what sustains it into the 21st century.

The impact of Crotonville stretches away from GE into leadership programmes in many other companies around the world. The easiest example of that is the impact of Crotonville on the BBC's Leadership Programme.

What we took from Jack Welch's insights became core elements of the leadership programme at the BBC. The strong brand image, the need to work on BBC problems and not generic problems, and the introduction of action learning sets, designed to encourage key executives to fix their own problems, were all parts of the Crotonville ethos. The then BBC CEO Greg Dyke was as heavily involved in the programme as Jack Welch had been. Greg personally launched most of the programmes and visited the residential base at Ashridge Business School (located north of London) over 100 times, and amongst other tasks, he led free-ranging Q&A sessions with participants, based around improving the organization. Conclusions were turned into actions that changed the way the BBC operated. What Jack Welch called 'Work-Outs', for example, the BBC called 'The Big Conversation' which was an integral part of the whole 'Making it Happen' change agenda (Dyke, 2004: 216–19). Greg also built a coherent top 400 executive team called 'Leading the Way Group' to own and deliver the change agenda in their separate parts of the organization. This was the first time in the BBC's history that such an integrated, cross-divisional group of senior executives had been created. Many long-standing senior executives met each other for the very first time at these sessions.

Greg Dyke summed up this experience, which has the leadership programme at its heart:

> In two short years we convinced most of our staff that we really wanted change, that we wanted to empower them, that we wanted to be better leaders ourselves, that we wanted everyone working for the BBC to have more rewarding and more fulfilling working lives. They knew we weren't doing this just to be nice. It was the means of achieving the ambition we all shared for the BBC: to become 'the most creative organization in the world' and as a result make the best programmes and provide the best possible services to our audiences. But, most of all, I hope we persuaded them that we cared. (Dyke, 2004: 220)

Like Welch's efforts at GE, the BBC's leadership programme was not delivered in isolation but as an integral part of cultural change and (in Welch's words) the 'inspirational glue' that held it all together. The overarching aim was to build an organization that was fit for the evolving purposes that being a media organization in the 21st century entailed.

What can we learn from Crotonville?

1 It is futile establishing the trappings of a leadership centre like Crotonville unless you have the supporting infrastructure and business credibility. Jack Welch 'owned' Crotonville. He was there many times a month, and commissioned a helicopter pad to ease the commute from NYC and the Fairfield, CT, headquarters. He spent hours teaching the senior leaders his vision of leadership and values, and authorized many of the action decisions that emerged from those discussions. Its success is not an indication of its power in itself, but of its power in context. Jeff Immelt continues that tradition and has redesigned the complete experience to fit a new agenda and a new context. He is also a regular visitor. When GE held talks with the French company Alstom in the middle of the takeover process, the critical, high-level meetings were at Crotonville. At least part of the reason was to emphasize the developmental culture in the company and to show that learning was deeply embedded in the culture.

2 The curricula are very important and deeply considered. They have gone through substantial change over the years – as indeed they should. But it was not just what was being taught that was so important. You could argue that how it was being taught was as significant. The no-holds-barred, action-orientated development, with its focus on debate and discussion rather than delivery of content, was equally as important as the content and the skill development. In other words, process was just as important as product.

3 Indirect messages are important. Getting delegates to cook the evening meal for each other has strong messages about compromise, teamwork and service. The messages emerge from the process rather than being forced on the group.

4 GE never did a strict return on investment for Crotonville. The consistent view over the decades has been that the pay-off extended for years and years beyond the event. In addition, it was extremely difficult to quantify the resonance that Crotonville created across the company. This was not just for the thousands who went through, but also for the thousands who knew about it, and were impressed by it, and saw its outputs first hand. In some ways, staff pride in working for a company that could sustain a place like Crotonville builds up an acute sense of commitment and belief in GE, which is almost unquantifiable. The corporate 'good' that emanates from such a centre reinforces and helps sustain the value systems. The big messages for staff and for customers are deeply embedded in that place.

5 Crotonville was successful and continues to shine because it has continuously remade itself. This is not simply about refreshing the curricula, or repainting the walls – it is much more fundamental than that! Crotonville has been successfully rethought and reimagined on at least three separate occasions. These were not hastily concluded events, but detailed process discussions involving many people throughout the company over a considerable period of time. The reimagining process that Peter Cavanaugh oversaw was extremely thorough and painstakingly precise in what it wanted to achieve. This process of change was drawn as an elaborate tableau that graphically describes the journey. The resulting image that encapsulates that complex journey for Crotonville was framed and put on the wall of the Centre as an illustrated narrative journey – some seven metres in length that is now part of the history of the place.

6 It is true that the physical infrastructure of Crotonville was remade over the decades. This was necessary as it needed to be refreshed. But the physical infrastructure had the same attention to detail paid to it as the curricula themselves. For example, the repackaging of the iconic White House was considered and deliberate. It broadcast a message way beyond the simple change of use. Classrooms were fundamentally redesigned to be more flexible spaces, and the centrepiece of Crotonville under Jack Welch – the Pit – is now far less a centrepiece because of its lack of flexibility as a teaching and learning space. It has become an historical artefact rather than a core space.

7 There are now new teaching blocks, new accommodation, and new landscaping of the site. There were no places for quiet reflection on the Crotonville campus in Jack Welch's day! But they are there now as embodiments of a new type of learning. In spite of these massive changes, the soul of Crotonville and its deep connections into the company remain the same.

8 Crotonville expresses something profound about the beliefs and values of GE and the tight linkages between the various GE businesses. This leadership centre has been built slowly and systematically over the years. GE is Crotonville just as Crotonville is GE; there is no sense at all that it is remote from the business or in any way out of touch. It feels right, and it feels connected. What Crotonville represents is certainly not for every organization, however, and copying the outward trappings is expensive and possibly futile. Indeed it should be resisted because it represents an enormous investment and needs huge commitment over many years.

9 Crotonville is one physical location, but it also manifests itself throughout the GE world. Crotonville courses exist in many countries, and one of Steve Kerr's achievements was to globalize the idea of Crotonville and make it tangible in all of GE's key centres. This has been dramatically extended in the new regime. So the presence of Crotonville resonates powerfully in GE centres worldwide.

10 In many ways, Crotonville is a brand. There are many ways to brand learning and leadership development, and this is one very successful example. It is impossible to separate leadership development in GE from Crotonville, and this creates a unique buzz around leadership development and makes all leaders conscious learners for GE. The notion of giving leadership development real status and a tangible presence is definitely worth emulating. Crotonville is only one of the ways you could do this.

11 Crotonville has been deliberately designed as an experience. This begins even before you drive through the gates, and it is intended that you will continuously be surprised by the experience. For example, the vegetable gardens grow much of the produce that is prepared in the Crotonville restaurants. The 9/11 Memorial, which stands on the shore of the lake, embodies GE's commitment to service (it was presented by the New York Fire Department in recognition of the leadership training that GE delivers to senior fire service personnel in New York every year and has done since 9/11). And it is also a place designed for reflection and silence. Therefore, it is both a symbol and a statement, as well as an integral part of the site. That one symbol has a powerful and dramatic impact on the whole site.

12 Crotonville is not isolated from the company as a whole. Senior executives teach regularly on all the programmes, and each week a senior executive is based at Crotonville, both to teach and to be available to coach and mentor course participants. That person is a part of the Crotonville mix and is highly visible throughout the week he or she is present.

13 Attention to detail is very important. The Crotonville journey begins at the point when you are notified that you have a place on a course and continues through the post-programme activity. No aspect of that journey is ignored and every aspect is debated and deliberately adds to the quality of that experience.

14 Crotonville is in permanent renewal. The map that is handed out to every visitor and participant has a simple message: 'GE Crotonville, founded in 1956, reimagined every day.' That is the strongest guard against smugness and complacency. The challenge of rebuilding Crotonville is a continuing task!

Crotonville is so much more than an off-site leadership centre or even a corporate university. It represents the brain of the organization and the place where GE comes to realign, refresh and move forward. It is a deliberately challenging environment, and it still has an aura about it of excitement and challenge. I spoke to one participant from South America and he said that he had heard about Crotonville ever since he joined GE and had attended Crotonville courses locally, but 'being here is something completely different'. In spite of the fact the gentlemen's club aspect has gone completely and the clientele are as diverse as the countries in which GE operates, it still manages to retain its magic and allure. That has nothing much to do with the physical location – however attractive – but everything to do with attention to detail. No aspect of the Crotonville experience is left to chance, and the journey from notification, to post-course connections and challenges is examined in minute detail. Everything has to fit, and the image of the place and the expectation that it builds in the minds of participants has to become a lived reality or the place would fail. It would be naive to underestimate the enormous achievement of the staff there under Peter Cavanaugh's watchful eye and Raghu Krishnamoorthy's strategic direction. Susan Peters, SVP of HR, achieved what she set out to do, and that was to build a Crotonville that is fit for purpose and at the heart of the company. Crotonville is no longer Jack Welch's vision; it is firmly in the grip of Jeff Immelt and delivering what he requires of it for the future.

Conclusion

There are a few watchwords at the heart of this experience. The first is surprise. It is important to create continuing moments that beguile the participants and trick them out of any sense that they have the place worked out. Some of the teaching is direct – it does what it says it will do; but some is decidedly challenging, such as working with a string quartet in close proximity, cooking for your colleagues, furnishing art from twigs! Here the messages are more complex and more profound. The meaning is metaphorical rather than direct. You have to work it out.

The second word is challenge. There is much reinforcement about GE and its mission, but participants are challenged in a direct way to rethink, realign and transform not just what they do but how they do it. Everyone leaves with an agenda for action that is a step up from where they started, and their manager will be waiting back in the workplace to ensure that this is followed through.

The third word is alignment. There is alignment between what GE wants to achieve and what Crotonville delivers – between the image of the place and the reality that is experienced by participants, and between what it means to be a leader in GE and what the courses embody. And this is not a secret process. Thousands of customers come to GE to improve their leadership. In fact, leadership development is part of the package when you buy from GE. So customers and company are also aligned.

The leadership philosophy that is summed up in the three-word tag line 'we all rise' applies to the company and its key customers. This is an onerous responsibility for Crotonville. It is, in some sense, the living embodiment of what the company means. This is an incredible achievement that has helped to sustain the company for the last 60 years. There is no sense that this place is out of time and a relic of a different past. It feels right at the heart of the company and embodies its DNA. No other organization can copy Crotonville – it is too embedded in its parent company. However, there is a huge amount to learn about how to deliver better leaders, and how to make good and consistent leadership a key element of what makes an organization tick.

References

ATD Research (2015) *2015 State of the Industry*, Association for Talent Development, Alexandria, VA

Bartlett, C A and McLean, A N (2006) GE's talent machine: the making of a CEO, Case Study No 9, November, Harvard Business School, Boston, MA

Cappelli, P (2008) *Talent on Demand: Managing talent in an age of uncertainty*, Harvard Business Press, Boston, MA

Cohen, E and Tichy, N (1997) *How Leaders Develop Leaders,* The American Society for Training and Development (ASTD, now ATD), Alexandria, VA

Dyke, G (2004) *Inside Story*, HarperCollins, London

GE (2016) Life at GE, Website, www.ge.com/careers/culture/life-at-ge

Greiner, L (2003) *Steve Kerr and His Years with Jack Welch at GE*, Marshall School of Business, University of Southern California

Von Butler, H (2015) *The Guides*, GE Capital, Germany

Welch, J (2001) *Jack: Straight from the gut*, Headline Publishing Group, London

Leadership on the edge   03
Discomfort as a learning experience

Just remember, Antarctica wants to kill you.
ROBERT SWAN'S ADVICE TO 2016 EXPEDITIONARIES BEFORE
EMBARKATION

*I had mounted an expedition to the South Pole without having ever
really been camping before.*
SWAN, 2009: 12

There are many endurance programmes designed to both test and
strengthen leadership and teamwork. The whole concept of 'outward
bound' goes back to the mid-20th century. The organization which
bears its name was established in 1941 by Kurt Hahn and Lawrence
Holt and was designed to build social skills, whilst developing and
maturing young people. It is closely aligned to the current Duke of
Edinburgh's Award, which sets a series of tests for young people in
outdoor skills in which hundreds of thousands of young people have
participated.

The logical extension of this philosophy and approach into leadership development for adults was not very far behind. It is now almost
a cliché when people discuss navigating rivers with minimal equipment, transporting objects from one location to another using only
the resources of a designated team, or even navigating – with only
basic equipment – to locate a specific remote waypoint. Many people
undertake such development experiences as an end in themselves or,
more likely, as a component part of a more orthodox classroom-based
programme.

This chapter addresses the model of leadership development in extremis. Is it effective? Are there long-term benefits, beyond those of having an experience outside one's normal comfort zone? Can this kind of development actually change lives and act as a critical inflection point for a career?

To test this, I participated in an expedition to Antarctica organized by Foundation 2041 (2041.com) which was founded by a remarkable individual – Robert Swan, OBE – who also led the expedition. I joined over 100 intrepid souls from all over the world (40 countries) many of whom had never seen snow, let alone navigated or even participated in a severe winter ecosystem such as the Antarctic. We were together for two weeks, which included seven days on the Antarctic continent or its surrounding islands. I interviewed many people in some depth and spoke to every single participant at some point.

The aim was to gauge whether the nature of that experience led to something more than could have been achieved in any other more benign location. But the real essence of the research was to estimate how much the impact of that unique experience turned into enduring behaviour change for the participants. This is the desired, but elusive, conclusion that the vast majority of leadership development programmes wish to achieve.

This end point had to be set against the cost, complexity and risk of such an endeavour. To put that into perspective, the ship that took us to the Antarctic was leased for US$1 million. That was just to get the ship and crew and Quark staff there and back and feed us all. There were 10 Foundation 2041 staff, plus 29 staff working for Quark – the expedition managers and the charterers of the ship – as well as a ship's crew of 59. This was not an endeavour to be taken lightly, nor a programme to be put together hastily. It was also not something that the participants decided upon at the last moment. Many had to seek sponsorship and gather together the not insignificant cost over years and in dribs and drabs. For the majority it was an investment and commitment that took at least one year to realize. Therefore, the sense of anticipation in the group when we arrived in Ushuaia at the southern tip of Tierra del Fuego in Argentina prior to embarkation, was palpable. Many were in a mild state of shock, realizing that they had actually made it this far and Antarctica itself loomed large.

What is Foundation 2041?

It is impossible to answer that question without reference to the man who established the Foundation – Robert Swan. Robert's biography is extraordinary. He is still the only human being to have walked to both the North and South Poles unaided; in other words without dogs and without being restocked at waypoints. Everything needed to get to both poles has to be pulled on sleds by the expedition members, and as there was a commitment to leave everything as they found it, all the waste and disused cans and boxes had to be lugged along as well, and disposed of once they arrived back at a place that could process it.

In one sense, Swan's trip to the South Pole was the fulfilment of a childhood obsession that started at the age of 11, when he saw the movie *Scott of the Antarctic* on a black-and-white television set. He raised the US$5 million required to mount the expedition over two years and walked with two other people to the South Pole at the age of 26. With a different team he negotiated the North Pole some 10 years later. It was clear that these dramatic experiences, that no other human being has replicated, together with his eyewitness accounts of what climate change was doing to the Poles, led to an interest in the environment and the preservation of Antarctica. He became the world's strongest advocate for preserving Antarctica in its undeveloped pristine state, and an incessant lobbyist for protecting the planet.

He became involved, quite naturally, in the debate around the Antarctic Treaty that was signed, initially in 1991, and finally concluded with the signature of Russia in 1998. The inclusion of Russia on the list of signatories was no chance event. During those seven years between the first set of signatures and that of Russia, Robert spent his time and energy cleaning up the 1,500 tonnes of rubbish left by Russia in the Antarctic. All signatories to the Antarctic Treaty had this obligation as a key responsibility, and all had complied apart from Russia which, at the time, was in political turmoil as it embarked on the process of disengaging from the USSR. The extent of Russia's waste pile made them highly reluctant at that time to sign up to any kind of commitment. So Robert took on the job of clearing away the Russian waste, and when that was completed Russia had no alternative but to come on board. They signed the Antarctic Treaty in 1998. It was a high-stakes endeavour, and pretty much a thankless and unpleasant task, but it delivered Russia into the Antarctic protection fold and meant that all of the countries that claimed any kind of interest in the Antarctic were signatories to the same treaty.

Robert had dramatically demonstrated the depth of his commitment to protecting the unique ecology of that area. But the treaty, however long fought over, was never set up to last in perpetuity. It expires 50 years after it was first signed, ie somewhere between the years 2041 and 2048. The name of Robert's Foundation serves as a permanent reminder of what is still left to achieve: the designation of the Antarctic as a wilderness area for all time. Ironically, that same year has taken on a greater significance recently. It is highlighted as the pivot point for climate change. That is the year – if nothing is done – that we tip into irrecoverable global warming with a five-degree average rise in temperature across the globe, or it could be the year when our efforts to control carbon emissions begin to bear fruit and the increase in average temperature around the world stabilizes.

The explicit aim of the Foundation is to preserve the pristine state of the Antarctic by ensuring that, when the treaty comes up for renewal in 2048, there will be overwhelming support to protect that wild, undeveloped continent for all time. Robert's way of ensuring that this will happen is to expose a significant group of potential leaders from all around the world to the Antarctic at a formative stage in their personal and career development. This process is designed to indelibly mark the expedition participants' leadership journey with the stamp of the unique and powerful Antarctic experience. By 2041 and beyond, the former expeditionaries will have risen from their positions when they participated into roles with both seniority and power. The hope is that they will stand and speak with one voice to defend and to protect the Antarctic, and ensure that any agreement reached will last, this time, forever. So leadership, learning and the Antarctic are indelibly fused together.

There is already a 1,000-strong cohort of alumni who have participated in these expeditions since 2003 and who still strongly identify with the Foundation and its explicit aims. There is little chance that any of those alumni would defend the destruction of the Antarctic at any point in their lifetimes. The issue and the object of the Foundation is a very simple one. In 2041, or thereabouts, there will be a sufficient number of senior people in high places whose voices will be heard strongly and forcibly in defence of the protection of the Antarctic. By 2048 Robert Swan will be in his nineties. He will need to have his vision perpetuated and articulated through those 1,000 or more alumni from every corner of the globe. It is a daring and ambitious aspiration with leadership at its core. As I said in the opening of this chapter, Robert Swan is a remarkable man.

Leadership and the Antarctic

With the idea of preserving the Antarctic came parallel ideas around sustainable leadership. Were there links? Could each idea help illuminate and support the other? In his book, Swan attempts to define his case more clearly:

> My most cherished hope is that the idea of sustainable leadership, developed during tracks and expeditions, can in some small way be applied to the biggest environmental test facing us today – how to keep the planet human-friendly and hospitable to life, reversing the degradation of the industrial era. (Swan, 2009: 6)

So the leadership skills developed in the programme will be developed in a context that will build a commitment to sustainable development and hold everyone to account. In other words, the environment will be used to develop better leaders who, in their turn, will be able to articulate the message of preservation more loudly and with more influence. It is a simple idea, but does it work?

In my interview with Robert Swan aboard the *Ocean Endeavour* in March 2016 during the return journey on the Drake Passage, he explained to me that leaders, above all, need a fantastic story. He said, 'In the noise of the planet, there is huge competition to get people's attention, and Antarctica is still a very big deal. It still has romance and mystique.'

Therefore, it gives all the participants a fantastic leadership story that will help them grab people's attention. The imagery also acts as a complex metaphor for other sorts of journeys and therefore has the power and potential to engage and anchor profound life lessons using that imagery. One of the reasons why the place resonates so strongly and generates stories that stick in the mind is because of its special place in people's consciousness and its special status as the one remaining pristine area left on earth.

Robert also believes that this process actually refreshes participants and gives them inspiration and conviction to move forward. It is akin to entering a different, very strange and magical world, having been shaken about and buffeted by the Drake Passage. As you have to pass through the Drake Passage – 48 hours on the roughest sea in the world – to get to the peninsula, you realize that Antarctica does not yield its secrets easily. There is no alternative way of getting there without that gut-wrenching journey from South America. This builds expectations and creates a space for preparation and engagement. The group is, therefore, somewhat self-selected by their courage and determination to get there, and their belief in the potency of the endeavour.

Disconnection and dislocation are very important ways of stimulating thought and encouraging new ideas to emerge. There is a deliberate process of systematic confusion and subsequent realignment that resolves itself in establishing new long-term plans and medium-term goals. The place itself also tends to generate trust and support. Participants spontaneously help and look after each other and offer encouragement when the going is tough underfoot or the waters churn. And participants sense the power that trust builds, and draw strength from that support. There is a realization that big things happen by small gestures and tasks, at least in that harsh environment. It was clear from my observations that the expeditionaries were having different kinds of conversations and living more raw and intensive lives. The issue, however, is how far that spirit carries back in to the more work-a-day world.

Two enduring outcomes from past expeditions include: the education station that was built by James Bray in North Carolina in an old railroad car that was hauled into the mountains and set up as a remote, connected classroom for its community; and the education station built in the Himalayas by Paras Loomba to help increase literacy in remote, inaccessible villages. There are many more that occurred only because of that leadership experience.

Yet, in spite of significant achievements by participants, expedition after expedition, when I asked Robert what success on this expedition meant for him, he replied, 'We return to dock at 6.00 am in Ushuaia and everyone is safe'. And I asked him how he wanted to be remembered. Not as the person who saved the Antarctic! What he said was, 'As someone who tried'. The essence of the whole expedition and its leadership message is encouraging people to try, and to believe in their power to make a difference. The leadership development model was built around affirmation. Every participant left the ship knowing the value of their potential contribution. Each person set out to do something in their own special way, however small, in global terms. However, the enduring belief established on that expedition was that 1,000 small initiatives all add up to a significant contribution that could reverberate on a global scale.

The journey

According to Robert Swan, 'the Leadership on the Edge Program is the golden thread that ties all of the activities and presentations together throughout the expedition' (Foundation 2041, 2016). The programme is a combination of presentations, teamwork and lectures, alongside journaling and reflection. The idea is to turn the experience of being 'on the edge' into strong personal learning. The life-changing development will build enduring competences and a mindset that will help people both to endure future challenges and to build a sense of purpose. The changes are designed to sustain the participants throughout their career by offering tools and techniques based on self-belief and a trust in people. The programme also stimulated debate on the whole issue of climate change and sustainability amongst a potentially powerful cohort of people.

So the presentations, given by experts, were imbued with the environment, and the theory and abstract models came alive in the reality of the location. In some small way the group came to live the science, history, biology, geology, and see everything through the lens of the Antarctic. Climate change and sustainability were thrown into a dramatic perspective and came alive. Theory became lived experience. There were 20 or 30 formal lectures available to the expedition group that included leadership development workshops. These were supplemented by the same number of presentations, delivered by members of the expedition, who wanted to share their own personal stories, learning journeys and plans for the future.

Each participant was given a journal and there was time allocated during the day and evening to note down thoughts about the experience in a tangible way. In addition, two specific times were allocated whilst on the ice for individual, quiet reflection. The journals were designed to track the learning and the insights on a day-to-day basis and act as a frame of reference once the expedition was over.

On the final day in Antarctica before the ship turned north to begin the return journey towards the port of Ushuaia, all the participants were encouraged to trek through the landscape of ice and snow and climb up onto a ridge overlooking the spectacularly beautiful Neko harbour. Once there, they were asked to sit quietly and reflect on the sum of their learning, and then to write down their thoughts, both in their journal and on a postcard. The postcard was sealed into a self-addressed envelope with the promise that it would be posted to each person six months after their arrival home. In some ways, then, the participants were asked to define their leadership insights and ambitions and then be challenged six months later to measure the degree to which they had achieved their targets and aspirations. The postcards were designed to create a moment, six months hence, to take stock and review the journey that each individual had taken from the ship back to their day-to-day lives and onward for that time.

The opportunity to learn from the myriad experiences on offer was completely integral to the whole package. This was designed to be a journey of self-discovery in tandem with the discovery of the Antarctic. The only dominant variable, outside everyone's control, was the weather! Fierce storms could appear from nowhere, but you could also awake to blue skies and sun. The lure to the ship's deck, or into the little rubber dinghies called Zodiacs – that carried passengers from ship to shore or on two-hour-long explorations of the waters, icebergs, coves and ice shelves of the area in which the ship was anchored – was irresistible. This meant that any programme on board the ship was always subject to the weather. It could be extended when it was impossible to disembark, or contracted when there was nothing more powerful than the urge to get off the ship and onto water or into the ice and snow on land. Every moment counted and no time was ever wasted, but every plan was tentative. Again, it was a kind of metaphorical experience about never wasting the great moments, or being thrown by adversity. Both these came in quick succession, every single day.

A chronology of the expedition

It was a carefully designed journey rather than a series of random events. Each discovery day on Antarctica would be in direct contrast to the next day. Rigorous activity was contrasted with quieter reflection, individual effort with team processes, technical skills with relaxed opportunities to observe, flat landscapes with rugged hills. The consistent elements were ice and water.

The group assembled in Ushuaia the day before embarkation. Some people had taken the opportunity to arrive early and explore the stunning landscape of Tierra del Fuego, whilst others arrived at the last possible minute. For many it was a long (at least 40 hours) and complex journey to get to the point of embarkation. This extended assembly process meant that participants could meet at least some of their colleagues, receive documentation and have their kit checked. No one was allowed on the ship without sufficient warm clothing to be able to survive in Antarctic conditions. Those with insufficient clothing were either loaned kit for the expedition or sent into the town to buy additional items from the many stores selling winter sports gear. Ushuaia is not just an embarkation point for Antarctica, but the base for trips into the mountains that surround the town's natural harbour.

The following day (Monday) was briefing day. The entire expedition assembled in a large room and a detailed briefing on all aspects of the expedition was undertaken. The underpinning philosophy of the expedition was articulated and participants had the opportunity to meet each other and listen to the Expedition Leader Robert Swan alongside the other presenters. He shared his approach and philosophy and then acted as the host, introducing those who would be delivering expert input on climate change, personal leadership development and project development.

Each member of the expedition was allocated to a 10-person team. Each team had a name based on a famous Antarctic explorer – Scott, Shackleton, Amundsen, etc – and those teams were grouped together around large tables and given the opportunity to introduce themselves to their fellow team members. The teams were important and time was spent on team familiarization and team processes. It was imperative that the team members supported and helped one another as they moved over the ice and climbed the hills. Everybody remained in their group for the entire expedition. As a group of 10 filled a Zodiac, it was important that the groups stayed together, and were ready to disembark together and help one another through the land-based tasks, in order that they could get back on the Zodiac together at the end of the day. This was for safety, but also drove the participants towards team achievement rather than individual prowess. Therefore, those groups became a significant feature of the daily routine, and each team member was entreated to work closely with the other team members. The impact was striking, support was offered without compulsion, and the groups helped one another when the going got tough or when individuals got anxious. Many found the mutual support instantly reassuring, and what was freely given was often gratefully received. This meant that team identities quickly established themselves and it made the process of acclimatization and preparation much easier for everyone. One participant noted:

> I was not sure about the team thing at the beginning, but it became very important and I looked automatically to my team for support and we really encouraged each other. By the end I really loved my teammates. They were a special group and we shared a lot together.

Embarkation was at 4.00 pm on day two following the series of presentations. Once in town and waiting for the signal to embark, groups gathered around their national flags and had photos taken. Many carried not only national flags but posters from sponsors that were to be used in Antarctica for location shots or a photograph with Rob Swan. The diversity of nationality represented was astonishing. The second largest national grouping after US citizens were the Indians – 19 participants – who made an instant and lasting impact on the dynamics of the expedition. To give an example of the diversity, the first 11 nationalities on the list were from: India, UAE, Canada, Kuwait, United States, Russian Federation, UK, Vietnam, Australia and Singapore.

Setting sail was scheduled for 5.00 pm. The first dinner together on board the ship took place at 7.30 pm as the ship sailed down the sheltered Beagle Channel before entering the rough seas. During the night the ship headed south and began to negotiate the notorious Drake Passage – it was like stepping inside a washing machine.

The Drake Passage is a right of way into Antarctica. It is a difficult and challenging experience and it lasts almost 48 hours. Reactions vary from acute sickness and being confined to bed, along a continuum to those few who have an ability to tolerate and even enjoy rough seas and get through that part of the journey with no obvious or appreciable side effects. What is indisputable, however, is that the boat rolls significantly and pitches violently. It is no small achievement weathering the Drake Passage. Many participants are genuinely terrified at the prospect, but put themselves through that experience because of what lies at the other end. That takes a degree of courage and acts as a pre-selection process for members of the expedition and is a demonstration of their determination and commitment, to say the very least. There is a genuine sense of relief when the ship turns into the relative calm of Antarctic waters and the real adventure begins.

By day four the ship has emerged from the violence of the Drake Passage into the smooth Antarctic seas. The programme of leadership development and scientific briefings began in earnest that day. Day five is the first day that the participants are able to step foot on Antarctica. The pattern for each day was to anchor in one or two locations during the day and move to the next location during the evening or overnight depending on distance. The briefing for the next day's location was carried out during the evening before dinner whilst the ship was sailing. The essential trajectory is to move ever further south until the ship is on the edge of the Antarctic Circle, moving in zigzag fashion down the Antarctic Peninsula towards the main mass of the continent. The group went from Deception Island, with its derelict whaling station, to Brown Bluff, and on to Portal Point and Wilhelmina Bay. The remaining locations were Ronge Island, the Lemaire Channel and Port Charcot, and finally the sublimely beautiful Neko Harbour and Paradise Bay. That final location was also the day of the polar plunge. Those who wished to do so (and virtually everyone participated) leapt from the Zodiac embarkation platforms into the sea, suitably buckled into a harness in case of difficulty. Each dive, plunge or simple collapse into the $-2°C$ water was filmed for posterity! It was almost like a rebirthing ceremony: a sign of change, renewal and achievement.

On the evening of day 10, the ship turned northwards and began its return journey through the Drake Passage before arriving in the calm waters of the Beagle Channel on day 12. Day 13 was disembarkation day when people made their way from ship to airport or lingered in Ushuaia.

There was a final celebration whilst the ship moved quietly along the Beagle Channel. This included celebrating some exceptional achievements by participants, and looking at the photo and video montages captured by those professionals on board. The large group from India also made that final day their own by organizing a festival of colours, where participants were smeared in bright coloured paint, some from head to foot.

What does a day look like in the Antarctic?

The days have a similar pattern which is ultimately dictated, in terms of the detail, by the weather. Good weather pushes the group out onto the ice as fast as possible, bad weather delays disembarkation.

The day begins early, normally at daybreak, when participants are urged to get out on deck and witness the new sight that befalls them. There can be icebergs of sublime beauty, seals, penguins or whales in the sea, or some spectacular, majestic scenery. The further south the ship headed, the more ice and snow built up on the decks, making passageways treacherous. That did not stop anybody making their early morning pilgrimage to the fore-upper deck. Following breakfast, half the group would get changed and prepare to disembark in the Zodiacs. Normally the first group would land and undertake walks and exercises. The Zodiacs would return and take the second group on a two-hour cruise to explore the nooks and crannies of the area where the ship was anchored. Obviously the Zodiacs could explore the seashore, sea ice, the sea life, and the silence. Part of each Zodiac trip was deliberately designated as a time for thought and silence. The outboard engine was cut and the Zodiac drifted quietly through the landscape. Participants were encouraged to put their cameras down and simply absorb the atmosphere and the detail of the place where they found themselves. Each Zodiac quickly lost sight of the ship and often of each other. To bob gently in the swell, taking in the over-powering atmosphere was integral to the experience and a key part of the leadership journey. There was so much group and team inter-action, that silence and self-reflection was a powerful antidote and stark contrast to much of the day, and also an act of respect for the pristine beauty of the location and its inhabitants.

Zodiacs then took that group to shore for their session on land and collected those who had experienced the land activities for their excursion on water. No more than 100 people can land on Antarctica in any one location. This is designed for safety and to protect the environment. There is also a bio-security programme, so all boots and footwear are cleaned when returning to the ship so that no bio-matter is transferred from the ship to the land or from land to land. The idea was that nothing was left behind on Antarctica, not even microorganisms!

The activities described took up a full morning and, if the weather held, a similar activity was organized for the afternoon in a nearby location and with different objectives. Prior to the evening meal, there were lectures on leadership and related activities. After the evening meal there were additional lectures or activities, often led by the participants themselves. The days were full and exhausting, both physically and intellectually, and no two days were even remotely

similar given the changing landscape and starkly contrasting locations. The deeper the ship went into Antarctica towards the Antarctic
Circle, the more profound the impact on individuals. That is why the
two opportunities to journal and reflect whilst on the ice took place
in the second half of the expedition. On the last day at Neko Harbour,
before turning northwards, the experience of writing a postcard to
yourself to be mailed in six months was a profound and emotional
experience for many. Not one person shunned the opportunity to sit
quietly and reflect; on the contrary, many had to be nudged to get up,
walk down the hill and return to the Zodiacs!

The elements of the leadership programme

There were three distinct leadership sessions programmed into each
day of the expedition, lasting over 10 hours. In addition, one-on-one
time was available for more specific coaching. To some extent, the content of the first two sessions could be described as structured leadership development, familiar in other programmes outside the Antarctic.
Indeed, most of the content that was delivered was taken from more
traditional leadership development. Nothing was specifically put
together for the expedition, although a unique blend of content was
curated. It was the social and physical environment, together with the
remoteness of the location, which created a very different and specific
response to the conventional leadership content.

These sessions comprised some content that was designed to help
individuals reflect on their own leadership journey, using the model
developed by the Authentic Leadership Institute. This was based
around a workbook that had to be filled in at different points. The
balance was a more experiential piece that emphasized a number
of leadership insights, together with activities to engage and extend
those insights. Its aim was to help the experience gel into real personal development and it was designed to encourage thought and
action.

The third element was a model for project initiation and planning.
It involved encouraging the participants to engage in developing their
ideas into a project that could be implemented on their return. They

had a short, high intensity time to formulate a robust idea with solid outcomes that could be 'pitched' to prospective funders at some point going forward. So the aim was to develop 'pitching' skills alongside a project planning model, which was designed to help participants take the abstract experience of the expedition into something more concrete that would be measurable and deliverable. Not everyone had a neat and tidy idea by that stage, but a surprising number had specific plans that they wanted to explore and develop once they returned. Whatever the circumstance, most participants found the model simple to implement and practical.

Across the whole expedition, there were clear designated opportunities to think, reflect and mature as a leader in and around the ship and on the ice. In other words, the first two elements of leadership development motivated participants to do something and set goals, while the third helped shape that something into a potentially viable project plan.

More detailed examination of some of the participants

An engineer from the UAE

Malek works for a large oil company. His background is engineering and he became part of a next-generation leader programme at Tisch College of Citizenship and Public Service at Tufts University in the United States. This is a celebrated course of between 20 and 30 students with massively diverse interests and backgrounds. It offers a huge support network across the globe. He was greatly influenced by the book by Jonathan Tisch called *Citizen You: Doing your part to change the world* (2010) which focuses on developing and encouraging social entrepreneur skills. Tisch is the long-serving CEO of the Loews hotel group and an active philanthropist.

Malek was committed from that programme onwards to making his contribution to change the world! He grew up in Abu Dhabi and went to Tufts without ever having seen the campus, and it created a passion for social entrepreneurship. His first college project was for a grass roots NGO. Working at the NGO sparked an interest in the environment and it prompted him to complete a PhD in this field, and this in turn led to his role at the oil company as part of the alternative energy team. So the expedition to Antarctica was a logical next step in his leadership journey and part of a coherent plan for his career.

A student from the United States

Morgan's leadership journey was made up from a number of significant events emerging from her childhood years to adulthood. For example, travelling outside the United States for the first time, her naivety was taken advantage of and she was scammed out of her travel tickets. This was in a country with which she was unfamiliar, and whose language she only spoke stutteringly.

She managed to cope, however, and work out her next steps. The whole process was harrowing but a fantastic learning experience for her. She got herself out of trouble by using the very basic Spanish she had and by seeking help.

She also had to deal with her team's disappointment when, as captain, they lost the final of a women's football competition. She learned that, at a time of bitter self-recrimination, there is a need to focus on what has been achieved rather than what has not been achieved. Positivity really helped to settle her teammates and enabled them to move on.

After taking a leadership position in her sorority she struggled, as she had made promises during the election campaign which she found she could not keep after having been elected. This taught her that she should always seek out the bigger picture, and also take a realistic view on what she was capable of before committing to anything specific.

So although one of the youngest participants, she had already considered her leadership journey and learned from critical leadership incidents and was ready to move forward and learn more. Antarctica was a dramatic leap for her and an explicit part of her leadership journey.

A consultant from Singapore

Nhan has done a number of things in her life that have had a big influence on her leadership skills and her attitude to leadership. This trip, however, offered her the most exciting opportunity yet. It convinced her of the need to believe in herself, and to trust others if she was ever going to be a leader who could make a difference. But she also learned that leadership by acclaim rather than instruction or command is the most effective kind of leadership. When she was stuck at a point on the glacier and unable to move without slipping, two people came to her aid without her ever needing to ask for help. They stepped into a leadership role and took command of the situation and offered assistance. Leaders by choice, not compulsion.

She was also impressed when the guide on a climb to the highest peak in Indonesia, after they struck very bad weather, helped each person individually and offered different support depending on the need of the individual. His leadership was effective and he rose to the challenge and proved that he was both patient, adaptable and caring. In spite of the weather the guide ensured that everyone made it to the top.

She learned a lot on this expedition about how to tell stories and engage people emotionally. During the expedition she had worked out an agenda for herself going forward after Antarctica with a series of targets. Being part of the expedition was both a consolidation of what she had learned before and a rich learning experience about leadership.

A teacher from the UK

James used the expedition to inspire him to continue his role on promoting sustainable schools with greater commitment and enthusiasm. He now feels that he has an international group of colleagues who work with him, feed him ideas and offer support. In that sense, the programme broadened his perspective and encouraged him to be ambitious and take his ideas forward with commitment and determination.

A senior NHS executive from the UK

Ghazala has been impacted greatly by the experience. The big moment of insight for her, which reinforced the impact of the expedition and made the message hit home about climate change/global warming, was seeing the giant tabular Larsson icebergs. She felt that they had powerful majestic presence and beauty. Global warming could create such presence as the icebergs broke off from glaciers and slowly floated away. Drifting past them in the half evening sun, standing on the bow was for her a deeply impressive moment. The beauty of the environment was coupled with the energy and positivity of the team. This became very infectious.

Then the experience of the leadership course really helped her work out her next steps. She is now committed to taking the sustainability issue into the heart of the NHS. She has already 'planted' the idea of including sustainability in the NHS clinical training programmes. It was met with support and will be incorporated in her NHS region. She will be presenting the same idea to the Chief Dental Officer when she makes her inaugural visit in May. She hopes that the idea will be taken up nationally, with her region acting as the pathfinder. She has also obtained funding for a year's Fellowship in Leadership and Management, dealing specifically in Sustainable Clinical Care.

This is a demanding and powerful agenda and she has started with great enthusiasm. This would not have happened without her attendance on the expedition. The pledges made on board the ship have been fully met back in the day-to-day working environment.

An elementary school teacher from the United States

Persis came with a colleague and had less than three months to fundraise for the trip – they reached out to their school business partners, family and friends to do this. They had a hard time raising the money. A lot of people said no, that they needed more time to bring the request to the 'higher ups', etc. Fortunately, they kept pursuing all their contacts and went beyond the school business partners and reached out to family and friends, and friends of friends, etc. In the end, all of the little donations they received added up to be enough for them to travel.

The motivation to go was strongly aligned to her students. She works in a deprived community school and, although there is a beach only 20 minutes away, most of her students have never been. There is

Leadership on the edge

little aspiration. When she asked her class what the best thing was about their town, they replied, 'The gas station, minimart, Wal-Mart, and Dollar General'. Her passion was to bring Antarctica to those students in order to show them what else was out there in the world.

She wanted to encourage her students to have dreams and aspirations, and then to pursue them, even if they did not know what the end result could possibly be.

On her return she began to share her experience of Antarctica with them. This made her realize just how much that journey to Antarctica could affect her kids. They were spellbound by the pictures and videos. They asked questions that shocked her – when talking about the long flight there, one student raised her hand and said 'Wait, you had to pay to go on the plane?' This prompted a teachable moment (always valuable to seize those opportunities) where she talked with the students about what ticket costs cover (fuel for the plane, maintenance, salaries, etc).

She also shared some of the stories she heard, and passed those on to the students as well. For example, sharing the story of the Himalayan town that had only just got solar power was a chance for her to help the pupils count their blessings. It led naturally to a discussion about all the things that they had to be grateful for. Her big idea she described this way:

> I hope my journey to Antarctica is helping my kids with their life journey... I hope I have opened their eyes to the world around them, that they can see that if they really want something, they need to work hard for it, and that the world is a magical place. I want them to feel as if they can make a difference... I want them to feel powerful and hopeful. I know that this journey is just beginning... to say that it was worth the effort would be an understatement. Not only was the experience itself indescribable, but the impact on my current and future students will be indescribable as well.

An oil and gas engineer from the UK

Dev's journey to Antarctica started three years ago when a dear friend returned from this expedition and announced 'it changed my life!'

That planted the seed. Bringing the expedition to reality was a combination of factors, some personal and some career-orientated. He was sold on the opportunity to surround himself with excellent people, in a truly remarkable wilderness, to discuss a topic that has always been of interest to him: climate change and sustainability. However, he was apprehensive about exactly how 12 days at sea would affect him.

When he heard Robert Swan speak for the first time at the participant welcome in Ushuaia, he felt the hairs on his arms stand up. It gave him a sense of awe and inspiration, and made him determined to immerse himself in the programme and trust that the emotional journey would lead somewhere special. He felt connected and truly present perhaps for the first time in his adult life. That enabled him to search deep inside himself to try to unravel what makes him tick. He found the presence of others very important, and the fact that he felt that he could share moments of insight with others led to an accelerated learning experience. The conversation and debate on climate change energized him. His learning journey was rich and fruitful and he felt that he had built a toolkit for the future.

He left Antarctica with a strong desire to do something different with his life. He was more comfortable showing his vulnerability and using that to connect with people at a deeper level. He also changed role. His remit now is to promote greener and more sustainable businesses with the UK government.

In addition, he has launched a campaign called 'The Great Alpine Energy Challenge' which aims to be the first bike expedition across the Alps that produces zero waste, utilizes renewable energy and promotes sustainable food systems. Dev was inspired by Antarctica but accepts that inspiration comes with a responsibility to inspire others.

Did the initial promise of change last?

I carried out some longitudinal research with the group above, and others, and asked if they had kept to their action plan or been distracted by the pressures of the day-to-day. The results were pretty impressive. As you can see from the discussion with Persis, the impact is both immediate, long-lasting and will impact on other lives.

Every person I contacted had done something, and many talked about a sense of 'obligation' having been through such a dramatic experience and of wanting to give something back as a result. There have been presentations, projects and sharing of experiences across the globe and a real sense that this is a community which continues to grow. Some on the expedition set out to do their bit to change the world. Two of the Indian contingent did something impressive in the Himalayas. Pratul Narayan Singh and Shaivya Singh Rathore set up their 'Leadership on the Hills' programme modelled and inspired by their Antarctic experiences and the work of the 2041 Foundation. They integrated four components in their month-long expedition: teaching, leadership development, community engagement and trek-king, under their motto of 'Teach. Learn. Explore.' and they persuaded 10 other volunteers to accompany them to establish and run the base camp for a month.

The learning centre was established in Biyanli in Uttarahand in the Gharwal hills of the Himalayas. They worked with the local village community and taught 60 village children computer literacy, maths and English language. The team then spent the weekends trekking in the foothills around the camp. A local teacher will staff the centre for most of the year and a local volunteer base will be established. It should become a long-term example of the legacy from the 2041 expedition.

The core and generic leadership skills that emerged from that group on the expedition were:

- courage to confront difficult things and rise to challenges;
- humility to know when to ask for help;
- agility to think much better on your feet;
- a strong sense of obligation to others and to the planet.

A feeling emerged that participants needed to earn their membership of this community by behaving in an appropriate and perhaps more selfless way.

Follow-up and conclusions

There are clear indicators of what tends to work and what does not. My focus was on trying to articulate those elements that led to enduring change in the participants. I wanted to tease out the elements that contributed to that change.

The most important 13 elements were:

1 The location and the challenges have to be authentic and take the majority of people out of their comfort zones, but to do this with a raft of support. The participants were anxious but not afraid. Trust was quickly established and it stretched from the participants to their leaders. Professionalism and trust were the watchwords for the entire expedition and they were fundamental to the overall success of the programme.

2 The experience only works when periods of reflection are deliberately in-built. Once you start this process it tends to develop its own logic. If you do not kick-start it, then it is unlikely to gain traction amongst most people and the whole event becomes task-orientated and short-term.

3 In some way leadership has to emerge, not be forced out. The leadership required when out on the ice has to align fully with the messages being delivered in the ship's classrooms. It does not matter which follows which, so much as that each aligns with the other. This means that instinct and natural choice have their own contexts, and that models and theories need to have a locus in reality to strengthen and reinforce their impact.

4 The actual model of leadership being used matters less than the context, and some overarching frames to articulate that context. For example, the concept of 1 per cent change resonated throughout the group and allowed them to take a more confident perspective on their own development. Aiming for a 1 per cent change was achievable and became a much talked about starting point to aim for. More generally it became clear on the ship that all models when delivered in context can work. So the important issue was to make the experience authentic and, in some sense, make people want to change. Once you have achieved that, individuals will choose the tools that work for them. Everything around the experience is more important than insisting on one dominant model of leadership. This is an important insight with far-reaching consequences.

5 The group needed to gel and support one another as an absolute minimum bedrock for genuine, individual change to occur. It was like building a safe space for experimentation and challenge. Without that, there would have been less learning and shallower commitments and far less honesty.

6 The emotional experience needed to emerge in order for behaviours to begin to change. And this was only possible when there was time to reflect on the experience. It was a process of taking the ideas inside and building meaning over time.

7 Everyone needed an action plan in order to process the experience and take it back into the real world. It was important, at some point, to focus on action and what happened once back into the more regular day-to-day world. The action plan needed to be prepared whilst still on the ship, to resonate and build commitment.

8 The environment did matter. The task of dealing with solitude and confronting exceptional and desolate beauty made a huge impression on everyone, and therefore played a significant role in helping people develop an openness that, in turn, made them more willing to change.

9 Reflection was a critical element of the mix. By encouraging journaling, the process of reflection came logically and was unforced. In retrospect, making time to journal, and building in quiet reflection, were important elements in encouraging a fresh perspective, personal reassessment and commitment to action.

10 Formal content was necessary but it had to align with the totality of the experience. Some elements of that content emerged from the experience itself. They fitted the context. The team realized that they should not try to control and shape that experience too much. There is a difficult balancing act between offering sufficient structured content to get people thinking differently, and giving them frames to understand what is going on. This balance is the alternative to overwhelming content that seeks to impose meaning

on the wider experience. The classroom content had to align with the strong emotional experience out on the ice.

11 The lack of communication with the outside world had the effect of throwing people together and binding the teams. With few outside distractions, the focus was, naturally, on the journey and on your team. It also allowed participants to slow down and disconnect for a few days.

12 There was a genuine, tangible element of discomfort and risk. Antarctica is an inherently dangerous place. This encouraged people to treat the environment with respect and awe. It also threw people into tight groups who needed to support and help one another. One very quick storm, caused by the katabatic winds (Weather Online) that blow up very fast from nowhere and with little advanced warning, was a powerful reminder that the environment was not benign and should never be taken for granted. The support shown in adversity had a marked impact on the groups. Support was always given freely without anyone having to ask. In straightened circumstances, the stronger or the more experienced immediately offered their help to the less confident or those struggling.

13 There is real evidence that well-chosen and well-structured experiences in a special environment actually lead to conditions where accelerated learning can take place. But the environment alone will not do it. Structure needs to be applied and care needs to be taken to build a genuinely challenging intellectual as well as physical environment. Experiences need to be processed and internalized to make real sense and to contribute to lasting change.

The best conclusion, and a new perspective, came from one of the participants: 16-year-old Payton Sierra. She lives on the Pine Ridge Indian Reservation in South Dakota and, before winning an award for her writing that led to the adventure to Antarctica, she had never left the United States and only visited three other US states previously. This extract from her poem sums up both her experience and that of 120 people from 40 different countries:

This boat...
It holds the world.
So many different countries and people,
Different cultures and belief systems. ...
So we're meeting new people,
Learning new things;
And creating our own paths. ...
The switch of determination is on.
And this light that we are all creating will burn so bright,
That eventually the world will have to pay attention.

Payton Sierra, 16 years old, Pine Ridge Indian
Reservation

References

Foundation 2041 (2016) Website, 2041.com

Swan, R (2009) *Antarctica 2041: My quest to save the earth's last wilderness*, Broadway Books, New York, NY

Tisch, J (2010) *Citizen You: Doing your part to change the world*, Crown Publishers, New York, NY

Weather Online, Katabatic wind (from the Greek: katabaino – to go down) is the generic term for downslope winds flowing from high elevations of mountains, plateaus, and hills down their slopes to the valleys or plains below, www.weatheronline.co.uk/reports/wxfacts/Katabatic-winds.htm

Rethinking executive leadership development

DeakinPrime

The context

DeakinPrime is a subsidiary of Deakin University, which is one of Victoria's key Universities with primary campuses in Geelong and Melbourne. The focus and function of DeakinPrime is to leverage the expertise of the university for the benefit of the private sector primarily in Victoria. A key element of this is to offer leadership development and other executive programmes including technical skills for the financial services industry on a tailor-made basis. It is run by Chief Executive Simon Hann.

DeakinPrime, like any university offering executive development, worked in a relatively traditional way. The programmes used external experts and Deakin Business school staff to offer a mix of lecture and discussion over a few days to focus on the key areas of development such as strategy, leadership, marketing, etc. DeakinPrime decided to shake up its offering and move into a new mode of working that would better meet the needs of existing and new clients. So this was a university remaking itself and rethinking not just how executive development was delivered but the purpose behind it. It therefore finds an appropriate place in this book as an illustration of what can be achieved if you listen to customers and adjust your offering to meet the changing world of business. This new approach, however, did not come out of the blue but emerged as a happy congruence of three elements that were by no means unique to Deakin University. And it was that congruence that made the need to move forward so compelling.

Firstly, they had undertaken research on effective design for L&D programmes including leadership development. This had given them some ideas on different approaches and tuned them into what was going on outside Deakin. If more effective models were being developed that challenged the way things were delivered in DeakinPrime, then in many ways it would be foolish to not work with this newly acquired knowledge. This research emerged at the time when there was more general discussion about the outcomes of previous more conventional leadership development programmes and the feeling that they could do more and get better results. There was real incentive to move forward and some excitement that they could do something, in their terms, that was innovative and mould-breaking.

Secondly, the prominence of the 70:20:10 model offered the chance to apply that blend of learning in situ, with stretch assignments and coaching support, to an entirely new programme. The great achievement of the 70:20:10 model is that it is not a prescription about what you have to do, but a challenge to use all your resources to focus on one learning goal, and extend its impact and effectiveness. In a new book by Jos Arets, Vivian Heijnen and Charles Jennings (2015) the authors explain 70:20:10 and outline its significance:

> 70:20:10 is a descriptive reference model, showing that learning is a result of working (roughly around 70 per cent) and with others (roughly 20 per cent) and is not limited to training (roughly 10 per cent). It's simply a way of describing how adults learn at work. (Arets, Heijnen, and Jennings, 2015: 36)

70:20:10 reflects how people learn in the real world, not as a series of abstract ratios, but more as a statement of the way we interact and the way work is changing. The practice of work is increasingly a learning experience that requires us to engage with colleagues or resources to make sense and make decisions. To say that learning is mostly from work and from others – sometimes completely informally, and sometimes using structured models like forums or communities of practice – is increasingly uncontentious. Exploiting these processes makes the actual time in the classroom (whether face-to-face or online) far more productive and effective.

Finally, the arrival of new technology applications offered the chance to deliver something that was a better mixture of face-to-face and online learning, and created the opportunity to extend that more coherently into a model that could build true personal learning into the mix.

The big idea behind this initiative was to design a new kind of bespoke programme that was more clearly focused on what went on in the workplace and that would promote lasting change. It meant a complete rethink of the way that DeakinPrime approached the development of a leadership programme.

The unique opportunity that presented itself was a programme targeted at a group of 120 senior staff in Deakin University. A review had indicated key leadership competences that needed to be improved as a matter of urgency. The review showed that there were a number of significant gaps in this group's leadership approach, and the group's basic management techniques also needed to be improved. The cohort comprised both academic as well as general staff.

This group was willing to try a new approach and the university was prepared to fund the programme. This happy coincidence meant that they had all they needed to do something completely different to meet an identified need. The new programme was launched in June 2015 and has made steady progress since then.

What is different?

There was a real drive to do something different. This was based on two key perceptions. The first emerged from the availability of large amounts of research – some quoted in this book – that indicated fairly unambiguously that the vast majority of leadership development programmes failed because, in spite of rave reviews from participants, they did not actually deliver sustained change. This spurred on DeakinPrime to deliver a programme that was focused on building permanent change in the participants which, in turn, could offer

DeakinPrime an entirely new way of building and delivering bespoke content. The second was the knowledge that what they delivered traditionally really rose to the challenge of helping leaders deal with an increasingly uncertain and volatile external environment. These two elements dominated their thoughts and helped rethink what they should offer and how it should be delivered.

There were a number of fundamental differences in approach between what they did this time and what had happened previously. In the previous model, they built learning programmes which were very much content-focused and content-driven. Most of the planning and discussion was around determining the appropriate content. And when it was delivered, everyone experienced the same content at the same time. There was no choice – people sat through content that could be highly relevant or almost totally irrelevant. Because of the nature of the delivery model – people sitting in the seminar room listening to a presenter – there was nothing that could be done about this. The assumption was always that most of the content would be useful to most of the participants for most of the time. This is a not uncommon approach and a limitation of conventional delivery. Indeed, most of the content was delivered in those kind of face-to-face workshops. There were, however, a few opportunities for very conventional e-learning which was not core and delivered mostly at the fringes of the programme. The only online experience on offer was conventional e-learning. Learning was, clearly, completely separate from the day-to-day work and any relevant linkages had to be constructed by the learner. It was also designed so that the sole focus was on the individual participant with very little team or group work.

The new approach aimed to turn this on its head. The focus was on personalized learning based on individual goals and needs. The participants themselves defined much of the content, and the delivery was varied and blended. It also reached directly back into the workplace where a concerted effort was made to encourage the line managers of all the participants to offer intense on-the-job support during and after the programme, to ensure that the learning was in context and that permanent change could emerge. The content was in much smaller chunks and delivered regularly to learners. Much of this was not created for this programme but curated from their own and other open learning resources that were available freely outside the university.

The emphasis shifted from learning in the classroom to learning at work, and from doing to the learners to doing with the learners. And there were many online technologies using both synchronous and asynchronous techniques to facilitate learning in the workplace and to align with day-to-day work issues. So discussion forums, based around problems and challenges, plus webinars focusing on specific topics, punctuated the delivery of resources. The key emphasis was not on pulling people out of work into the classroom but to build an enduring online community that could offer mutual support and expert input. In this way, learning was integrated into the workflow and the biggest emphasis was on the group's ability to solve its own problems collectively with or without help.

This can be summed up below:

Previous model:

- content-focused and content-driven;
- no choice of content;
- all learners experience the same programme at the same time;
- content is delivered in face-to-face workshops;
- the only online activity was conventional e-learning modules;
- learning separate from the day-to-day job;
- sole focus on the individual with little team or group work.

New approach:

- personalized learning based on individual goals and needs;
- participants define much of the content;
- blended and varied delivery;
- line manager support for all participants;
- bite-sized, curated content delivered regularly;
- emphasis on 'on-the-job' learning;
- multiple use of online methodologies with webinars and discussion forums;
- an enduring online community built;

- learning integrated into the workflow;
- focus on the group, not the individual.

These design principles led to two very specific outcomes that had been articulated from the beginning and were core to the programme. The first was an emphasis on behaviour change for the participants. Emphasis was put on working with each participant to identify their personal learning goals at the outset of the programme. These plans were expressed in terms of behaviours that the participant wanted to change. There was, however, space built into the programme to address emerging needs as the programme progressed.

The second outcome was that the group was required to work on organization-specific 'wicked problems' that would lead to positive organizational change. Action Learning Projects were set up that targeted each organization-specific 'wicked problem'. This term was first used by Keith Grint to describe problems that are not susceptible to solutions by 'experts', ie they are complex and there are no correct answers (Grint, 2005: 1467–94)

The purpose of this was, on the one hand, to get the group to feel that they could change the organization for the better, not just change themselves; and on the other, to develop a process for dealing with thorny problems inside the institution, as a model going forward.

The core principles

The underpinning model behind the programme was adaptive leadership (Heifetz, Grashow and Linsky, 2009). The idea was to help leaders respond flexibly and creatively to the changes in their environment and recognize that change and leadership were inextricably bound together in contemporary institutions, and increasingly shaped the nature of work. The second dominant design principle was the explicit recognition that the whole working environment that leaders faced in Deakin University and elsewhere was chaotic and overwhelming. Existing development had not addressed that changing work environment or offered much support to leaders to deal with it. The programme had to offer leaders a new approach or mindset to be able to cope with it.

The mindset change required was identified as a shift from a fixed mindset to an adaptive mindset. The theory of fixed and adaptive mindsets was first set out by Carol Dweck in her research of young children. It has been widely adapted and applied in other contexts. (Dweck, 2010: 16–20). This focus was therefore on developing the participants' ability to respond to change positively and to cope with complex and changing demands on them. The aim was to encourage the organization, not only to be more flexible and react more positively towards change, but also to build skills in the participants to respond with a greater flexibility of approach to the issues that they confronted.

> It matters whether people believe that their core qualities are fixed by nature (an entity theory, or fixed mindset) or whether they believe that their qualities can be developed (an incremental theory, or growth mindset)… I show that an emphasis on growth not only increases intellectual achievement but can also advance conflict resolution between long-standing adversaries. (Dweck, 2012: 614–22)

The fourth principle was that the programme would be practical as well as theoretical. The programme needed both leadership and management elements. In other words it covered both the whys as well as the hows, and the opportunity was provided throughout the programme for practical implementation of ideas and tools in the workplace. Therefore, there was a specific and consistent attempt to narrow the gap between learning and work and give participants the opportunity to test out the theory in practice, and then report back to their colleagues or line manager.

Structure and critical success factors

Core research on adaptive mindsets was used to define and structure the programme. That initial research identified the six critical success factors for the programme. They form a neat framework for this programme but also the many others inside and outside DeakinPrime.

The six are: behaviour change, personalization, contextualization, experimentation and reflection, reinforcement and, finally, collaboration.

The focus on behaviour change is to ensure that participants modify their practice, and ensure that this change lasts longer than the duration programme. Contextualization is around framing the programme in the real world of work that the participants experience on a day-to-day basis. Experimentation links to reflection. It was seen as important for the participants to build in time and be encouraged to try out new ways of working and reflect on their success or otherwise. Generally developing the habit of reflection as part of their leadership practice was a deliberate core outcome of the programme.

The process of continual reinforcement was designed to ensure that changes in work practice became habitual. It was also an underpinning design principle that all the components of the programme aligned and reinforced one another. This coherence tended to encourage more permanent changes in behaviour. The programme was built around the concept of deep collaboration between colleagues. If one of the outcomes of the programme was to successfully develop a strategy for tackling some of the core wicked problems that affected the university, then this had to be achieved through partnership and collaboration. It was also hoped that, once these pathways were established, they would become a permanent way of working and allow more rapid solutions to emerging problems. If this way of working proved successful, then the resulting practice would allow teams to work together to help each other achieve their individual goals and targets, as well as improve the organization as a whole.

The programme was divided into five core phases:

1. Initiation phase

This was when the context for the programme was established. The core business strategy was defined, and sponsorship for the programme at the most senior levels in the organization was sought. In this phase the importance of achieving the '70' component of the 70:20:10 model was stressed (Paine, 2014: 61–74). This is the 'experience' element, where learning takes place during the course of work. The basic discussion was about how the programme and its learning could be firmly incorporated into the daily work rhythm of the participants. This was fundamental to the structure and approach for the whole development, and emerged before a single piece of content had been developed or conceived.

Specific tasks included setting up meetings with key stakeholders in order to explain the context, and analysing the challenges to gain commitment to the programme as a whole. In addition, a number of HR workshops were run to explain the aims of the programme and solicit support for the endeavour. A half-day seminar for the entire University Executive Team was also organized in order to gain insight into the challenges that the group faced, to allow their free comment and discussion on the way that the programme might develop, as well as to gain their commitment to proceed. 'Welcome' videos were created alongside a campaign that was aimed at committing senior executives to the programme.

2. Discovery phase

In this phase, the needs of each participant as well as the profile of the group were worked out. A participant survey was also carried out as a basic needs analysis and a scoping exercise for the programme as a whole. A whole raft of 360-degree feedback exercises were organized together with detailed debriefing for each participant to formulate both individual and group profiles. These had a positive focus, encouraging the recipients to move forward and build an adaptive mindset, ie see the feedback as helpful data to establish an individual change agenda, rather than react negatively to what could be seen as personal criticism. These first two phases lasted for one month.

3. Engagement phase

This was when the participants created their own personal mastery plan. This phase lasted one month as well. Essentially each participant looked at the feedback they had received, and their own agenda that they wanted to work on during the programme, and built their own plan of learning. They looked at personal outcomes which would determine whether the programme was a success for them, and thought deeply about their own work context and what support they might require to achieve their aims. To help this process, a one-day workshop was organized for participants with three core aims: to help with the self-assessment of practical skills; to work out a Personal Mastery Plan (PMP) in order to develop an adaptive mindset; and to focus on practical skill development. Finally, a calibration session was organized to look at the overall scope and structure of the PMPs and ensure that they were fit for purpose and achievable in the time frame.

4. Action phase

This is the heart of the programme and lasted six months. The focus was not on content but on changing habits and mindset. This was locked in with new skill development. Integral to the success of this phase were six small group coaching sessions. The aim of these sessions was to build a strong individual commitment to trying out new things at work and learning from their outcomes, but undertaking this as a shared experience with colleagues and soliciting help and support if necessary. In this phase strong relationships were established with colleagues, and a number of new ideas were explored that could assist work-based experiments and help to ensure better outcomes.

It was important during this phase that individuals defined and reinforced their commitment to the group as a whole. These small group sessions helped establish the collective will to change and share the experience of change that the new approaches created. Throughout this phase, content was delivered in small chunks. The content focused on key leadership competences such as how to influence others. The programme ran in monthly cycles. Every month there was one small group coaching session and then a combination of webinars, simulations, discussion forums and curated content, followed by diploma units for those who wished to pursue a qualification from the programme.

In addition, on a weekly basis, there were coffee and self-reflection sessions that ran alongside the action learning projects and peer coaching sessions, where groups shared problems and challenges and coached and supported each other. The programme also established cross-project team buddies. Meeting your buddy was an opportunity to review your progress and discuss the outcomes of the learning in an informal way. Some of these elements, such as peer coaching and the buddy system, continued into the next phase.

5. Super charge phase

This was the final phase and was designed to last 12 months. This is where the learning was embedded and mastery of new skills and approaches occurred. Participants were mandated to build in regular reflection sessions on their own, as well as seek to work as a more effective senior management team. This is where action learning sets were established alongside the more regular management meetings. The groups worked on organizational problems as well as individual change agendas. Each participant's line manager had a key role in this phase. Essentially the line manager had a critical role to ensure that the changes that had been discussed and worked on in the previous phase became embedded in new work processes and practices.

The programme therefore concentrated on organizational change, built around personal development agendas and more effective leadership. To achieve this, a relatively large budget of around A$800,000 (US$500,000) was required. The budget took account of the fact that it was funding not just a single leadership programme but an entire remodelling of executive leadership development. The outcomes of those processes would therefore stretch beyond this initiative and into an entirely new way of looking at bespoke executive development. In some ways then, this was an investment in re-engineering the way that DeakinPrime tackled one of its most important work streams. The whole process involved learning an entirely new philosophy and approach to leadership development, not as a theoretical model but as a practical working example.

The programme had the entire senior management team from the university as participants (with the exception of the vice chancellor) and the cohort was challenged to address six of the most 'wicked' problems that the university faced. The action learning sets that were set up for this purpose had between 12 and 15 participants, with a deliberately diverse membership drawn from right across the cohort. One intended by-product of this process was to fracture the departmental silos and help participants see that they could contribute to solving whole university challenges. They were encouraged to work on building the university as a whole, rather than simply their part of it. This created a genuinely cooperative atmosphere and increased the sense that what went on in the university as a whole affected everybody and was also the responsibility of everyone to manage.

The course was built around cohorts of 25 members. Each cohort was divided into coaching groups of five, and larger action learning sets of 12 to 15. So some elements of the programme were delivered as full cohorts. The coaching groups were small focused teams where members probably got closest to their colleagues. This was balanced with individual learning, and the larger action learning sets that moved the focus from personal agendas to university-wide issues.

The delivery was a combination of external consultants and facilitators together with top learning experts. All those working on the programme were briefed on the overall shape and the desired outcomes. Just as the participants were encouraged to take responsibility for university-wide issues as well as their own departmental or individual tasks, those teaching or facilitating on the programme were required to think about the programme as a whole, and align with it, rather than simply focus on their own specific area of expertise. Everyone involved in delivering or managing the programme was encouraged to be part of a coherent design and delivery strategy. This was time-consuming but critical to the success of the programme which had to appear completely aligned. This meant that much more time was allocated to the design phase and the building of appropriate activities for the groups than is normally the case in leadership programmes, where the emphasis is on getting the content right, rather than the process of learning.

In addition to this, regular pulse checks were built in to ensure that the programme was on track. The outcomes were shared with participants to encourage a co-creation model and to build in their commitment to make it work. The evidence of success and emerging challenges is constantly gathered so that DeakinPrime has a pretty clear idea of how the programme is working. Structure allows for modifications en route. So it is always dynamic and relevant. However, a formal evaluation will be carried out at some point that will focus on the enduring impact and permanent changes that have occurred in the organization as a result.

What is already clear is the fact that personalization and contextualization were very high priorities for the programme, which increased the motivation of the participants and their perception of the value that they took from it. It was made to feel as if it were 'just for me' and 'just in time'.

It is noticeable that a new terminology has emerged into common parlance in the university as a result of this programme. For example staff talk regularly about 'wicked problems' and 'leadership for the greater good'. This represents a tangible shift in organizational culture. The conscious focus on leadership has improved decision-making and staff motivation and engagement. In many ways, the process of witnessing the senior management in the organization trying hard to be more effective leaders creates a positive atmosphere in itself.

In addition, the throwing together of staff from quite different parts of the organization, eg academic and administrative staff, has built strong cross-university partnerships, and has resulted in interesting conversations around the university as well as generating imaginative solutions to some of the problems that the university faces. There is also evidence that the methodology used in the programme is now being picked up and used by participants with their own teams. The open nature of the programme, and the bite-sized resources used, make it ideal for this purpose. Small elements of content can be used in discussion and development because they are easy to extract from the programme as a whole.

Outcomes

There were a number of outcomes directly attributed to the programme which indicate that it was achieving its core purpose. Setting out to identify personal learning goals and getting commitment from the individual learners to deliver on those goals led, in some cases, to marked behaviour change. And certainly noticeable changes in behaviour were picked up by direct reports and therefore reverberated through the university as a whole.

Tackling significant organizational challenges through the use of action learning sets changed staff attitudes. Instead of being overwhelmed by complex problems, there was a better 'can do' attitude amongst most senior staff. The process of working on significant challenges during the programme encouraged the same people to tackle new, emerging problems when they arose rather than wait until they became disruptive.

The biggest change, however, was the alignment and integration of those two processes. For the first time, perhaps, individual leadership change reflected and reinforced changes in the organization, and change in the organization, in turn, reinforced the need for leaders to change. This was perfect symbiosis and an enormously enduring outcome which will help the institution adapt to the challenges of the next 10 years and ensure that staff in the institution embrace that change in a positive way. This is a remarkable achievement.

Core lessons to take away

1 If you want different outcomes for your learning programmes then you have to build a different way of learning. It is as simple and stark as that. In other words, tinkering does not necessarily work. In this case the programme team began with the end in mind and worked backwards. Almost every aspect of the programme was changed from the model they had used previously. The result was that much more time was spent in the preparation and development stage, and the participants were much more involved in defining what they wanted. This required a totally different relationship with the target group. They had to be willing to work hard on what they wanted, and trust that the development team would deliver on that.

2 A focus on behaviour and culture change cannot be developed by programmes that only focus on the individual rather than the group or the organization. A large part of the process for

individual change required strong teams, and a focus on the organization. This was because individual commitment and empowerment emerged and was sustained by the group processes. In some ways, it is counter-intuitive that the group focus led to individual change. But this is an important lesson.

3 The establishment of self-managed groups that supported each member and work on organizational and individual challenges is an enduring outcome from this programme. Post-programme, the groups and the bonds that held them together endured. This required careful engineering. The coaching groups, for example, were kept small so that each member could be given individual attention and the group dynamic could develop. The action learning sets, on the other hand, were kept large in order to gather together a diversity of view-points, and to encourage a number of options and a broad debate.

4 It is possible to make leadership development more about changing mindset and changing the organization, and less about a focus on the individual in isolation. Many of the outcomes were due to group empowerment and the momentum that was developed. If it is clear that things are changing around you, it is harder to resist and opt out. If the focus is only on individuals in isolation, it is easier to disengage.

5 Getting early buy-in from the top of the organization is critical for success. The commitment of the entire senior team, but especially the sponsorship of the vice chancellor, was of lasting significance. This programme defied expectation about what a leadership programme might look like, and the increasing time on the initiation phase needed continued commitment and support. Once the programme started, it was that sponsorship that ensured the engagement of line managers and the agreement to implement the organizational changes recommended.

6 The powerful learning emerged from group members and the developers, not external teachers. There was a management team that kept control of the programme at all times. They invited the external faculty to work with them and buy in to the logic of the programme as a whole and not cede responsibility to those

external providers. It was important for the organization to retain control. Ultimately, the programme had to meet the expectations of the sponsors, and the developers had to continue to be involved from the beginning to the end. The use of pulse checks on a regular basis ensured that the development group remained in touch with the reality of the programme.

7 Building trust between participants was essential. That was the only way that those on the programme would open up and make commitments to change and spend time supporting each other. But the trust relationship extended to the programme sponsors as well. Their willingness to go with a new approach and give it time to work was important. This also meant that the individual participants took shared responsibility for the success of the programme as well. The organizers managed to get away from the idea that this was something being done to people and built an environment where there was a kind of collective responsibility.

8 The course had to remain aligned with the reality of the working environment of the university at all times. It was important to reflect back to the participants what had been achieved at each stage, and vital for the organization as a whole to acknowledge progress. This was particularly true for the action learning sets. When big organizational change decisions were agreed, not only was acknowledgement required, but there also had to be agreement, above all, on speedy implementation of those solutions.

9 Coaching – in this case in small groups – was essential to the success of the programme. This was where thorny issues were debated and where commitment to change was negotiated. The small coaching cohorts grew stronger and more effective as the programme progressed. Without them the programme would have lost momentum, trust relationships would not have been established so quickly, and the outcomes would have been less significant.

10 It is always difficult to get buy-in by line managers. In this case their direct involvement was an integral part of the structure and process. You could argue that behaviour change would not have occurred to anything like the degree that it did without their

commitment to work with their direct reports. Only with protracted use, and on-going change, did what occurred on the programme become habitual. The fact that line managers cared made a disproportionate difference in terms of the time that was allocated. This meant that when the action plans were drawn up by the participants, they knew that represented a quasi-contract between them and their managers. It revealed a commitment to deliver and a commitment to change. The fulfilment of the plan and the ensuing noticeable change was at the heart of the programme delivery. Without this it could have fallen apart. The consequent discussions between participant and line manager took that relationship onto a different level that was sustained beyond the programme.

References

Arets, J, Heijnen, V and Jennings, C (2015) *70:20:10: Towards 100% performance*, Sutler Media, Maastricht

Dweck, C S (2010) Even Geniuses Work Hard, *Educational Leadership*, **68** (1), pp 16–20

Dweck, C S (2012) Mindsets and human nature: promoting change in the Middle East, the schoolyard, the racial divide, and willpower, *American Psychologist*, **67** (8), pp 614–22

Grint, K (2005) Problems, problems, problems: the social construction of 'leadership', *Human Relations*, **58** (11), pp 1467–94

Heifetz, R A, Grashow, A and Linsky, M (2009) *The Practice of Adaptive Leadership: Tools and tactics for changing your organization and the world*, Harvard Business School Publishing, Boston, MA

Paine, N (2014) *The Learning Challenge: Dealing with technology, innovation and change in learning and development*, Kogan Page, London

Leadership as a catalyst for change

05

The example of the NHS

The context

Leadership development programmes have traditionally been single mode delivery. They are mostly classroom based, continue outside the workplace and require each person to move through the programme lock-step. There are many reasons why this model is no longer fit for purpose (Corporate Research Forum Report (Pillans), 2015), and there is now evidence of alternative models that blend different modes of learning. These are beginning to gain traction and often deliver more impressive outcomes.

If you search through leadership development programmes delivered in companies large and small, it is almost impossible to find single mode delivery systems, ie comprising one type of learning for the entire programme, with no variation in style or approach (Osguthorpe and Graham, 2003: 227–33). The vast majority of them offer a combination of methodologies and media mixing, perhaps lectures combined with small group work, one-on-one coaching and detailed case study work. So why include a chapter that appears to state the obvious, ie that learning (and leadership development is included here under that generic umbrella) is usually a mixture of modes and therefore is mostly blended!?

The answer is partly about quantity but mostly about quality. Above all, however, it is about impact. If you take a pretty traditional three-day face-to-face leadership programme that suggests articles to read, either pre- or post-programme, it could be argued that this is 'blended learning'. This same th   gramme might well include: a formal lecture, some discus   content and then a small group exercise that offers s   d skill development. You may argue that this is a 'blen.   Boone, 2015: 275–83). If we pursue this logic, we are re   ncept of blended learning to a meaningless catch-all term tl.   -defined that it ceases to be useful. It is important, therefore, to   h specific and clear about what is meant by the term, and why i.   till valid and useful. If you want to use leadership development to : transformational change, then the nature of what you blend and how you blend it together is extremely important.

The literature on blended learning is huge. Most of the discussion centres on university-based academic programmes. If, however, we focus on texts that look at blended learning in the workplace, a more valuable definition is available than one that focuses only on university undergraduate degree programmes. An early protagonist is the 2005 e-book *The Blended Learning Cookbook* by Clive Shepherd. He later produced a 2008 edition and then a hard copy version in 2011. That in itself indicates some enduring value!

In the first chapter of this book, Shepherd defines blended learning as 'a mixture of e-learning and traditional methods' but acknowledges that 'this definition is unhelpfully restrictive... about so-called "traditional" methods' (Shepherd, 2005: 14). He revises the definition for the 2008 edition to amplify the variety of options in the blended mix:

> A blended learning solution combines education and training methods within different social contexts for learning (self-study, one-to-one, group) with the aim of increasing learning effectiveness. It may also mix the learning media used to deliver the solution (face-to-face, online, offline, etc) as a way to optimize the efficiency of the solution. These choices are made in response to particular learning requirements and audience characteristics, as well as practical constraints and opportunities. (Shepherd, 2008: 16)

This is a good working definition that has stood the test of time and will form the basis for the discussion around blended learning in this chapter. Shepherd uses his words carefully. He talks about increasing 'learning effectiveness' and 'optimizing the efficiency' of learning.

This is a mix of pragmatism, ie overcoming practical constraints of budget or time and place, together with opportunity; in other words, creating an effective mix of methods that focuses on getting the outcomes you set out to achieve. This is an important point: if you want to change people or change organizations, then you have to consider the learning methodology and approach extremely carefully.

The focus of this chapter will be on a practical example of a suite of leadership programmes that have amplified the learning effectiveness and impact of leadership development by consciously selecting a combination of methodologies and media in such a way as to maximize the impact of the learning and consolidate the effect on the organization. Good design should also take account of the specific circumstances of different learners or groups of learners, and enhance both their ability to learn and the scope of the impact of their learning. Recognizing those two constraints – the need to increase the impact of learning and the ripple effect of the learning from individual to organization, and doing this in a way that takes account of the circumstances of different target groups – is at the heart of many development decisions. Therefore, the concept of blended learning, as defined here, is relevant and helpful in thinking through the process of developing leadership programmes that achieve what they set out to deliver.

The best leadership programmes focus on maximizing impact and therefore choosing models and approaches that achieve this end. They also have to be built in a way that allows appropriate access to the target group, and aligns with how and where they work.

A good example of the way this is done is embodied in the huge, five-stage leadership programmes being run by the NHS Leadership Academy in the UK. These programmes are delivered by a number of partners who vary according to programme. Two of the core programmes, the Elizabeth Garrett Anderson Programme, leading to a master's degree, and the more advanced senior management programme, the Nye Bevan Programme, are run as a partnership between the NHS Leadership Academy and a consortium led by consultancy firm KPMG. There are an additional three programmes: one that is self-paced and online and introduces the basic concepts of leadership, a second that caters for the newly appointed or aspiring leader led by the Hay Group and an aspiring chief executive programme. All programmes deliberately recruit and partner partici-pants from the administrative side with their colleagues on the clinical side. This traditional divide in healthcare systems was consciously bridged in these programmes at every level.

NHS Leadership Academy programmes

I met with Louise Scott-Worrall, who led the consortium that co-designed and co-delivered the Nye Bevan and the Elizabeth Garrett Anderson programmes, and I received input from Karen Lynas who is the Interim Managing Director of the NHS Leadership Academy. The two programmes are run in strong partnership between the two individuals and their organizations and form part of the five-step leadership development programmes on offer.

Karen is a long-serving NHS senior officer with vast experience of how the NHS works. She joined the NHS through the Graduate Management Training Scheme. Louise is in charge of the KPMG-led consortium responsible for implementing the second two programmes of the leadership initiative on behalf of the NHS Leadership Academy. She is herself a former NHS practitioner and was trained as a podia-trist with expertise in biomechanics. She started in higher education training student podiatrists. That proved to be her stepping stone into KPMG where she joined their further and higher education team. She transitioned into the 'world class skills' area and contributed her spe-cialist healthcare knowledge to that team.

In 2013, Louise set up a bid team to respond to a request for tenders to establish the NHS Leadership Academy's academically accredited leadership programmes. The tender was in direct response to the recommendations of the Francis Report (2013) which had examined the extensive failings of the mid-Staffordshire NHS trust and made 290 recommendations, many of which had pan-NHS implications. This is explained in more detail later in this chapter. The Report had demanded the dramatic improvement in leadership to combat some of its core findings. The Report exposed a negative culture in the Trust that led to professional disengagement, poor governance and no forum for the voice of the patient, which in turn led to a lack of focus on standards of service and the wrong priorities. The Francis Report was a significant lever for the leadership initiative.

Essentially the report pointed to a whole system failure, and contained broad recommendations aimed right across the NHS. Better leadership was one element that required significant attention.

The idea behind the five leadership programmes, together with a continuing professional development for the most senior leaders in the NHS, was to create a professional cadre of leaders who would inspire and impact across the whole of the service, whether in a clinical or a non-clinical context. The hope was that, as numbers of alumni grew, the programmes would transform human resource practices in the NHS and lead to better communication, greater innovation, increased efficiency and higher job satisfaction. The achievement of these aims would lead directly to an increase in the quality of the patient experience – the ultimate outcome. This whole endeavour was extraordinarily ambitious.

The report argued that the issues in hand did not require a wholesale reorganization of the Trust or the NHS, but a 're-emphasis of what is truly important'. It listed these overarching priorities in the report's executive summary as the need to focus on building a commitment to common values throughout the system by all who worked within it. This required readily accessible, fundamental standards, together with a clear understanding of what compliance entailed. This meant, at the very least, no tolerance for non-compliance and the rigorous policing of those fundamental standards.

In addition, the report demanded openness, transparency and candour in all the system's business. This required strong leadership in nursing, together with strong support for leadership roles and a level playing field in terms of accountability. This meant that performance information had to be accessible and usable by all, which would allow effective comparison of performance by individuals, services and organization (Francis Report, 2013: 66).

The report emphasized the fundamental need to change the culture of the NHS and embed a clear set of values for all staff. In addition, there was an identified need to encourage much more cooperation and mutual support between clinical and non-clinical staff, hence the decision to recruit from both 'sides' of the NHS and set up mixed cohorts.

There was also a specific recommendation (recommendation 214) that called on the government to establish a leadership college to raise the standards of leadership across the NHS as a whole. This recommendation was part of a suite of eight recommendations that linked leadership with the need to establish a common culture and values.

The government's response to the report was outlined less than a year after the Francis Report. This was in the form of a publication entitled *Hard Truths: The journey to putting patients first* (Department of Health, 2014). This report accepted the conclusions of the Francis Inquiry and agreed to the implementation of all its recommendations. It responded to the leadership recommendation by saying, amongst other things:

> The role of training and of leadership development is critical in both reinforcing the expected standards, and in supporting staff to address issues within their own practice. In addition to formal training, it is vital to recognize that one of the most powerful means by which all staff providing care learn how to behave, is by observing the behaviour of others. The behaviour modelled by leaders and peers is very often the most powerful source of what is or is not acceptable. (Department of Health, 2014: volume 1, 93)

The commentary on recommendation 214 in Volume 2 of the government response accepted the recommendation in full.

The NHS Leadership Academy, supported by NHS England, responded to the recommendation by developing a leadership model for the NHS and a suite of development programmes, tools and interventions to support a change in culture in NHS leadership through a national network of local delivery partners. It researches and champions the professionalization of leadership.

The Academy provides a suite of programmes, some academically accredited, which map against a leadership career, irrespective of professional background. This establishes the need for prior training and development before applying for significant and vital senior roles, and creates an expectation of sufficient experience, knowledge and a minimum level of academic achievement for leadership roles. The Academy works with partners and in-house experts on developing a model for leadership, based on research evidence and best practice (Department of Health, 2014: volume 2, 183).

At the time when the reports were published, the NHS had no real concept of what was required to be a great leader. And there was a huge gap between NHS Boards and the operational management, which also needed to be bridged. This was the general conclusions from both the Francis Report and the government's response. Subsequently, NHS England re-published the NHS Constitution for England (first published in 2009), which contained the six values of the NHS (NHS Constitution, 2015: 5).

They are:

- working together for patients;
- respect and dignity for all;
- commitment to quality of care;
- compassion;
- improving lives;
- everyone counts.

They embody a widespread commitment to how leaders should behave. The values define a strong leadership ethos based on strong communication, respect for colleagues and customers, improving the customer (patient) experience, and raising standards of service across the whole organization. They could apply to any organization if the words were tweaked slightly.

The Inquiry also organized seven 'Forward Look' seminars. These were stakeholder debates examining key themes emerging from the Inquiry and seeking a more local perspective on them. They covered areas such as 'Patient Experience', 'Methods of Regulation', 'Organizational Culture' and 'Training and Development of Trust Leaders and Managers'. The latter brought together a group of around 40 participants, by invitation, chosen for their 'personal experience and insights' (Harvey, 2011: 12).

The seminar concluded that people in first-line management roles needed more support than they currently received, and that better preparation was required for executive directors, including those in their first CEO posts. In addition, it was agreed that a network of informal support was necessary for senior leaders, and better opportunities were required to share leadership and management development tools and approaches. This would all require ongoing investment in training and development (Harvey, 2011: 36–37).

The seminar findings reinforced the Francis Report recommendation on leadership. In order to fulfil the Inquiry recommendation, an invitation to tender was issued for a leadership programme development that would work closely with, and be led by, the NHS Leadership Academy (which had been established in 2012). This response was later accepted by the government in its commentary on the report in *Hard Truths* (Department of Health, 2014: 183).

KPMG assembled a team that had NHS, KPMG consultancy and academic experience and that understood the requisite NHS values. Their bid was successful and they were appointed in March 2013. The KPMG-led consortium team reported to Karen Lynas, the then Deputy and now Interim Managing Director of the NHS Leadership Academy.

The KPMG team co-developed and now co-deliver two of the core leadership programmes.

The NHS leadership suite of programmes

At the time of writing there are five NHS Leadership Academy professional leadership programmes and one continuing networking programme. The first programme is called the *Edward Jenner Programme*. It is named after the distinguished scientist Edward Jenner (1749–1823) who developed the smallpox vaccine and is known as the father of immunology. This programme builds leadership foundations. It is entirely self-paced and on open access for all who want to develop their core leadership skills. Content is free to access and delivered online. The main target for the programme is newly qualified staff and those seeking to move their careers forward toward first-line leadership roles. The course comprises 21 sessions of roughly 40 minutes' duration and it leads to the NHS Foundation Leadership Academy Award.

The second programme is the *Mary Seacole Programme*. This was named after Mary Seacole (1805–1881) who set up care facilities behind the British front lines in the Crimean war. The aim of the programme is to help staff lead (like Mary Seacole) with compassion, resourcefulness and practicality.

Staff wanting to enter this programme have to apply online or be nominated. It requires 10 to 12 hours' work per week and originally lasted 12 months. It comprises both online and group work and funding is available for those nominated. It is aimed at staff either in first leader roles or aspiring to those roles. Successful completion gives participants an NHS Leadership Academy Award in Healthcare Leadership.

The next level up in this suite of leadership development opportunities is the *Elizabeth Garrett Anderson Programme*. It is named after Elizabeth Garrett Anderson (1836–1917) who was the first female to qualify as a physician and surgeon in Britain, the first dean of a medical school and eventually the first female Mayor in England (of Aldeburgh, Suffolk). It enables participants to learn to lead like Elizabeth Garrett Anderson, with dynamism and a drive to challenge the status quo. Applications are made online, and it requires 15 hours a week of study and workplace application spread over 24 months. It includes online learning, action learning sets and residential study. This programme includes specialist input from global partners. It is aimed at all staff who lead other leaders or who lead complex teams, or who are aspiring to do so, and, like the other two programmes, is targeted at both clinical and non-clinical personnel. Graduates of the programme receive an NHS Leadership Academy Award in Senior Healthcare Leadership, as well an MSc in Healthcare Leadership, which is jointly accredited by the University of Birmingham and Alliance Manchester Business School.

The fourth level of the suite of programmes is the *Nye Bevan Programme*. It is aimed at senior healthcare staff in or aspiring to reach senior executive level roles. It is named after one of the most important ministers of the post-war Labour government and the chief architect of the National Health Service, Aneurin Bevan (1897–1960). The programme helps participants learn to lead like Nye Bevan with a bold vision and wide-ranging influence. Again, applications are made online and 8 to 12 hours per week of study is required for 12 months. The programme uses online learning, residential blocks, and group learning. This course leads, on successful completion, to the NHS Leadership Academy Award in Executive Healthcare Leadership. Both the Anderson and Bevan programmes include a number of global partners to add additional weight and gravitas to the academic component. These include the Harvard University T H Chan School of Public Health, Erasmus University Rotterdam and the University of Pretoria. The final step of the suite of programmes is for aspiring chief executives, and the programme is a collaboration between the Academy, NHS Improvement and NHS Providers.

In addition to these five-step leadership development programmes there are a number of additional programmes to complement them, such as a newly appointed Chief Executive Programme, Executive Directors Support, Ready Now, Return to Work Mentoring, and NHS Graduate Management Training Scheme.

How the programmes are structured

The Mary Seacole programme is the first rung of the leading care suite of three structured courses. It is nine units in length, which are organized in four- to five-week blocks. The whole programme is structured around an online virtual campus, and is designed to allow maximum flexibility so that participants can juggle the programme around their work and other commitments. A lot of the programme is delivered online, and those online elements can be exercise-based, involve watching video interviews or situations, or reading an article by a leadership expert. Every participant is allocated a tutor and a tutor group, and participants are expected to get involved in debates and conversations with colleagues via the online portal. Participants are expected to post comments or ask questions around a number of key topics. The allocated tutor can also provide one-to-one support either online or via the phone.

There are three tutor group meetings during the programme that are located regionally, and there are also three leadership workshops based regionally which give participants the chance to develop their leadership skills and explore leadership challenges. To be awarded the certificate, completion of four assignments is required.

The Anderson Programme, which is the next stage in the leadership journey, is a master's level course. It is the largest programme offered by the Leadership Academy and spans 24 months. It is a partnership between KPMG, Alliance Manchester Business School, the Health Services Management Centre at the University of Birmingham, the NHS Leadership Academy and other academic and technology experts. Both universities jointly accredit this master's programme.

There are seven modules which focus on leadership at three levels: individual, team and organization. So module one has a focus on the individual, module two on the team, and module three on the organization. Module four's focus is on leading across organizations. Module five considers leading across teams and module six returns to the individual role of the leader. Module seven focuses on the development of research methodology skills and knowledge and the completion of a major, critical healthcare leadership case study, which is the participant's master's dissertation.

Participants access much of their learning content via an online portal (the Virtual Campus). They work in cohorts of 48 participants and are supported in tutor groups of 16. Some of this support is face to face on a one-to-one basis, some is in tutor groups (either face to face or virtually via online meetings). Importantly, throughout the programme participants are required to implement their learning in the workplace. Workplace application is a fundamental element of the programme, which is also formally assessed via work-based assignments that sit alongside critical assignments that assess the academic elements of the programme. There is a four-day residential workshop in Leeds to launch the programme and further residential blocks later in the programme. These are combined with a programme of action learning (see Chapter 9) so that participants can work with fellow participants from other ogranizations to problem-solve and develop their leadership skills, whilst at the same time gaining a broad understanding of the issues faced by their colleagues. These groups are deliberately mixed clinical and non-clinical staff, so that there is broad appreciation of the challenges facing everyone at that level, regardless of where they work.

The Bevan Programme again includes the KPMG-led consortium in partnership with Alliance Manchester Business School and the University of Birmingham but with additional academic expertise provided by the Harvard T H Chan School of Public Health, the University of Pretoria and the Erasmus University in Rotterdam. It is focused around the challenge to improve delivery at a personal, unit and systemic level. It has a self-managed approach to learning, which involves participants setting two persona goals, and assessing each other in small groups as to their achievement of their learning. It also enables participants to share their development with their peers to create a supportive and flexible learning environment. In this way a senior team can support its own development. This will stretch beyond the confines of the programme. It also includes design input from major KPMG corporate clients.

There are three core modules: knowing yourself and others; broadening horizons; and making the case for change. Again this is based on self-managed learning with learning sets. There are 12 compulsory days of face-to-face residentials, facilitated by the set adviser. The virtual campus complements these face-to-face sessions with simulations, webinars, videos, surveys, electronic journals, books and tutorial discussion boards. Participants attend one 5-day residential workshop and two 3-day residential workshops from a list provided. With the assessment taking place at a two-day residential workshop situated towards the end of the programme. The participants assess each other and decide who has achieved their learning goals in the programme and who has not. Peers, in other words, determine success or failure in the programme.

The Aspiring Chief Executive Programme is based around a Hay 360 diagnostic tool. Individuals are rated by their line managers, peers and direct reports to get a rounded view of how they are performing. Depending on what emerges, the programme will be tailor-made according to those identified needs and individual preferences. Participants on the programme can select masterclasses, workshops, and executive coaching assignments in any combination appropriate for the individual participant. It has no end point, as the programme is designed as a continuing support structure for senior leaders in the NHS.

Four hundred and thirty-five participants from the first two intakes of the Bevan Programme have already graduated. As of May 2016 there are 29 live cohorts going through the Anderson Programme (1,309 students) with 12 cohorts to date having graduated (366 participants). The overall aim is extremely ambitious. It is to make a deliberate, widespread and measurable impact on the quality of leadership in the NHS. This should, therefore, contribute towards the efficiency and effectiveness of the NHS as a whole and ensure wide uptake of the NHS values.

The aim is to develop much more awareness of cross-boundary issues and therefore ensure more cooperation and partnership. Much of the learning is applied directly to the workplace. They are demanding programmes. The Anderson Programme, for example, can require up to 15 hours a week study in addition to a full-time job and other external commitments. Scenarios are available for the team to work on. These look at realistic and difficult issues in the NHS with no obvious right answer, and the group debate and agree their recommendations going forward. The best possible outcomes agreed by the group are then compared to the views of experts who have considered the same scenarios. This is a more valuable way of engaging with real problems than simply being told what experts would do.

The residential elements of the programs are designed to stretch participants. The Bevan Programme has three residential blocks. One is four days long; the other two lasts two or three days. Participation in the residential element is mandatory in order to achieve the award. This is the place where strong bonds are formed and the students get used to sharing their views openly and engaging in debate. Having the residential components helps build a learning community and makes people more willing to share their views in the online forums as well. Line managers are involved at every stage, and participants are not only endorsed and/or sponsored by their line manager in order to participate but also share progress and challenges along the way. Line managers have a specific duty of care to ensure the success of the participants in the programme to the best of their ability.

The initiative is designed to develop the skills of the participants – not for their current level, but for the level that they aspire to. The aim is to create something that can evolve as the NHS evolves, so that professional leadership qualifications will be like nursing qualifications or other medical-based qualifications. That is, they will be designed to keep up with advances in clinical and other practice and require ongoing professional development. This is not just an isolated leadership development suite of programmes aimed at the relatively small number of individuals who go through them, but an attempt at fundamental cultural change that resonates through every aspect of the NHS. This is leadership development as a change agent – leadership as a disruptive influence that is designed to empower and influence staff beyond the numbers who directly participate. There is much to admire and possibly emulate about these programmes. In particular, the commitment of the whole organization to make this work, and the endorsement of senior leadership from the outset. All participants know the importance of what is at stake and the emphasis is both on the individual contribution and the organizational impact.

They are designed to marry state-of-the-art leadership development, with personal insight and challenge alongside career development. From the initial impact measurements carried out, the programme is more than meeting its targets and the ripple effect throughout the NHS is beginning, but the full wave of change could take a number of years to manifest itself in systemic change.

The programme asks the particpants, in many ways, to put themselves on the line by responding openly and frankly to really challenging questions that are aimed at the heart of an individual's commitment and beliefs. For example, if you are asked 'Can I say that the service I deliver is good enough for somebody I love to receive?' – any reaction is emotional as well as intellectual. And participants are continuously challenged to explain how they know that what they do really works. Where is their evidence? Does it really prove their case?

Components of the blended learning mix

If we take the two core leadership programmes, Anderson and Bevan, the component mix is complex and challenging (NHS Leadership Academy, 2016). Each participant has to juggle a study programme that combines online learning with work-based problem-solving, face-to-face seminars, tutorials and learning sets (Bevan) or action learning sets (Anderson). Rigorous academic study needs to be set against case studies and scenarios based on the NHS where pragmatic day-to-day decisions have to be taken. The programmes require discipline and commitment, and the individual needs the support of both colleagues and line manager to succeed. Often belief systems and practices that are deeply embedded are challenged and replaced by new sets of behaviours. This is the highest level of leadership development.

Both the Anderson and Bevan programmes share many common features as well as a common philosophy. The main differentiator (apart from the level) is that Anderson is a two-year master's programme while Bevan is a one-year postgraduate level advanced programme.

Both programmes have multi-partner delivery – in other words different parts of the programme are handled by different organizations, with KPMG as the consistent lead partner overseeing both programmes and ensuring articulation and linkage. National Voices, the coalition of health and social care charities, represents the voice and input of NHS customers (ie patients) and they are important partners in both programmes.

There is strong academic underpinning from five world-class universities. This is obviously a fundamental part of any programme that leads to a master's degree. However, their role goes beyond the validation of the academic content. They share their research and expertise with the students and provide high-level content for the academic modules that form the core part of the Anderson programme. These eight modules are delivered online via a virtual campus. Participants share latest thinking and establish their own building blocks for continuing learning beyond the programme. The virtual campus is also used for online tutorials, academic input, readings and other resources for study, plus computer-based simulations to develop practical skills across individuals and groups. The virtual campus also acts as a home base that tracks progress in the programme down to individual element completion.

In addition to the academic modules, there are four face-to-face residential workshops for each cohort. Both programmes seek to develop skills and promote changes in work practice, as well as build a wider context for participants that transcends their day-to-day role. These workshops make the most of having the participants together in one place. They focus on changing leadership behaviour by concentrating on experiential and simulation-based learning activities. In the Bevan Programme, for instance, the participants act as a Board and run a simulated NHS Trust where their decisions have direct consequences on the Trust's performance. These workshops complement the 11 full-day action learning sets located in regional clusters that develop personal leadership, and help share issues across workplace or work role boundaries. The sets help individuals resolve personal leadership issues but also explore and rehearse being able to work successfully in leadership groups more widely, where diversity of view, challenging individuals, and difficult problems to resolve are the norm.

The sets help explore what works and does not work in relationship building and team development, and therefore develop enduring skills beyond the overt problems that the set is tasked to resolve.

There are also workplace-based exercises to reinforce the application of the learning in the day-to-day routine. Also online tutor groups reinforce the learning and offer a forum to deal with any challenges and issues. These are delivered via the Leadership Academy virtual campus. This also acts as a repository for the programme resources and so continues beyond the programme as a location for content that can help deal with on-going challenges.

The Anderson Programme topics have been structured into four-week blocks, each of which has specific learning outcomes attached. There is flexibility within each block so a student can move quickly or more slowly through the material as long as it is completed within the stipulated time period.

The Anderson and Bevan programmes are cohort-based. Anderson's 48-participant cohorts move through the programme together and are required to work and support each other (as do Bevan's 49-strong cohorts). In addition, each participant is allocated a personal tutor who will regularly review the participant's performance and help resolve any academic, work-related or personal issues that impact on progression.

There is a conscious effort to relate what is learned to the practical exigencies of the workplace, so participants look at what they can use in their workplace that helps them perform their role more successfully. Both programmes require a large and continuing commitment of 10–15 hours per week of study. Some of this is workplace-based and during normal working hours, and some is outside working hours either alone or in small groups. So an element of the programme is scheduled, but other elements are flexible in terms of when, where, and how a module is completed.

The participants are encouraged to share their experience with their manager at regular intervals and practise the new skills they have learned systematically over the course of study. There has been a significant effort to develop a broader pan-NHS perspective as well as to strengthen the working of local NHS communities. Therefore, it is not simply a question of improving individual performance, but also working practices across the NHS as a whole. Fundamentally, the end result of all of this investment comes down to a simple question: has the patient had a better experience?

The Leadership Academy Award is not about success and achievement but rather about learning and impact. It is given in recognition of sharing participants' application of learning in practice, and their impact as a leader.

The Bevan Programme has similar structure. It is aimed at the next level to the Anderson Programme, this time at aspirant directors from a clinical or non-clinical background who will develop the knowledge and skills to perform at board level. It also delivers a formal award at the end.

The curriculum covers both leadership skills and specialist health sector knowledge, aimed at approaches and behaviours that will deliver patient-centred outcomes. There are three principle strands in the programme that are woven together: personal learning, which is reviewed and assessed in an action learning set; face-to-face learning in a residential workshop; together with the online virtual campus elements which deliver continuous learning and provide access to resources throughout the programme. It is more reliant on self-management and self-development than the Anderson Programme, as that is a core part of the skill set that the programme is seeking to develop. So the individuals are required to take full responsibility for their own learning and provide evidence of mastery and progression throughout the programme. This evidence is always work-based.

The programme also includes a significant component of assessment by peers. This reflects the need for the participants to hold themselves and others to account – one of the key recommendations for senior leaders that emerged from the Executive Summary (Francis Report, 2013). The main way of delivering this is for peers to give and receive feedback on assignments both formatively and summatively. Ultimately, the cohort decides as a group who will be recommended for the Healthcare Award in Executive Healthcare Leadership and who will not. So ultimate success or failure is determined by their peers.

Like the Anderson Programme, Bevan is cohort based. Each cohort is made up of 49 participants, divided into seven self-managed learning sets, each with its own adviser. These groups are diverse and cover a range of both clinical and non-clinical roles. The number chosen mirrors the kind of executive team that the participants will be familiar with. Making their group perform successfully translates back directly into work practice. Each is encouraged to develop its own way of working, much like any senior executive team. This set is established as the bedrock of the programme, and a supportive home base to which the participant returns throughout the year of study. It acts as a support network and sounding board.

Like Anderson, there are a number of face-to-face residential workshops. At one of these, the groups receive feedback from a panel of patient representatives together with frontline staff. The workshops were designed to be highly experiential and participative, in order to make full use of the time that the entire cohort is able to meet.

Bevan is built and structured around a number of core learning outcomes. The first revolves around making a reality of the NHS Constitution. The second focuses on creating the right conditions for frontline staff, irrespective of their background. The third is about systems leadership, helping participants work across and beyond organizational boundaries. The fourth concentrates on the skills required to operate successfully at board level and the fifth is about engaging patients, service users and carers from all backgrounds to work better in a complex environment. The sixth is designed to help participants develop knowledge and networks that will support them post-programme and throughout their future career. The seventh helps each individual reflect on what it is like to be on the receiving end of th ~ leadership, whilst the eighth examines and works on the cond' ~essful teamwork. Underpinning all these outcomes it to diversity and inclusion. Participants are enco nge existing practice when it is found wanting, and ta ation spanning view of what the NHS needs to do to ir. d commit to a cycle of sustained improvement.

In addition to the esta ed and prescribed curriculum, each participant chooses two p nal learning goals and is tasked with providing the evidence of achievement in them. It is a one-year programme, and so far over 85 per cent of participants who enrolled have successfully completed the programme and received the award.

Why each component was selected

The CRF Report on the state of leadership development, asks a simple question: is leadership development fit for purpose? (CRF Report (Pillans), 2015). A deliberate blended learning approach goes some way to ensuring relevance and fitness in function and structure. But to answer the question in the context of the NHS Leadership Academy's suite of programmes we need to retrace our steps, and look again at the Francis Report that provided the logic and impetus for the leadership initiative in the first place.

In the letter to the secretary of state which forms a preface to the report, Robert Francis QC, the chairman of the inquiry, states:

Building on the report of the first inquiry, the story [the report] tells us first and foremost of appalling suffering of many patients. This was primarily caused by a serious failure on the part of a provider Trust Board. It did not listen sufficiently to its patients and staff or ensure the correction of deficiencies brought to the Trust's attention. Above all, it failed to tackle an insidious negative culture involving a tolerance of poor standards, and a disengagement from managerial and leadership responsibilities. This failure was in part the consequence of allowing a focus on reaching national access targets, achieving financial balance and seeking foundation trust status, to be at the cost of delivering acceptable standards of care. (Department of Health, 2014: 183)

This is clearly more than a leadership issue, although failure of leadership does go to the heart of the problem. As the government's formal response to the Francis Inquiry acknowledged:

The Inquiry highlighted failures of leadership at all levels of the NHS. It rightly identifies the importance of a clear leadership framework and the need to ensure that clear standards are in place for the most senior managers.

Developing a strong, positive culture of leadership for the NHS is the responsibility of all leaders; and there is a particular role for the NHS Leadership Academy in ensuring that the right values and behaviours are driven through leadership development at all levels. (Department of Health, 2014: 186)

There is a linked series of issues around poor behaviours reinforced by negative culture and a habit of 'turning a blind eye'. Therefore, any increased leadership capability needs to be balanced by attitude, culture and behaviour change. The structure of the two leadership programmes, described in this chapter, makes a concerted and explicit effort to address all the issues and deliver on the specific mandate that is given by the report.

The elements of the blend are like strands in a fabric. As they are woven together, the completed cloth is far stronger than any single strand out of which it is made.

If we look at some of the elements of the Anderson Programme, these linkages become more obvious.

Table 5.1 Components of the Anderson and Bevan leadership programmes

Programme element	Function in overall aims
Academic study	Increasing depth of understanding of leadership in a health service context. Implementing best practice from around the world.
Action learning sets	Building networks, developing respect, building trust and self-healing for the organization. Living shared values; holding members accountable for their actions.
Online resources	Access to expert content, opportunities to debate issues and seek solutions with peers. Opportunities to reflect and take considered views. Merger of theory and practice.
Face-to-face workshops	Building networks across the organization, learning by doing, observing good and poor practice. Looking at systemic issues. Seeing the big picture. Listening to health experts and share top expertise. Focusing on group work.
Tutor support	Focusing on individual responsibility and individual competence. Challenging the individual to take ownership of his or her own learning, clear understanding of the bigger picture. Ensuring changed behaviour is supported.
Simulations	'As is' experience; practising in a safe environment, understanding alternative perspectives. Operating in real time. Learning by doing.

The special contribution of blended learning

How does the blended learning approach described in this chapter differ from another more typical leadership programme?

The answer is all to do with the way the programme is constructed. A blended approach starts with the end in mind. In other words, you look at the outcomes you expect from the programme and then align the learning mode to each of those outcomes in turn. The aim is to create the best opportunity in each circumstance to deliver those outcomes. Certain processes suit certain learning formats. Each element of the programme is therefore crafted separately, and different providers are selected for their expertise in different modes of learning.

There is no slavish model to follow or a recipe for the optimum blend which takes a small amount of 'a' and mixes it with a dash of 'b' and a little 'c'. It is more an approach that is uniquely crafted for the specific circumstances inside the organization. The fundamental question you have to ask yourself is: how best can we make this greatest impact?

As the stakes are high in many instances, and there is pressure on leadership programmes to make a noticeable and profound change to the way organizations are run, the value of taking a blended approach is increasingly obvious. And as new learning technologies come on stream and provide more and more choice for delivery, there is an increasingly urgent need to engage in blended learning from that output and outcome perspective.

Core lessons

1 There is no single model for leadership development. Success comes from the variety of learning opportunities that the student is offered. These are blended into the programme as a whole. But what is offered, is offered from the point of view of providing the best outcomes, not simply variety for variety's sake.

2 Action sets, whether based on action learning or self-managed learning, have enormous potential to help sustain leadership communities and allow self-management of problems and challenges. A group that is able to hold each other to account can be a very effective tool in the delivery of real change in an organization.

3 Everything should ultimately focus on improving what goes on in the workplace. This is done best through small interventions over time rather than huge one-off initiatives. The lasting impact comes through changes in the value system, behaviours and approaches. This all needs time to develop.

4 There is huge value in adding academic rigour and insight to leadership programmes. The intellectual and research-based

underpinning gives substance to the entire operation and allows the programme to easily achieve credibility. However, it should be a part of the mix, not the exclusive content.

5 Bringing in an organization like KPMG (in the NHS example) allows the commissioning body to step back from the day-to-day running of the programme. The managing organization can add value by taking a more dispassionate view and their insights can keep everything on track. Meanwhile the commissioning body can look at evolving the programme, managing the measurement of impact, and maintaining the strategic alignment with the parent organization.

6 Ultimately, demanding programmes require some sort of accreditation. This helps sustain motivation and allows the participants to take on more substantial research or work-based projects than they might have if no qualification was offered. The prospect of a postgraduate certificate or a master's qualification adds enormous perceived value and sustains the programme over an extended period of time. It also helps set external benchmarks and standards.

7 Tutor groups and personal tutors, or coaches and mentors aimed at individuals, can keep those participants on track by helping sustain motivation. It also allows a strong element of personalization in the learning experience, the setting of individual goals and targets, and the chance to problem-solve in situ in the workplace.

8 It is very easy to focus on the residential workshops and choose really good locations and fine facilities so that an exciting and challenging learning environment can be built that makes each participant feel special as they engage with it. It is equally important, however, to develop a similar vibrant, online community through some kind of online portal. This can then be much more than just a means of getting content to the participants. It can be an area to practise, select resources, debate and discuss with peers, and perhaps support the leader post-programme. It allows continuing and regular engagement with colleagues online. This kind of environment allows for an element of flexibility in terms of when and where to study, so the programme can fit in with busy working weeks and different patterns of work.

9 A stepped approach from the foundations of leadership to a support programme for the top executives is ambitious but allows development over a number of years and a chance to uncover and work with talented individuals from their very first steps into leadership through to top jobs. As in all such programmes, it will aid retention and build commitment across a number of roles.

10 Providing the vision is strong and the coordination effective, it is possible to have a number of distinct suppliers for one programme but still ensure that it is perceived, and operates, as a homogenous whole.

11 Using quality simulations that are instantly credible and deal with familiar issues brings the learner into the programme instantly. Telling a story well not only engages the participant but turns abstract concepts into lived experience that can be debated and processed. The time and effort spent on getting those simulations right appears to have a significant knock-on effect across the programme as a whole and act as a glue to cement the various aspects of the programme into place. It is impossible not to engage emotionally with those simulations, and therefore by inference with the programme as a whole. They have the raw quality of lived experience and using actors and realistic sets brings not just the simulation but the whole programme alive.

References

Boone, J (2015) Leading learning organizations through transformational change: making the case for blended learning, *International Journal of Educational Management*, **29** (3), pp 275–83

Corporate Research Forum Report (Pillans, G) (2015) *Leadership Development – is it fit for purpose?*, Corporate Research Forum, London

Department of Health (2014) *Hard Truths: The journey to putting patients first*, Vols 1 and 2, TSO (The Stationery Office)

Francis Report (2013) Executive summary, *Report of the Mid Staffordshire NHS Foundation Trust Public Inquiry*, Para 1.119, TSO (The Stationery Office)

Harvey, Dr S (2011) *Forward Look Seminars*, The Mid Staffordshire Foundation Trust Public Inquiry Report, Crown Copyright

The NHS Constitution (27 July 2015), Crown Copyright

NHS Leadership Academy (2016) Programmes, http://leadershipacademy. nhs.uk/programmes/

Osguthorpe, R T and Graham, C R (2003) Blended learning environments: definitions and directions, *Quarterly Review of Distance Education*, 4 (3), pp 227–33

Shepherd, C (2005/2008) *The Blended Learning Cookbook*, Saffron Interactive, London

PART THREE
Changing the Paradigm

Any time, any place leadership   06

BP's digital leadership development

Digital age learning at BP

It is possible to translate existing models of leadership development into a digital format. This means, essentially, extracting each conventional component and making it digital. So a face-to-face lecture becomes an e-learning course, a seminar transitions into a webinar, etc. This is a crude and largely unimaginative method of moving into the digital space. In an unpublished doctoral thesis, Peppe Auricchio (2015) of the Spanish Business School IESE investigated the likelihood of this transition, and the speed at which it would replace more conventional learning models in Executive Leadership programmes. Two of his key conclusions were: firstly, that preconceptions about online learning are slowing the adoption of blended learning as a model for corporate leadership development; and secondly, that the affordances of a blended learning model do not align with the needs of executives and the objectives of their development. This is a particularly bleak prognostication for moving leadership development online and is based on interviews with 41 corporate learning leaders from Europe and North America.

The translation from one mode (essentially face-to-face) to another (largely online) clearly has limitations that are particularly stark in the leadership development sphere. The issue of resistance to online can be broken down, but there are justifiable prejudices around online learning, largely born of negative experiences. Online learning is often lonely and boring and, for executives, finding blocks of spare time to sit at a screen is usually all but impossible. It can be pointless as well.

Cramming in conclusions, and learning in theory, does not relate well to the real experience of leadership on a day-to-day level. There are ways that these prejudices can be overcome, and there are examples of this elsewhere in this book. You can make this interesting, rewarding and useful. But the second conclusion, that new models do not align with the needs of executives, is far more critical.

The major insight here is the huge incidental benefit that taking participants in a programme out of the workplace, and keeping them together for a number of days, can engender. The opportunity for networking with colleagues, and the opportunity to develop a strong leadership community, clearly fulfils a fundamental need and expresses a crucial – but often undefined – outcome. The online programme takes much of this opportunity away and, therefore, does not meet an explicit and important need of executives. The focus is on content delivery and the onus is on the individual to fulfil the requirements of the programme in isolation. Development, it turns out, is much more than simply good content, and the formal structure of delivery such as lectures, presentations and seminars, needs a strong informal and social element to deliver lasting value. These benefits accrue in the gaps between the formal elements of the programme, and in the casual conversations after dinner. The translation model pushes that to one side in favour of the need for rapid deployment, and economies of scale that reduce per unit costs. Auricchio argues that this could be a false economy.

Capgemini: from virtualization to digitization

There is an alternative model that has the potential to be much more successful. That is to transform the learning experience rather than simply to translate it. It means exploiting the available communications technologies in order to build something that bears little resemblance to what has gone before. This thinking was outlined by the French consultancy Capgemini as a two-stage process at their corporate university on the outskirts of Paris (Capgemini, 2016). They referred to it as an initial process of virtualization (the process of translation from one mode to another) leading to digitalization (the transformation of the learning process).

Capgemini breaks up the elements of the shift into five distinct processes. These take you from a translation approach to a radical rethink of learning facilitated by the digital tools available: transformation. The first is the shift from an e-learning model to developing digital and social learning frameworks. Rather than taking an existing course element that delivered content in a face-to-face setting and dropping the content into an e-learning format, instead you look at what the session was trying to achieve and rebuild it using new approaches and exploiting opportunities for social learning. In a sense, then, the focus shifts from content creation and delivery to a focus on what learners need and when, and on a more deliberate interaction with the business and the direct experience of the leader.

The next shift is from the concept of 'massification' – ie getting as much learning as possible to as many people as possible in the fastest time – to the concept of personalization. This requires an entirely different and more learner-centred approach. This means tailoring what is on offer to the specific, and possibly unique, needs of each individual leader. To achieve this there has to be a more profound understanding of needs together with a completely open structure for the learning channel so that relevant material can be selected by the learner at the moment of need.

You have to move from the individual to the model of the organization as well. This transition involves getting out of a siloed departmental approach to structuring courses and curriculum that reflect the existing organizational structure, and beginning to look holistically at the company and the broader cultural and strategic aspirations. In other words, to have learning which embodies the future rather than reflecting the past.

Linked to this is the need to help the organization develop a different kind of leader. The move is towards agile and transdisciplinary teams rather than reflecting existing structures and hierarchies. In other words, anticipating a new way of working and using the technologies available to model this. It is possible now to develop programmes that help leaders taste what the future work organization and work process could be like, rather than reinforcing the current models.

The final part of the jigsaw is getting away from an approach that is only concerned with putting content online, to one that uses the connected nature of the digital experience to build strong learning communities. This is fundamental, and counters some of the negative reactions that Auricchio's research revealed. It is possible to build very strong online learning communities, and develop teams that can work successfully together to share their learning, and co-create the experience.

Most organizations are locked into 'translation' mode as Auricchio's doctoral thesis showed. In other words, thinking in terms of old models of learning, and then digitizing that process largely to cut costs and reach out to more people more quickly. The real opportunities, however, could lie in the process of transforming the learning experience, bringing learning closer to the workflow, and being able to instantly accommodate the needs of the learner. This is an attractive proposition where learning merges into a performance support and troubleshooting process; a framework where access to help can occur in the moment of need. This is a hugely challenging aspiration generally, but particularly hard for leadership development which has clung on – more tenaciously than other programmes – to traditional face-to-face and residential delivery for reasons that Auricchio elaborates in his doctoral thesis. There are indications that new models can work as Capgemini reveals. To make this abstract discussion more tangible I investigated a new approach to leadership development by the petroleum company BP, and this chapter is built around an in-depth interview with BP's Director of Online Learning, Nick Shackleton-Jones, together with other relevant resources. The programme was conceived and developed by his team; however, he was the primary instigator of the endeavour.

Leadership online at BP

This represents a living example of how these ideas might work in practice. The context is a radical rethinking of how the company could deliver both a first-level leadership development programme, together with a leadership course aimed at senior leaders in the company. The aim was to target those staff in transition to new leadership roles, as first-time leaders and as senior leaders. This approach allowed access to appropriate development at the time of appointment, ie when it was most needed. The traditional model was to place someone onto a development programme at the time of appointment. This meant that only a proportion of leaders received training, and in many other cases a delay of several months before they were able to attend a course and get the development required. Obviously any programme designed to help someone with a transition into a new role will work best the nearer it occurs to the actual date of appointment. This new approach guaranteed immediate access.

In many ways the design emerged out of the underpinning principles for these two programmes. The principles were built from in-depth conversations with staff from both target groups (senior leaders and first-time leaders). That was the starting point – not curriculum or any attempt to impose an idea of what people needed, but a process of listening to how people defined their challenges in their day-to-day work environment. From this process, seven conclusions emerged that were then reflected back to the groups. These then became the structuring principles for the learning programmes and helped determine how they might be put together and how the learner would experience them. The starting point was, therefore, almost the opposite of a conventional course development process. There the delivery method is fixed, so the discussion is all about appropriate content and the best structure to deliver this.

The seven principles

1 A need to align with transitional needs, ie be available as soon as anyone was promoted into a first-line or senior leadership role. And this helped determine the way the content was organized. It was simple to access and based on checklists and video insights. It was also applicable, rather than wordy and theoretical.

2 The programmes had to reflect the reality of the *always on* smartphone and tablet culture, and be available wherever the participant was, and whenever access was required. People of all ages use mobile devices to get help when they need it; the new approach had to work in a similar way.

3 They had to be totally flexible to reflect need, not a linear process of learning. The content was structured entirely around the tasks and concern of transitioning leaders, and it was this principle – not the digital format – which resulted in the successful outcome.

4 Both the solution design process and usage were user-driven, by which is meant that the programmes embodied the real world of leaders in BP, not an abstract paradigm of what leadership ought to be. To ensure that this was indeed the case, a user group stayed with the learning team across the whole development cycle. It eventually became the initial group of critical friends who worked through the programme for real, after it had been developed but before launch, to ensure that it fitted the context in which the target group was working.

5 The content itself was primarily resources and guidance, structured around tens of interviews with existing staff in those specific roles. The learning team had to make sure that what they built reflected the challenges and goals of the people who were interviewed.

6 Wherever possible, the voices of those key staff that had been through those transitions in the company were used in the programmes to deliver a strong layer of authenticity. This was not theoretical and abstract, but practical, and reflected the world as experienced by the participants. Much of this content was delivered on video, so users could see and hear the views of colleagues. This created credibility and authenticity. None of the responses were scripted.

7 The digital tools were open and available for anyone to use. There was no selection process. Anyone new to that role was contacted directly and encouraged to participate, but anyone contemplating such a role or curious about what was being said was also free to take part. In theory, this meant that a new, junior member of BP staff could access a programme for senior leaders and understand a bit more of their world and what their main drivers and challenges were.

The target groups were fairly self-evident. The total leadership population was around 25,000, with a maximum cohort of 1,500 people transitioning to leadership roles in a particular year, and, in addition, there were 200 or so more senior staff moving into senior management. This gave the two programmes a maximum cohort size of under 2,000. In reality, however, and much to everyone's astonishment, over 20,000 staff actually accessed those programmes – 10 times the theoretical cohort. This was one important indicator of intrinsic value. It was discovered that staff already in that role, those contemplating promotion, and the managers of first-line managers all participated. The logic and the messages from the programme therefore spread widely and quickly around the company. The 'no barriers to entry' decision worked better than anyone could have reasonably expected, as well as minimizing the administrative overhead of selecting and enrolling participants.

How were the programmes organized?

BP has four core leadership values that are consistent throughout the company and at every level of leadership. Leaders in BP are expected to:

- build enduring capability in their teams;
- lead through the BP values;
- energize people;
- deliver maximum value to BP.

The obvious way of structuring the two programmes would have been to use those four values as the headline names for a course of four separate units. The feeling in BP was that these four leadership values were high level and needed to be translated into day-to-day leadership reality, so rather than structure the programmes, they formed a backbone to them. This helped solidify the values and help the target groups work out what the values meant for them in practice, and in context. It was made obvious where each leadership value aligned with and underpinned the content. The actual structure, however, was based around the discussions with the user groups. What emerged from the conversations with the first-line leaders was a need to focus on what those staff actually did. This became the structuring logic: managing the transition; managing self; managing peers; managing my team; and managing senior staff, including my own manager. It was summed up in the rubric as: managing upwards, sideways, downwards and inwards. Easy to remember and logical, and also aligned perfectly with the experience of leadership of that core group.

It was easy to see where specific help could be found as the structure reflected their day-to-day work. So, as they took their first steps into a leadership role, guidance and support was available for each new step and each emerging challenge. And because it was online and freely available it was possible to access the content at any time and on any device. Important content did not take the form of 'bite-size nuggets' but rather useful resources such as one-page guides, checklists, demonstrations and infographics. Because the content was also designed for usability, it could be accessed at any point, even just before going into a difficult meeting, for example.

The first-line leaders' programme was specifically designed for that transitioning leadership group, so the content was not conceived as a chocolate box of goodies to pick and mix, but a systematic walk-through of all the issues that these individuals were going to confront. On the Hub, which represents the gateway into the content for the programme, the focus is on practical support and tools that would help. The overall structure of the programme is included across the top of the page, detailing the big ticket items that will be covered: a new team; decision-making; managing performance and leadership expectations. There is also a section on the language of leadership. The structuring principle is becoming a leader, then managing yourself and managing your team. There are no big theoretical sections or complex models, just help and support in the form of text, graphics and video.

In addition to the resource-based content, the team also designed a native app, designed to 'nudge' leaders into positive habits and encourage them into a weekly feedback loop. The app calculated their daily engagement score based on specific and anonymous feedback from their team members.

What did the programmes look like?

The fundamental structure then for both programmes was an adaptive portal on the internet, together with a phone or tablet app which focused on feedback and support. The portal delivered content comprising mostly short videos, checklists and guides to action. The app gave a very truncated version of the guide, but focused on polling teams, scooping up data and directly helping leaders alter their behaviour to systematically improve their performance. So the app delivered a summary of content and acted as a tracking device for feedback on how a participant was doing. The portal was for more reflective and concerted learning. It was designed to create a deep experience, which the app then reinforced. The overall leadership development programmes combined both portal and app, not one or the other. They were designed to work together seamlessly and reflected the actual working experience of the participants. Sometimes they had the time and space to sit and access content, and other times they needed quick guidance on the run. So one element of the programme demanded a relatively fixed place and a focus on learning; the other allowed the participants to roam freely and implement what was learned, and get some feedback on their performance. It was a continually refreshed cycle of moving back to the portal, and then onto the app, and so on as the programme proceeded.

Because the programmes were open, the entry point could be chosen by each participant. So someone with a specific challenge could leap in at the appropriate point and try to resolve the issue or work out how to deal with it. Or they could decide to work more systematically through the content. Both programmes were designed to be accessible at the point of need and offered a more considered and coherent learning experience. The first-time leaders' programme aligned with a more formal, short classroom-based course that – due to the exigencies of planning and timetabling – often was not available until months after promotion. Both learning experiences were maintained and were seen as complementary. The idea was that the online experience should provide performance support, leaving the classroom free to focus on practical exercises. So, in principle, there was help available for the new leaders that stretched from day one through their first six months, before a more formal course became available to reinforce and summarize the core learning. It is still too early to tell if the digital endeavour has made the more formal course irrelevant or whether there is any need to ensure that the two separate programmes are more formally in alignment. At the moment they are designed as two separate experiences.

How does it work?

Essentially the digital leadership programme is a systematic attempt to offer two different leader groups performance support at the point when it is required most. In much the same way that people use Google or YouTube for help at the point of need, both programmes offer instant, performance support. Based on an analysis of the leadership challenges, in the context of how work is actually done in BP, resources are developed that are distributed using one of two platforms: the portal on the intranet and the smartphone in their pocket or handbag. This is a different approach to simply taking a large amount of leadership content and chunking it into manageable bites, which are pushed out to phones or other devices. It is a conscious move away from structured courses, to developing resources that inform and direct behaviour. It is rather like offering a leadership satnav as opposed to a leadership manual. This is what makes it radically different to what went before. It is not just the technology, but the complete approach that makes it fundamentally new.

This programme is not designed to cut out the intervention of the participants' line managers, or make their interventions somehow less relevant. On the contrary, it is specifically designed to encourage valuable conversation, and create a context where the line manager can offer support that reflects what is needed at the time. One of the core leadership values for BP is to 'build enduring capability' and this programme and its approach enables – in part at least – the more senior managers to play their role in helping their direct reports move into new roles with as little friction as possible. The line manager, therefore, is a key player in this development model. This is quite unlike face-to-face courses which tend to be self-contained and where the line manager is unaware of content and can see the course as something that detracts from work rather than enables work.

So if you take the 70:20:10 model of development (Paine, 2014) where learning providers are encouraged to focus on the 70 element of on-the-job learning, the 20 element of stretched assignments and extension to the 10 which is the formal course (in other words, taking a more holistic and integrated approach) the BP programmes fit that model well. Here, the 70 comprises the content on the portal and the phone, recast as on-the-job learning rather than formal e-learning, as well as the interactions with line managers supporting the assignments and challenges which are built into the learning. The *20* is the social media and peer interaction and support. The later face-to-face course represents, then, the final *10* per cent activity at the end of this process to reinforce and reflect on the transition.

The design principle

In order to develop a programme that radically breaks the mould of conventional leadership development, the approach to design has to change. BP uses a six-stage (5Di) design programme:

Stage I: Define

This was an important first step to define the results required, rather than outlining the learning objectives. Achieving learning objectives may not result in any performance change, and performance change is often best achieved without learning (as discussed by Atul Gawande in his book *The Checklist Manifesto*). In other words, focus was very much on 'What is the change we want to see around here?', as well as 'What will we notice that is different as a result?' Essentially you work out what changes you want to see and work backwards from there.

Stage II: Run research groups

The key message in stage II is to work with practitioners. The learning team identified BP people already in first-line leadership or senior leader roles. Through a series of structured research groups, they were asked to talk about their own transition, the problems they faced, and the kind of help that they would have wished for or found helpful. The discussion continued by reflecting on other concerns or challenges in the role. Early stage tasks, and reflections on the challenges and issues, were written up so that they could be tested and validated by the research groups. Therefore, the developments at every stage were closely aligned to what people actually did in their role, and concentrated on the real challenges that they faced on a day-to-day basis. This stage was all about establishing and remaining focused on context.

Stage III: Design

The team worked on two things at this stage. The first was to curate useful resources that meet the challenges that were identified in the previous stage. These included existing materials from BP's own resources that could be included in their entirety or adapted for the programme. In addition, external resources were curated that are freely available, such as TED talks, articles, and even book extracts. This stage also helped identify what resources had to be developed as part of the programme and what had to be adapted. The decision on what resources needed to be developed was the final stage, once everything that existed internally and externally had been identified.

At the end of this stage, there was a large and comprehensive list of existing resources, alongside resources that needed to be developed. The aim here was to be as far-ranging and as comprehensive as possible. Editing down to a more realistic pot of content came later.

At this stage a matrix of assets and formats was built. In other words, it is clarified at this stage what form the assets should take. Here decisions are taken on what needs to be video, or developed as an infographic or delivered as text. Owners for each asset were assigned, and these individuals and teams were charged with preparing the assets for use on the programmes.

Stage IV: Develop

This is the development stage of the programme where practitioners and digital designers built the necessary resources. Nothing got past the wary eye of the practitioners. They ensured that each asset was fit for purpose, and no more complex or convoluted than it needed to be to get its message across. This stage, for instance, was where it was decided if it is more appropriate that a text asset, for example, is replaced by a short video. It was all about what was fit for purpose, and what was more aligned to the overall content mix.

This same development model had been used successfully for the Discover BP programme designed for new entrants to the company and for the graduate programme, BP Advance. It fitted perfectly as the framework for the first level and senior leadership development programmes too.

Stage V: Deploy

The team drew on expertise in digital marketing and design to ensure that levels of awareness and ease of access were high at launch, sustaining the momentum of the campaign over a six-month period.

Stage VI: Iterate

The team drew on lean start-up methodologies throughout the design process, meaning that they worked towards a 'minimum viable product' which could be successfully launched and which could then be adjusted through a series of iterations based on user feedback and observation.

The digital offer

In addition to the leadership portals, BP has developed a YouTube-like system for sharing and retaining knowledge called the Hub. At the time of writing, the Hub contains approximately 2,500 short videos and has been accessed around 660,000 times. All of the programmes listed are accessible from the Hub. They form simple tabs across the top of the screen. Access could not be easier and does not require any permissions or forms or registration documents to be filled in.

On the first-level leadership portal itself, there is no mention of the word 'learning'. This is a portal that provides 'all the tools you need for your transition into leadership'. The headline buttons in the first-line leadership portal comprise: becoming a leader; managing yourself; managing your team; and BP leadership expectations.

The front page includes a number of interactive buttons to help you decide where to start if you haven't got a specific issue you wish to address immediately. These include: 'what people want from a manager', 'values and behaviours', 'leadership expectations', 'code of conduct' and then a number of buttons to help gather data that will animate the smartphone and begin to help you gain feedback on your performance. These include: 'top 8 leadership mistakes', '10 questions to ask your manager', '12 questions for your peers', 'questions to ask your direct reports', '14 things to check', and finally, 'three-month checklist'. There are also two buttons that encourage participants to download the leadership app.

This front page is designed to encompass the entire trajectory of first-line managers' programme as well as seduce and entice the participant to move into the programme. It is, therefore, a critical first point of call for the participant. It has to be both enticing and attractive, but also serious and comprehensive.

There are extremely difficult decisions to be made about what works and what does not work for this home screen. Therefore, it is the participant user groups who make the final decision about how it should be structured and laid out. They are the target group, and they have to be convinced enough to want to move forward from that screen and get involved with the programme. The hope is that the home screen will encourage the participant to begin the learning journey. Once the first item is accessed, they will be hooked and will proceed further.

There is nothing flashy or over-designed about the portal page. It is fundamentally workman-like and fit for purpose. It does its job, addresses the audience needs and entices the participant to take the simple first step of clicking on one of the buttons.

The app

The leadership app is designed to do three things. The first is to act as a leadership survival kit and cover core areas succinctly to help the leader at the precise moment of need, a sort of hitch-hiker's guide to leadership. Areas covered include, communication, dealing with conflict, gaining feedback, participating in and running more effective meetings, building motivation and developing your team, as well as more specific advice on policy and process. To some extent it replaces the corporate intranet. The second area takes the same challenges and helps develop skills associated with them. This area is the data-rich aspect of the programme, where you encourage feedback, and which allows you to see at a glance how you are doing.

Each element of the app has multiple suggestions or areas to consider. There are over 200 suggestions, hints and actions. They try to cover most eventualities experienced by the first-time leader and reflect the in-depth conversations with existing staff in those roles. The emphasis is always to be practical, helpful, and succinct.

Each element of the programme that is delivered in the app is col-our-coded. The button on the home screen concerning team develop-ment, for example, is dark red. The detailed hints and tips on team motivation are in the same colour to allow the user to make simple connections and navigate the software easily. The same design sens-ibilities and ambitions that consumers expect of apps they might find in the Apple app store were brought to bear on the design of the lead-ership app.

The app encourages the participant to get regular feedback from the team, automating the process of progress monitoring and in so doing providing the organization with a rich dataset relating to the performance of its leaders. Part of this feedback will be scored and related to leadership success. This score then compares the individual with the BP average. Therefore, it is a great motivator to beat the average. If you beat the average, and so do your colleagues, the average score rises and increases the level of challenge. Everyone gets better and it is, therefore, a win-win for the organization and the team! The app is also aware of the time interval between interactions. It can, therefore, gently nudge the individual into action by pointing out, for example, 'Regular feedback is a great way to improve. Choose how often you want to receive feedback.' Then, 'It is six weeks since you asked for feedback.' The user can draw the simple conclusion that it is time to gather feedback!

By continuously pitching the user on a number of dimensions (eight in all) such as 'engagement' or 'self-development' against the BP average, it is easy to see where they slot in and to take action if they are unhappy with the conclusion. They do this by setting themselves suitable targets and challenges, all chosen from the resources available in the digital leadership programme.

The app also enables leaders to understand the different things that motivate their team members, through a simple questionnaire. This is important, as successful leaders are inclusive leaders, under-standing that different aspects of work engage different individuals within their team – encouraging leaders to flex their style accordingly. The more you know, the better you can meet the team's needs and the better the team's performance.

The app gathers data on teams directly by asking questions and scoring responses. It asks the team to define what their top motivators are, for example, 'to help society' or 'to work autonomously' or 'be more creative'. This opens opportunities for conversations and potentially a change in the structure or the process of work, in order to play to that individual's strengths and thereby increase their engagement, motivation and performance. So the app behaves like a digital assistant – prodding, informing, and guiding the owner, and prompting action when necessary. 'Assistant' is the key word here. It does not tell – it suggests – and offers information and insight without drawing conclusions. This makes it simple to develop and directly helpful. It is not an artificial intelligence robot, attempting to programme your activity or tell you what to do. This would be wholly inappropriate (and impossibly expensive to develop) when a key function of the leadership programme is to encourage leaders to take responsibility themselves, and chart their own path to improvement, as well as to develop better working practices. Instead the app encourages the development of positive behaviours such as feedback gathering and inclusivity, which in turn provide a healthy environment for engagement, performance and development. This is far more effective and affective than leaving the decision process to artificial intelligence.

Measurement of outcomes

How do we begin to track the impact of such a radical new approach? The first metric is around usage. When large numbers of staff are electing to use the resource, you have to assume it has some inherent value.

We know that there is a well-researched causal relationship between improved engagement and business outcomes in any organization. If this product can improve engagement, it is likely to increase the effectiveness of the organization. Therefore, leadership feedback and evaluation is gathered on that 'engagement' metric. Because the system is digital, it is clear what is being used extensively and what is being ignored. It is also possible to track how long users spend on a particular item or even viewing a specific video. This in turn allows the learning team to build an activity map that reveals both the hotspots and the inert parts of the programme. This is not complex; adding something as freely available and straightforward as Google analytics to the portal can accomplish much of this data-gathering role.

It is possible, therefore, to pinpoint what is clearly working and what needs attention. Tracking that activity and linking it to changed behaviour requires a whole different level of evaluation. Just as the programmes were conceived as a series of outcomes rather than learning objectives, they need to be evaluated in the same way. Team members are asked what changes they notice in the behaviour of their managers. Line managers are interviewed about their capability-building role with direct reports. Some had been part of the programme; others – as a control group – had not been involved at all. What changes do they notice? Is engagement better, or are there noticeable improvements to the company bottom line? It is, therefore, possible to gather qualitative information as well as quantitative data around the effectiveness and impact of the two programmes.

Essentially this programme is trying to change mindsets inside BP. It is encouraging staff to develop a 'proactive and growth' mindset, to see problems as complex but not insoluble, and to be solution-focused rather than defeatist. At a time of massive change in the oil industry, this process, and the changes in behaviour that it encourages, will help energy companies rebuild themselves in the light of their changed reality.

Individual or community

Considered as a whole, the programme is not structured around the success or failure of the individual. It is deliberately organized around a community of learners who are encouraged to share insights, pose questions and communicate with one another. The huge team of first-line managers in BP has more in common, spread as they are across all of the divisions and all of the geographies, than staff at different levels in their own location. There has been a deliberate creation of cohorts who are asked to share ideas and experiences in basic online community settings. Every participant is encouraged to comment or share ideas at any point, in discrete communities. When this works well, the group begins with fairly unimportant initial conversations that grow in stature over time as trust is established and then crunch into real issues and problems. Leaders learn how to ask for help and support and solutions are shared.

BP knows that communities seem to flourish when they are thrown together to achieve a specific task, and then disband at the end. Building this insight into the development of leadership communities is the next stage of development. The company is learning more and more about building successful communities to problem-solve and manage change. There are powerful incentives to include communities for development in order to encourage and sustain behaviour change and fast adoption of new ideas.

Mentoring and expert input

Any programme as important and complex as this should offer expert support on demand. The programmes are experimenting with the idea of Instant Messaging 'an expert'. This involves using the internal instant messaging system linked to a database of experts who can respond to queries and questions. It draws on that requirement within the four BP leadership values to 'develop capability'. In other words, it is a fundamental responsibility of more senior managers to come to the aid, as quickly as possible, of first-line managers who are struggling at any point. This in turn helps build a knowledge base that automatically offers instant assistance or guidance to a participant who is struggling with a particular issue. In theory at least, each iteration of the programme will be more useful to the participants as the knowledge base grows.

The senior leaders programme

The senior leaders programme can also be accessed via a tab on the Hub home screen. And, like the first-level leaders programme, it is freely available to anyone to access. If you want to know what concerns senior leaders in BP, then you are free to click on the tab!

The approach is similar in design and layout, but has a completely different focus, as you would expect. For example, the challenges of senior leaders are more likely to revolve around resilience, decision-making and strategy. In spite of all this, the similar approach functions well and is equally as popular (given the much smaller community) as the first-line leaders programme. But what is not tracked is whether the accesses of the programme by staff who are more junior in the organization has created a shared understanding of the tasks and challenges facing senior leaders, and therefore helped build greater empathy and coherence throughout the organization. All of these programmes are designed to encourage BP staff to work and see themselves as one big team as it moves through its current difficult transition.

Points you should take away

1 Design with the user, for the user. Developing any programme, let alone a leadership programme, in isolation from the user community is shortsighted, and a potential recipe for being irrelevant and unhelpful. The user community stuck with these online leadership programmes right through the development phase and into operationalization. The continuity and contact proved invaluable.

2 Careful curation works. There is a huge advantage, not to say cost saving, when you incorporate freely available resources – whether from external or internal locations – into your programme. Increasingly, when anyone wants to learn something, they reach for YouTube or a TED talk. Building this kind of material into the programme is cost saving, but more importantly it creates a sense of familiarity and a recognition that the issues being covered are generic and widespread, and plugs the BP staff into a wider leadership community.

3 Performance support is better than content dumping. There is a tendency towards using technology to break content into ever smaller pieces in the belief that it will become more useful than large chunks. However, starting with a performance support mentality is a very good structuring device and a way of ensuring that the programme meets immediate needs. It also helps generate

some focus on what is important and ensures that the programme is not too long-winded or complex. It further defines the structure so that any content can be accessed and used quickly.

4 Basic data-gathering tools, such as Google Analytics, are sensible and cost-effective. The richness of the data available is gathered without the expense or complexity of an LMS. The delivery platform for the courses can, therefore, be totally familiar and integrated into the normal experience of working with the intranet. Separate log-ons or new user interfaces can get in the way of access, particular for busy people in leadership roles.

5 If you can build in instant feedback for the leaders, they will be able to see immediately the impact they are making on their team. This has to be a motivator! It does not take complex software or artificial intelligence engines to make this work. It requires collating responses to simple questions, and measuring those responses against the average for the company.

6 Developing a largely online learning programme for leadership development has many advantages. It is instantly available when it is needed and creates a resource that is freely accessible anywhere in the world. Because it is online it is instantly scalable. This is an attractive and cost-effective option. But that may not be sufficient to make the most impact. These programmes require some support, which could include mentoring, as well as receiving expert input. It is important to work out ways to provide this that do not get in the way of the flexibility of the programme. If you do not address this issue, the programmes themselves will be less valuable and their impact will be smaller than they otherwise might have been.

7 The programmes described in this chapter are highly innovative and only in first iteration. As more is learned about what works and what does not work, the programmes will become increasingly effective. Without copying the format, there is still much to learn about how you can run similar programmes. It is possible to develop similar stand-alone initiatives, but it is also possible to use these ideas as the basis for adapting or restructuring a part of a more conventional programme.

8 This process of learning online in a resource intensive environment has some value in itself. It is encouraging staff to manage their own leadership development and it can help build lifelong learning skills. Over and above this, the encouragement to share and curate resources for others, as well as to participate in online communities, helps establish a culture of learning across the whole organization. There is some evidence emerging from BP that staff like the control that this learning opportunity provides, and this process has more generic applications for other sorts of learning in all sorts of situations. It also develops resilience by providing a model for problem-solving and self-help.

References

Auricchio, P (2015) Exploring the Use of a Blended Learning Model in Executive Leadership Development (unpublished doctoral thesis, University of Pennsylvania Graduate School of Education)

Capgemini (2016) Internal paper from the Capgemini University, following discussions with Steven Smith, VP in charge of the Corporate University

Gawande, A (2010) *The Checklist Manifesto: How to get things right*, Profile, London

Paine, N (2014) *The Learning Challenge: Dealing with technology, innovation and change in learning and development*, Kogan Page, London

Leadership development as storytelling

07

Social leadership in a large company

Introduction and context

Every process that has been looked at so far is a modification and extension of existing practice. This can yield dramatic results if executed well, as the case studies demonstrate. However, there is pressure to do more and approach leadership development with fresh eyes in order to build something more radical that deliberately confronts the culture and practices of an organization. This is not common, and the search for a suitable example took some time. What results is a study of a radical approach to leadership development that deliberately took aim at cherished parts of the company culture: its inward nature, unwillingness to challenge leaders, siloed defence of one's 'patch' and poor communication. This is an experiment and shows that an individual and radical approach can work even in a conventional manufacturing company – probably the last sector where you would imagine such a development would be appropriate.

This example explores a radical new approach to leadership development that was carried out in a high-tech petrochemical company, specializing in developing resins, polymers and thermoplastic sheets. It is a large, complex company with a turnover in billions of US dollars and staff in the hundreds of thousands. It was born from innovation (using waste by-products from the petroleum industry) and continues to innovate today. The chief executive set the company a huge challenge in 2014, which was to double revenue over the following

10 years. He recognized that, in order to achieve such an ambitious goal, the company's entire culture had to change, and with it, indeed pivotal to it, were its leaders and the quality of leadership inside the company. In order to realize that target there would have to be a fundamental reconsideration of what leadership entailed and how it was delivered. The early view was that this was a collective process with leaders working together, rather than a process where each leader worked in isolation on their own development agenda.

The CEO commissioned a boutique change consultancy – Seasalt Learning, based in the UK – to help it develop its top 150 leaders. These executives were the key managers in the company. They were of a level of seniority heading up divisions or country markets, and between them they control vast resources and large numbers of staff. The leadership programme was in essence a cultural change programme, using leadership development as the pivot. One key objective of the programme was to transform the organization's frame of reference from a local single market perspective to an increasingly global and holistic viewpoint. In addition, this process was designed to unlock new revenue streams through innovation and experimentation across the entire value chain.

This programme is fundamentally different from a more conventional leadership development assignment in that, during more orthodox leadership development, the organization defines the content and the leaders are processed through that content with the hope that at least some of it will stick. In that way, leadership practice can be developed and improved. The difference between the more orthodox and this programme is that this uses a scaffolded model of social learning (Hogan and Pressley, 1997) for the core of the leadership development process. It makes the design of the programme interactive, participative and continuous. Julian Stodd, the designer of the programme, defines scaffolded social learning as:

> a design methodology that utilizes both formal and co-created social elements. The formal components allow the organization to feed in its side of the story, whilst the co-created community discussions are 'sense making', where we construct the meaning and relate it to our everyday reality. (Stodd, 2015a)

In this way, the participants define what they need, and work out how to achieve that change in small cohorts. These cohorts are set up to evolve into strong communities of practice and support. In more conventional leadership development, most of the effort goes into developing formal content, and the rest is spent on providing support and guidance to ensure the formal content 'sticks'. In this model only 25 per cent of the content is formal. What that means is that the prepared content is designed to challenge and stimulate activity and discussion rather than act as the main focus of the learning. The remaining 75 per cent of the content is co-created by the participants with the help of their facilitators. This means that the focus remains concrete and company-relevant rather than abstract and neutral. The support infrastructure provided has the important role of ensuring that learning takes place, and that the learning is shared and anchored inside the company rather than being abstract and dislocated from it.

What is the structure?

The target group of 150 leaders was divided into 10 cohorts of 15 members each, with a staggered entry into the programme so that tacit knowledge from earlier groups could be passed on to the groups following. This would enable knowledge to be shared, enhanced and then recycled back to the first groups and so on. The aim was to churn insight constantly throughout the larger cohort whilst ensuring that each of the smaller groups developed into a tight mutual support network.

The programme was delivered across 24 weeks and was divided into three distinct phases. The first, covering weeks 1 to 4 was about community building. Each cohort was charged with the task of forming a strong guiding coalition. The entire cohort is connected socially and plugged into the broader infrastructure for the programme which all the participants will share. At this stage smaller teams are established and trust is built. These small teams need a fundamentally safe and secure space in order to discuss issues openly. One of the key criteria for developing trust is that all participants acknowledge that nothing will be shared unless it is agreed to share it. This strong level of trust is a determinant for progress to the next stage. The rest of the programme requires open discussion, sharing written ideas and editing each other's work.

The second segment covers weeks 6 to 15. This is the power segment where the main work of the programme is outlined and executed. During this segment each cohort works on articulating the kind of leaders they need to be in order to deliver the transformation required by the company. This process is both collective and individual. What sort of leaders does this organization need? What kind of leader do I want to become?

From weeks 17 to 24 the focus is on narrative: telling the leadership story in a compelling way that builds individual ownership as well as collective agreement about the nature of leadership. This is all about embedding the learning over a longer period with limited, external support. This means that the cohort has to take a larger role in ensuring the quality of the output from the programme, and the commitment and agreement of each individual member. In one sense, the programme does not ever finish, as the new approaches and leadership behaviours become habitual and redefine the culture and outlook of the company. It is about practice, the generation of tacit understanding, and implementation of the approaches that were previously agreed. This is the point where the learning from the groups breaks out most obviously into the organization as a whole. And it is at this point that real change should begin to ripple throughout the company, and that the processes developed during the programme become self-regulating and deeply embedded.

In week 5 and again in week 16, there are two week-long off-site workshops. These sit strategically between the first and the second segments, and the second and third segments of the programme. The first week-long workshop was delivered in the Middle East, and the second one in China. In the first, the group worked on a complex business simulation that was commissioned for this programme and is designed to expose the challenges that the organization faces. It allowed the participants to practise the new kind of espoused leadership model they were developing, both in the way that they tackled the problems generated by the simulation, and in the way they worked with each other. They also built their key personal and group agendas for the subsequent weeks of the programme.

The second workshop places the cohort firmly in the real world of business. The cohort, either individually or in very small teams, worked with small start-ups in China. Over the course of the week they wrote case studies of those companies, describing what they found in terms of working practices, culture, expectations and work styles. They then determined what, out of all those insights from new businesses in a new environment, could be applied to their day-to-day role in the company. The week is designed to enhance and complement the work achieved in the middle segment and prepare the participants for the third segment. The participants looked closely at the conclusions they had drawn from the second segment, and they reflected on how those conclusions had been challenged by their new insights collected in a different work and social environment, which is outside their company's culture and existing processes.

What is the programme like?

Only a small amount of the content that is used is formal. This comprises beautifully designed stimulus material, which briefly outlines the relevant weekly topic and is designed to drive forward the week's agenda. The teams are encouraged to respond, explore or challenge the formal input. For example, one article posits the idea of an 'asymmetric competition' and shows how it has become the dominant model for modern competitive business environments. The cohort is then asked to explore that idea and give examples of where they think asymmetric competition could challenge their own company – initially – on an individual basis, but then by commenting on each other's responses as a collective statement. These formal responses are compiled weekly into a magazine that is published on the community site for everyone to share and compare. It can be refined and iterated, and is then made available for all subsequent cohorts. Each cohort then builds new knowledge on the back of the existing responses – this process delivers richer and richer results as more and more cohorts move through the programme.

The term 'asymmetric competition' was first used to describe plant populations: in other words when competition between individual plants is unequal or even one-sided (Weiner, 1990). The concept has been picked up by economists to describe a modern competitive landscape where companies both compete and cooperate. For example, Apple competes with Samsung in terms of phones they offer, but Samsung supplies key components for every Apple iPhone. It also applies where advertising for one brand actually changes the market as a whole for all the competing brands in that space (Carpenter *et al*, 1988: 393–412).

The generation of the weekly magazine compiled by the cohort is aided by a group of facilitators who are known as 'storytellers'. Their role evolves as the group becomes more confident in its own narrative ability. In the early stages, for example, the storyteller may – almost as a journalist – interview the team member and then write the emerging story for them. This can evolve into an editing role or even just compiling the magazine from the content that has been submitted. It can take any form, ie written content, video blogs or podcasts. But every participant is encouraged to produce something of note on a weekly basis that is compiled into the group response and published.

It was agreed before the programme began that each participant would be required to spend three hours per week on the programme tasks. The three-hour commitment was divided into 30 minutes to absorb the formal content, and then two and a half hours to respond to it. This response required research and investigation and then some kind of 'write-up' describing that person's conclusions. In this scaffolded model, for example, one person could choose a company as an example of asymmetric competition, and the next cohort would be asked to critique or validate this choice or build on the initial idea by finding specific other, complementary examples.

The process being exemplified loops between curation, interpretation, analysis and reflection. The discovery/curation phase means engaging with content: What do you notice? What is interesting out there? The interpretation phase is where the participant adds insight and value: How is it different? What has been learned from this? Then the analysis phase: How should I respond? What else do I need?

And finally, the reflection phase – embedding the learning and working out the wider implications: What should change as a result of these insights? What can I actually do now?

This cycle of curation, interpretation, analysis and reflection is repeated hundreds of times until that process becomes habitual and a clear way of interpreting and framing issues and concerns. It generates deeper thinking, more reasoned adoption of new ideas, and a coherent response to change, based on collective discussion and personal understandings. This process is seen by the company as core to their new leadership philosophy and approach, as well as illustrating the future direction of the company. So the concept of scaffolding becomes a core element of the active design process of the programme, and the key response process for the individual learner as they work their way through the material. It is essentially about discovery, leading to perception and then interpretation (Stodd, 2015b). In other words, it is a process of making sense that moves from outside: What is out there that is interesting and maybe helpful? – to inside: What have I learned, and what can I do with this learning? How will it help me or my organization? What will I do differently as a result?

Stodd defines scaffolded social learning as:

> a way of combining both formal and co-created components into one coherent learning narrative. The formal elements will be things like workshops, eLearning, mobile materials, assessments, podcasts, reading and so on. The co-created elements are those things that we do within our communities: it's the 'sense making' activity. (Stodd, 2015b)

He points out that this process is complex and sensitive. When you go out and curate, you are actually curating your reputation at the same time. An example of this could be asking the group to bring back examples of good leadership that they have discovered and share that with the group. This could be a book or an article, but it could also be a video or podcast or even a scene from a play or a film. In justifying what it was that made the participants choose such an item, they expose their beliefs around leadership. If the discussion is handled well, it is possible to emerge with precepts about leadership that could form the fundamental building blocks for what the organization needs going forward. Instead of being 'told' that this is the kind of leadership that is appropriate for this company, the group works it out for themselves and owns the conclusion, and sets a benchmark against which they can match their progress. The individual insights have context applied to them and they become tangible and useful as a result. In addition, the process for coming to a conclusion, models the leadership behaviours that the group wishes to adopt throughout the company. In working on what they mean by leadership, in this instance, they are living and demonstrating one aspect of the leadership practice. As well, the group is learning a huge amount about each individual member and their beliefs and value systems, as well as how they work together. Done well, this is a powerful model of self-development and organizational alignment.

The programme avoids third-party case studies. It was felt by the organizers that discussing case studies from outside creates distance and disengagement. The agreement was that case study discussion is based on static information which is, on the one hand, too abstract to change behaviour, and on the other imposes distance between what is being learned and what works in the specific context in which the learner operates. Case studies force the discussion inwards, so that all of the reference points are part of the case study, not the world in which the group normally operates. So the impact is limited, and the transfer of learning into work practice does not readily occur.

Who runs the programme?

There are three roles that are crucial to the success of the programme. The first is the role of storyteller. This is the person who works closely with the cohort, helping them tell their story in whichever form is most appropriate at that point in the programme. The role could evolve from delivering quasi-journalistic interviews, ie listening and then writing up the results, through to being more of an editor who helps shape the content. The role also requires the person to take the content and merge the various contributions into a single coherent weekly magazine.

The second role is that of community manager. He or she ensures that all of the nuts and bolts of the programme are in place. This person helps individuals get connected, deals with technical issues, and ensures that participants are fully able to participate in the programme. The community manager also has the critical role, initially, of helping the group to gel. This role is practical but also focuses on the building of relationships between individuals. The manager intervenes in order to first build, and then help sustain, that community. Here he or she is sensitive to the degree of help each individual requires and is on hand to sort out any tensions that arise between members of the community.

The third role is that of workshop facilitator. This is the most obvious and generic role of the three. This person's job is to facilitate the conversations in any workshop format, regardless of whether this is held face-to-face or remotely. He or she needs to ensure that the discussions are productive, and that the lessons learned are clear and unambiguous and owned by the entire group. He or she also ensures the transfer of learning, so that the group itself gets better and better at facilitation. It is important that members of the group learn the basic skills around facilitation so that they can take on more and more of this role as the programme progresses. These skills will also be useful post-programme as a mode of company-wide learning going forward.

Essentially the community manager role is much more hierarchical than the storyteller role. The community manager is in one sense 'in charge'. In this role they ensure the distribution of content and can direct the group and encourage the completion of tasks. This is in direct contrast to the storyteller role, which is completely outside the hierarchy. Storytellers interact with the group depending on what is required. Their role is based on how well they can assist the group and do what is necessary to help the group achieve its aims. The entire role is negotiated at both an individual and group level. It is possible for the storyteller to have an entirely different role in each cohort and to operate very differently with individuals in the same cohort. If you like, the community manager defines and protects the structure, whilst the storyteller acts as the glue that holds structure together. In more conventional terminology, the former has a programme manager level of responsibility, and the latter acts as a kind of group facilitator.

If cohort members have someone working with them, with that kind of storyteller role, it is very hard for them to make the excuse that they were not able to complete an exercise. In the final analysis, that person will listen to what each member has to say and write their response! This is one of the ways that participants are encouraged, step-by-step, into active participation. There is a point, at roughly week five, where individuals are either in the programme, ie fully participating, or they have missed the boat and cannot catch up. Both the community manager, and the storyteller have a key role in ensuring that the entire cohort is active, alert and embedded into the programme during the first, few crucial weeks.

The hope and expectation is that key members of each cohort will take on the storytelling and interpretation role. This is important going forward as the learning has to be shifted from purely tacit knowledge, owned by one person – or a small group of people – into an active resource available to the entire leadership community. To emphasize the criticality of this, the company CEO organized a dinner for those participants who had emerged as the most active members of each cohort and taken on that narrative role as the organization's storytellers. By doing this, recognition was accorded to those individuals who had emerged as the seekers of sense and the sharers of insight. They had become the voices of the cohorts and the organization recognized their commitment.

The final output from the programme is a book that is presented to each member of the cohort. It comprises the formal learning from the programme, together with the responses and stories articulated by the group. Each subsequent cohort has access to that cohort's 'volume' and can learn from it. As time progresses, each cohort builds on the achievements of the previous one, and therefore the knowledge builds and becomes absorbed into the leadership practice of the organization.

Each participant leaves with a tangible acknowledgement of the process that their group has been through and what it has achieved, and their own contribution is set alongside that of their colleagues. It also has the additional advantage of being a transparent summary of what the programme itself has achieved. If anyone wants to know what has been learned, and the reason why certain leadership practices have changed, or certain processes were modified or enhanced, the answer lies in the relevant book. Each book is different – apart from the 25 per cent of common formal content – from any other book produced by the programme. By externalizing the learning in this way, each member of the cohort has a clear view of the journey taken, as well as the lessons going forward. The books are hard copy. They are not folders of material, but attractive, case-bound hardback books. This creates a sense of longevity and value. The book concept also raises the bar for the participants. If a cohort's output is encapsulated in this way, there is a certain responsibility and sense of pride to ensure that the content is of high quality and high value.

The lessons learned

A programme such as this demonstrates how important it is for organizations to gear up to a world of increasing volatility, radical uncertainty, massive complexity and ambiguity. Formulaic answers and past assumptions do not hold good, and there is no simple way of defining leadership direction and strategy. This programme created an alternative power structure to that of the hierarchy inside the organization, and helped the leader – both as an individual and as part of the leadership team – to develop new ideas and new working practices to deal with this emerging climate. By the nature of the discussions and the experiences shared, leaders are encouraged to hold spaces of uncertainty open. They are encouraged not to move too quickly to conclusions without carefully thinking through both the intended and unintended consequences.

It also develops a significant layer of profoundly connected people who have achieved a degree of openness and honesty with each other that is much more tangible than pre-programme. This developed not only over the many weeks of shared insights, but also in the two weeks away from their home base where some pretty fundamental beliefs about business and leadership were challenged.

The participants also learned the basic skills of facilitation and storytelling and learned to respect the views and perceptions of their colleagues without rushing too quickly to a conclusion. The programme encourages cross-organizational dialogue and respect for colleagues, as well as bringing in new insight and ideas from outside. This is a radical approach to leadership that holds out a real prospect of transformation, both for the individual and the company. It sets up an environment that allows leaders time to reflect and think through complex issues with colleagues, whilst not offering simplistic frames or models as a crutch. And it achieves this within the workflow for the most part. The relationship between work and learning becomes deliberately blurred during the 24 weeks of the programme.

This process, therefore, challenges leaders without offering simple solutions and forces them to look to their colleagues for resolution, insight and collective action. It does not provide any answers. The participants have to work it out for themselves and hold each other to account. The programme has an extremely complex development structure, compared to more orthodox leadership programmes that focus on the delivery of content and then move on. It requires close attention to detail and intense hand-holding in the critical set-up phases, but it has the potential to deliver substantial transformation at individual and organization level. It is as much an organization change programme as a leadership programme.

Key issues to consider

1 Organizations are inherently conservative and can put up robust resistance to social and cultural change. The models in this programme need time to embed and strong and consistent support from the top to succeed. In spite of the fact that the demand on the participants' time during the weeks of the programme is minimal, it is critical. To succeed, the programme and its processes need to become habitual during the 24 weeks and then elements have to continue into the normal workflow.

2 All participants need to be visible to the organization and communicate conclusions effectively. It will not work if it is simply a closed discussion among senior leaders. Part of the way that the programme works is to raise the stakes for everyone. If senior

leaders know that what they write or share will be seen widely across the organization, it encourages deeper, more considered thought. If you compare this with a conventional classroom session, where the individual can tune out and with no real consequence, the contrast is obvious.

3 The key roles of facilitator and storyteller have to be absorbed into the organization at some point. These individuals need status and credibility in order to survive in those roles, and the new stories which emerge after the leadership programme concludes need to be celebrated and embedded. This is the most difficult moment of transition and it requires active intervention by the organization itself. The CEO lunches were one way of offering status and recognition to individuals who participated most strongly in the process, but there have to be others built into the culture of the organization as time progresses.

4 The curation model needs an outlet for sharing insights. Harold Jarche has written at length on the power of personal knowledge mastery through his *seek, sense and share* model (Jarche, 2014). The power of this programme is in taking personal insight and turning it into organizational insight, learning and action. This is a huge step, and it is complex; but without this process much is lost. The key element in that process is not simply finding something interesting, but making sense of it and assessing its relevance in personal or organizational terms. If others do likewise, that insight takes on a much more significant status in the organization. Essentially it moves from one person's opinion to a way of looking at the world for the whole organization.

5 Working from individual insight to team insight requires challenge and debate, not just tacit agreement. How this debate occurs, and how the group reaches any conclusions, is extremely important and requires careful facilitation. It should not be dependent on the loudest voice, and it should usually be based on evidence from inside as well as outside the organization. It should lead to experimentation and testing before running to widespread implementation. Individuals and small groups have to be willing to take this leap and share the results, good and bad.

6 This model presupposes that breaking down some of the vertical hierarchies of power and mechanisms of control is desirable and productive. Arguing the case for this is complex and difficult. Particularly in the early stages of the programme, these traditional power relationships tend to re-emerge. Someone has to be sensitive to this and able to draw the group's attention to how it is performing.

7 Participants need to feel that they can speak openly without any threat of humiliation or retribution. Trusted colleagues need to be discreet and respect confidentiality. Sometimes internal IT systems can feel more visible and transparent than external systems. On this programme the use of familiar technologies outside the company, such as WordPress and LinkedIn, generated more engagement than when an internal site, based on SAP, was created for the same purposes. Comfort levels for the participants need very close attention.

8 All participants need to be visible to their community. This means that all of their postings, stories and comments need to be acknowledged and the authorship made clear. As soon as the dialogue becomes anonymous, the trust built into the whole community disappears. Or, if there is any attempt by the internal communications team to own or massage the message, the power of that message disappears and it ceases to have resonance.

9 The real benefit to the organization of a programme like this occurs when graduates of the programme become seeded throughout the organization. In this way, their influence is widespread, and the network stretches horizontally across the entire operation. In other words, this works best post-programme when much of the cohort have completed their 24 weeks. But this is the precise moment when momentum can begin to dissipate. Therefore, significant effort has to be made to ensure the networks continue, promises are kept and lessons are shared widely. It is at this stage that the organization has to take responsibility. It is as if the ball is being passed from the external agents (Seasalt in this instance) to the internal managers.

10 This kind of initiative is a slow burn. The organization needs to keep faith with what it is trying to achieve over at least a year. If the demand is to show immediate results, or if its achievements are written off too quickly because they are not as impactful as the organization might have wished, the programme will ultimately fail. Programmes like this need to evolve and be embedded inside the organization so that the output becomes 'the way we do things around here' and then the required cultural change will emerge. One of the core lessons for the participants in the programme – do not rush too quickly to a conclusion – has to be taken into account by the organization in terms of the initiative as a whole. The idea of rushing to condemn a programme that embodies the idea of reflection and patience has an irony which is too delicious not to share!

11 Many elements can be taken out of this programme and applied to other types of learning structures or incorporated into more conventional leadership development. The concept of storytelling is rich and powerful, as is the regular challenge on everyone to respond to the formal content in a 'public' way so that it can be shared. Taking time to work out the big lessons that are emerging, and what to do about taking them forward, is also useful. Pushing responsibility onto the group to ensure that learning is relevant can be a necessary and demanding consequence of any leadership programme, and it almost guarantees ownership and tangible outcomes. There is also something very attractive about gathering together the body of knowledge that has been worked on and debated by an entire cohort over 24 weeks, and publishing the results in some shape or form for each person as a permanent record of their learning journey.

References

Carpenter, G S, Cooper, L G, Hanssens, D M and Midgley, D F
(1988) Modeling asymmetric competition, *Marketing Science*, 7 (4), pp 393–412

Hogan, K and Pressley, M (1997) *Scaffolding Student Learning: Instructional approaches and issues (advances in teaching & learning)*, Brookline Books, The University of Michigan

Jarche, H (2014) The Seek, Sense, Share Framework, Blog, http://jarche.com/2014/02/the-seek-sense-share-framework/

Stodd, J (2015a) Scaffolded Social Learning in Action: Exploring competition, Learning Blog, https://julianstodd.wordpress.com/2015/04/09/scaffolded-social-learning-in-action-exploring-competition/

Stodd, J (2015b) 10 Techniques for Scaffolded Social Learning, Learning Blog, https://julianstodd.wordpress.com/2015/03/20/10-techniques-for-scaffolded-social-learning/

Weiner, J (1990) Asymmetric competition in plant populations, *Trends in Ecology & Evolution*, 5 (11), pp 360–64

Making online learning an immersive experience 08

The context

When you think about online learning as part of a leadership programme, excitement is not the first word that springs to mind as you attempt to describe the nature of that experience. There is much talk of the transforming powers of virtual reality and artificial intelligence and how the next iterations of technology will create genuine learning assistants on our tablets and phones which will order and curate our learning based on context. As always the wonderful transforming powers of technology are just round the corner and rarely on the table. This is interesting, however, and that possibility and potential is the subject of a later chapter. Here we look at the evidence of what is possible today, and how online learning can be a critical element of engagement in a leadership development programme to both deepen and broaden the learning experience. Used well, online learning can also generate learner engagement and commitment to the programme in hand. In order to try to tease out the elements that work and what is necessary to pull them together, I talked to the CEO of LEO.

LEO is one of the UK's largest and most successful learning technology companies. It was one of the core partners in the NHS Leadership programme. It was there from the very beginning as a member of the KPMG-led consortium that successfully bid for the development and execution contract of the NHS Leadership programme. LEO developed most of the e-learning and simulation elements for the Elizabeth Garrett Anderson and the Nye Bevan programmes.

The company has vast experience going back many years in developing technology-based solutions as part of leadership development initiatives worldwide.

One of the lessons from big leadership programmes, such as the NHS programme, is that you require ambitious and global consortia to make the programmes work. KPMG led the consortium but it included, alongside LEO, five top-class universities: Harvard School of Public Health, Manchester Business School, the University of Birmingham, Erasmus University in Rotterdam and the University of Pretoria (see Chapter 5 for more detail). There was no lack of deep expertise, or academic underpinning, but turning that expertise into an exciting and engaging leadership development programme that was designed to minimize face-to-face time, and therefore reverse the traditional model, was challenging. The aim of the programme managers was to change leadership development from a 2:1 ratio in favour of classroom learning, to a 2:1 ratio in favour of online. At a stroke, the learning experience was not just executed largely in the workplace, but was more directly interwoven with work itself. To achieve a new dynamic balance, required much more effort and thought than simply translating the classroom process into a series of e-learning modules. As Chapter 1 illustrates, the translation of traditional mode into e-learning mode is a first stage development and rarely works as it should. This programme required something much more profound: a transformation of the learning process. This was the focus of LEO's contribution.

LEO cut its teeth in this area when it took on the development of high-end simulations that required new thinking in online learning. It did this over 10 years ago with a range of companies, most notably for the BBC. One of LEO's formative stages of development was as the primary contractor for an important online- and CD-based learning initiative for the BBC's 15,000 journalists. Its aim was to ensure familiarity with the BBC's newly published Editorial Policy. But it had to do more than simply get staff to read the policy (a notoriously difficult task in itself). BBC staff, like most people, find the subject of compliance boring and rarely engage with it until there is something to worry about, ie when it is too late! The aim was to embed the right behaviours from the beginning, so the process of working retrospectively to fit what had already been made into the compliance model, would have been seen as an old mode of operating. It was a huge challenge, under acute time pressure, to deliver successful training to a large number of people as quickly as possible.

As the news spread round the organization that Editorial Policy training would be both online and compulsory, the immediate reaction was the generation of howls of derision. This confirmed the expectation of the development team that there would be a marked lack of enthusiasm on the part of the target audience to participate. Whatever happened, this was a tough call. The way that the BBC and LEO confronted the expectations and tackled the topic offers lessons for anyone wishing to use online learning as an integral part of a leadership development programme rather than simply as a bolt-on or an afterthought.

It was critical, when tackling such a theoretically dry subject (however important it was for the organization), to create an element of surprise, in order to defeat the negative expectations as quickly as possible. In this instance, it was important to build interest and engagement as fast as possible from the first log-in. Engagement of the learner was one of the key criteria for success in this project. This was measured by time spent online, and from gathering feedback from participants in the face-to-face sessions that every team was charged with organizing. Their role was to firmly contextualize the generic learning. This meant that the implications of the new policy guidelines were clearly understood by all programme makers and journalists. In other words, they took the appropriate guidelines that reflected their role. And then within those teams, how the editorial guidelines impacted each team member, depended on their specific job. The guidelines had to influence and challenge the whole of BBC output, on radio, television and online.

The opening sequence of the programme was set in a BBC *Question Time* planning meeting on the eve of the Iraq war, when a suitable, balanced panel had to be chosen for that show. The programme offered a choice of 16 possible candidates with one or two almost agreed. As choices were made under time pressure by the learner, messages flooded onto the screen to increase pressure on the decision-making. There was a note from Number 10 Downing Street (the Prime Minister's Office) demanding a replacement for the Labour Party nominee at short notice with someone more robust in his or her commitment to the war. The learner, in the role of programme editor, had to decide immediately whether to agree, ignore or challenge the request. Once initial decisions were made, the learner's choices were scrutinized according to the new Editorial Policy guidelines and usually found wanting. So the exhortation was to try again. Eventually the editor of the programme appeared 'live' on video to explain the actual choices that were made on that date, alongside the reasons for the choice of each member of the panel. Finally, there was a discussion around how the guidelines related to that process and which of the guidelines was specifically relevant. When a user commented that she had broken into a sweat during the first 15 minutes of using the programme, the developing team knew that the motivation to compete and complete was firmly established.

By making the guidelines reflect real-world situations where extremely high stakes decisions had to be made, the content was relevant and engaging. Complexity was increased by adding time pressure to challenge users, and forcing participants to make real decisions in real time. As a result, motivation dramatically increased. The learner was hooked within 15 minutes, and the link between decisions in the real world, BBC output on TV, radio or online and the impact of the new guidelines was firmly established. That learning programme had a 98 per cent uptake, and equivalent completion rate amongst the target group. The cohort, within weeks of the launch, had demonstrated a high level of familiarity with the new guidelines. This was in marked contrast to the impact of previous editions. They were located at the bottom of a drawer in a producer or editor's office and had been there since the day that they were distributed. In the past, the guidelines were issued, filed away and only ever referred to when there was a crisis (ie when it was too late). The BBC went – almost overnight – from being highly resistant to the idea of e-learning, to e-learning becoming the go-to mode for fast and efficient learning on a large scale.

LEO went on to develop sophisticated awareness programmes for the BBC journalists who covered the situation in the Middle East, Iraq and Afghanistan, as well as outside the BBC. BP, for example, used LEO to develop a learning programme that deconstructed the

Texas Oil Refinery fire and firmly embedded the learning that emerged from that tragedy. The learning content that was developed worked in a similar way, with the same intention of engaging the audience and building deep insight from the start.

The development process

The interactive, online material for the NHS Leadership programme was developed by a strong team, in much the same way that LEO had worked on other initiatives. Essentially, each development team comprised someone from the NHS Leadership Unit, plus one academic partner, a KPMG manager and the LEO developers. Therefore, the technical expertise to build online learning was combined with deep knowledge of the NHS, alongside public health experts. These teams reported to a central design authority that kept tabs on each development segment. The development timescale was fast and furious: programmes commissioned in March were launched in October with some continuing development post-launch for segments that occurred later in the programme. These had to be ready for the students as soon as they reached that point in the programme.

The virtual campus

At the heart of the NHS leadership programmes is the virtual campus. This is an incredibly important element as it acts as a hub for learning and as the place to start from and return to as participants work their way through the curriculum. The virtual campus maintains a comprehensive record of how far the participants have got in the programme, and it acts as an elaborate signpost to and repository for all of the other resources that are available, including the face-to-face sessions. If the virtual campus had not built a strong community of learners, and had not been extremely learner-friendly in the way in which the resources were accessed, as well as completely transparent in terms of its role, the entire programme would have wobbled. Nice touches included an automatic check of the laptop being used, so that learners could see at a glance if they were about to have any technical issues when they attempted to use any of the resources available from the virtual campus. When all the indicator lights were green, the learner knew that everything would run without technical glitches. It took less than a second to access that information.

If, on the other hand, any of the system lights glowed amber or red on the desktop, access was provided to a dedicated help desk. The idea was to prevent the deep frustration experienced by users who could not understand why their system would not work properly, what was wrong, and what they needed to do to fix it. The aim was to create as seamless a user experience as was possible, so that the learner could focus on the task in hand and not be diverted by trivial technical issues that would get in the way of the user experience.

The virtual campus is Moodle-based (Moodle, 2016). In other words it was built with open-source software that was customized and redesigned to fit the look and feel of the programme and feed the resources to the users of the NHS programme. The function of the front page is absolutely critical. It is the first formal, identifiable contact with the programme, and in learning – like many other things – first impressions count. Uncertainty and confusion within the Hub would only be amplified for the learner as they went further into the course. The development team kept the look and feel very simple. It has a brief two-line synopsis of each module, and a link to the learners' personal e-portfolio, which is used to store workplace examples that demonstrate mastery of the various elements of the programme. And the system test indicator box is there on the front page as well.

Clicking on one of the modules takes you to a detailed synopsis of the contents, including all of its components and the likely time it will take to complete them. For example, if you only have 10 minutes, it is fairly pointless and frustrating starting to read a detailed article or begin a 40-minute simulation task. You can select the component that matches the time you have. All of this is designed to be friendly and helpful and support learners as they move through the programme. It acts as a starting point, a gentle nudge to complete a module, as well as an indicator of progress. It is also the access point for all the other resources and a schedule for the face-to-face elements.

The programme is built up of a number of discrete features chosen by the designers to fit the task in hand. The learner can be asked to read something, ask questions, watch something, play an interactive exercise, explore, listen, solve a problem, discuss an issue, or share an insight. Each of these tasks has a corresponding mode in the virtual campus. For example, this could be a piece of e-learning, an activity to complete offline, a video that has been custom developed, or one available from outside like a TED video. TED stands for Technology Entertainment and Design and is the name for a series of private conferences under that umbrella, the contents of which are widely available. All presentations are free to view and run for around 15 minutes each. Many notable ideas are disseminated and speakers' insights are gathered together in TED talks.

The learner can be asked to participate in a game or simulation, share something on social media, read a PDF, or access one of the two mobile apps. In addition, participants have access to – and are encouraged to use – the University of Birmingham's specialist health and social care online library. This allows them to search for and read specific resources, such as journal articles. Research questions e-mailed to the library are answered by a specialist librarian. It is even possible to borrow books via postal loans.

The principle design feature of the NHS Leadership programme is variety. It is organized in such a way as to engage learners and provide a stimulating online environment, rather than endlessly repeating identical study modules. The media can vary from video interviews, to dramas, tutorials, audio and even broadcast programme links. The virtual campus is the place for access to expert blogs, transcripts, e-books, journals and the Birmingham University's library. The e-learning was carefully standardized into either 10-, 20- or 40-minute activities. There were also psychometric assessments, quizzes and realistic real-world scenarios to grapple with. Other features included memory joggers, set books, assignments, reference documents and weblinks. A learner handbook for the course was also provided, as well as a facilitator handbook for those facilitating face-to-face or online seminars. This was designed to be a rich and motivating learning environment, but it was not the only element of the programme.

What else?

There are two other elements of the programme. The first is the tutor-led, collaborative online learning environment, together with the large cohort-based face-to-face workshops. The second is small group action learning sets that meet regularly throughout the programme. In addition, online discussion groups and forums are freely available.

There is, therefore, a combination of synchronous online content as well as face-to-face meetings. This 'live learning' is built around a series of workshops, two four-day residential events over the 24-month duration of the Anderson Programme, group seminars, and finally a high profile graduation event!

Learner-produced content is encouraged, and assessments with tutor feedback are mandatory. The learners are expected to keep learning journals, build e-portfolios and undertake assignments as well as gather work-based evidence of progress and learning. Learners are encouraged to generate their own commentary, be it via text or video, as well as write – towards the end of the Anderson Programme – a short dissertation focusing on some aspect of their role.

The final piece of the jigsaw is the smartphone environment. Two mobile apps were developed for the programme. The first is designed to update the learner. It contains news, alumni involvement and support, and is the place to find colleagues who can help or support each learner. It is an element that helps to build and sustain a strong learning community. The other app offers a swathe of on-demand support resources that are readily to hand, whenever needed. These include checklists, process reminders, flow charts, infographics and short articles. This is similar to the use of mobile apps in the BP leadership initiative (see Chapter 7).

There are three critical modes for the learner. The first is study mode. Here the learner uses a laptop or an office computer and concentrates on grasping new ideas and looking more at the theory of healthcare systems. The second is work-based learning mode. Here learners gather evidence of achievements and insights whilst at work and in the workflow. The focus is on putting into practice some of the existing learning. The third is interactive mode where the learner is in active discussion, either face-to-face or online with peers, or contributing to the blog, or tackling challenges. It is absolutely clear how these elements lock together, and the importance of engaging across all three modes. In fact, participation in all three modes is critical for the successful completion of the programme.

In many ways, therefore, the leadership programme is both a thing in itself, and a preparation for continuing professional development. It acts as preparation for all the modes of learning that the users may encounter across their careers. It also convinces reluctant or under-confident learners that they are capable of studying at a high level, and demonstrates the positive correlation between study and effective performance in the workplace.

Building a sense of reality

One huge question in a leadership programme of this complexity is how you keep it locked into the real world of work that the learner enters and deals with every day. It has to supply context that makes sense. This allows learners to move from what is largely academic and abstract, to confronting workplace issues directly. It is important that learners who are enmeshed in the day-to-day visceral reality of the NHS (or any other organization for that matter) get a sense that this programme engages with this reality. This is at the heart of the pro-gramme's effectiveness and is a critical pathway to keeping learners on track and motivated.

There is not one simple way that this is achieved, but a number of techniques are exploited. One is drawing regularly on NHS staff and asking them to share, on video, their own leadership experiences. These are called vox pops and comprise leadership stories from NHS staff that link the learners with people like them from whom they can learn.

Another element is the Video Wall. Here, there are brief videos from patients and carers as well as NHS staff, describing their experi-ences of the NHS system, and sharing their frustrations about the current leadership. One person talks about her specific experience as a patient following a skydiving accident; another discusses the diffi-culties of adapting to the wide-ranging challenges facing the NHS. The average posting is less than two minutes. So in a 10-minute ses-sion you can easily watch five or six of these commentaries and get a strong sense of the environment and the issues confronting those in the NHS and its clientele.

One of LEO's key roles was to build a simulated NHS Trust called Glenvern. This allows many opportunities to put the learner in the hot seat and experience what it is like running an NHS Trust 'for real'. Small teams on the Bevan Programme run Glenvern and make decisions related to funding and direction and then watch the consequences. Learners are leaders responding to conflicting pressures in the Trust, in A&E or elderly care, for example. Where do you put your resources and why? On what basis do you make your decisions? What are your driving objectives? Scenarios are dramatized using actors and NHS facilities, to create a sense of realism and build the pressure on learners. This part of the programme goes back to the heart of the issues in the Mid-Staffordshire NHS Foundation Trust that led to a government inquiry into its failures. There, decisions were made on the basis of balancing the budget rather than providing quality patient care. By working through the simulation, the learners run the Trust Board and make big strategic decisions that affect the overall success of the Trust in its community. And of course this is precisely what many of them will be doing on leaving the programme. The simulation acts as an opportunity to put the academic theory to the test and revise the learning on team working, decision-making, etc.

There are major, scripted film dramas emerging from the Glenvern NHS Trust simulation. They are shot in realistic locations and use professional actors to create both the illusion of reality, and a strong sense of tension and drama. They look like high quality TV drama and they run extended storylines that allow the leader to get closely involved with the lives of the participants. There is an extended scenario, for example, set in the A&E department of the Trust hospital, where things are going badly wrong and roles are confused. The learner has to interject and make decisions in real time as the drama unfolds. Again, this is a useful exercise for the individual who is asked to take a leadership role in the scenario, and also serves as a richly fertile ground for discussing as a group.

The programme uses the power of storytelling to engage and motivate the learner. What might be dry abstract questions about where to allocate funds, become dramas that appear to impact the lives of 'real' people. There is much that has been written about the power of storytelling and its importance. For example, the chapter that Terrence Gargiulo added to the book he edited, *The Trainer's Portable Mentor* (Gargiulo, Pangarkar and Kirkwood, 2008), is called 'Seven strategies on how to use stories to increase learning and facilitate training'. He argues that stories are fundamental not just to learning but to encourage the participants to think more clearly and make better decisions (Gargiulo, Pangarkar and Kirkwood, 2008: 227–34).

Stephanie Reissner and Victoria Pagan in a recent book, *Storytelling in Management Practice* (2013), focus on a research project that explored the effectiveness of storytelling as a tool. The book reveals the dynamic relationship between any story, the person delivering the narrative, the audience and, most importantly, the organizational context for its delivery (2013: 4). The book helpfully distinguishes between the purposeful deliberate use of storytelling when it is a conscious tool, and its use in more spontaneous and intuitive contexts when a leader decides, almost on the spur of the moment, that this could be helpful in getting the message across (2013: 3). This is both a practice of sense making, but also sense giving (2013: 64). These distinctions are helpful in an online learning context.

There is, however, a significant body of literature that simply endorses the power of storytelling without providing any evidence of its effectiveness. For example, the book *Lead with a Story* by Paul Smith (2012) ends the first chapter with the statement: 'Experience is the best teacher. A compelling story comes a close second' (2012: 4). He provides no evidence to substantiate the statement. He also claims and celebrates the fact that 'storytelling has retaken its rightful place in management's bag of leadership and influencing tools' (2012: 5). When, how, where and why are the questions that spring to mind and need answering!

In the NHS Leadership programme these dramatic stories have a clear purpose to:

- lock the programme into the lived experience of participants;
- offer them the opportunity to make decisions and see the consequences in a safe space;

- engage the learners in tackling complex problems that impact on the NHS;
- create narrative continuity from one module to the next;
- draw learners into the programme emotionally by exploiting the power of narrative to engage.

The scenario feedback can be complex and detailed. One discussion panel on the screen shares this with the learner: 'Throughout this scenario, you have seen a series of dilemmas faced by a ward manager. At each stage you have seen the results of your decision. Let's now reflect on what these decisions represent. At each stage you were presented with two options. Whilst neither was necessarily correct or incorrect, one always gave you the opportunity to challenge others. You also indicated your comfort with the decisions. On the axes we have plotted your responses. Read the description associated with each quadrant in order to learn more about what this means' (NHS Leadership Programme).

The feedback showed where each learner was located – in a quadrant made up of two axes: not challenging... to challenging, and comfortable... to not comfortable – based on how they respond to the choices given. This approach is not designed to tell the learners what to do, but to allow them to explore their own 'natural' leadership approach and style, and perhaps modify their behaviour in the light of this feedback. This output of this data also provides a rich source of discussion in a tutorial or can be used as one of the wicked problems that an action learning set has to tackle.

In another scenario related to a team meeting, the learner is asked to take on the role of Abigail Elliott. Abigail is a member of the team and an occupational therapist. The meeting is being chaired by Annette Costa, who is a relatively new leader. The dilemma is posed when Annette asks if anyone in the team has any concerns they wish to raise.

'Abigail does remember an initiative being discussed with the acute hospital regarding discharge planning prior to Annette Costa starting her new role as team leader. This appeared to be important at the time and she knows that discharge planning has not improved.' What should Abigail do?

The choices are: to not raise this as a concern and search out a copy of the discharge planning initiative; to not raise it as a concern, but to check with some members of the team informally after the meeting to see if they remember this initiative; or, to raise it as a concern straight away at the meeting, and ask if the team has an agreed objective around their relationship with the acute trust and/or discharge planning.

The consequences of each of these choices then follow through the rest of the scenario, which leads to feedback similar to that discussed above. Each of these scenarios is realistic and debates a dilemma that will be familiar to many of the learners. It also helps the participant understand the bigger picture – in this case when and how to intervene in a meeting – in a safe environment where choices can be tested and analysed.

The importance of the learning team and the cohort are strongly evident throughout the NHS Leadership programme. When the participants are acting as the Board of the Trust and making their decisions, others are observing their behaviour. The peer group assesses whether individuals stay on the Board, or whether they are replaced if it is agreed that the person is not performing well. That ability to judge peers and sometimes make hard decisions is a core competence that should be carried into the real world of the NHS once they leave the programme. Again, failing to take action when leaders witnessed unacceptable decisions and poor performance was a key aspect of the failure of the Mid-Staffordshire NHS Foundation Trust.

What is the impact?

The scope of the leadership programmes is substantial. By 2016, over 3 million hours of learning and 4.5 million hits on the virtual campus. There have been over 200,000 participant posts and 1.18 million views in the forums linked to the programmes (LEO data). As a clear indicator of the status of the programme within the NHS, the CEO of NHS England has made a point of presenting the certificates in person to the graduates at the award ceremonies.

What many learning professionals will tell you is that graduation ceremonies, and statistics detailing participation rates for learning programmes, are almost irrelevant because the only data that really matters concerns impact and sustained change in the NHS. It is still too early to offer definitive conclusions: obtaining this evidence could take up to five years, as cohorts of graduates seep into the four corners of the NHS and begin to link up their individual spheres of influence to make systemic change possible. But the early signs are good, and concerted action is taking place on the ground as a result of the programme (according to Piers Lea, CEO of LEO).

Over 95 per cent of participants increased their understanding and developed their leadership skills, and 97 per cent claimed to have applied their learning to the workplace. This is having a direct impact on the way the NHS is run on a local scale. One Nye Bevan participant claimed: 'The Nye Bevan Programme has given me wings. Not the sort you get from a leading energy drink but the sort that has enabled me to meet new and inspiring people, and to appreciate the difference I can make to move my career forward in the NHS.'

Another participant claimed: 'It has challenged me and in turn I am challenging others, especially those people that I work closely with but also those I can and do influence.'

There is clear evidence of the impact programme graduates are having on their teams, and, in turn, on the quality of the services to patients. Over 35 per cent of those responding to post programme questionnaires confirmed promotions, acting up, or role enhancements as a direct result of the programme, and this tended to occur within a month of graduating. Graduates say that if they meet fellow graduates, they immediately switch into more productive conversations (conversation with Piers Lea).

In other words, the programme is teaching a new kind of discourse that will lead directly to positive change once it is more firmly established inside the culture of the NHS.

There will be a major impact review of each element of the leadership programme in 2017 as part of any re-funding proposal, which will add flesh to the evidence already gathered.

Issues to note

It might appear that the kind of immersive online experiences described here require massive budgets to deliver. Clearly this is not a cheap option, but there are many other factors leading to success than simply the size of the budget. Amongst the ones that this example reveals are the need for a team approach. Scriptwriters are only as good as the storyline which they are given. The development team need an almost visceral understanding of the environment that they are building scenarios from. Retaining that taste of reality requires more than talented writers, directors and producers. The experts from the NHS had to be involved at every stage.

Secondly, the topics must be sharp, and focused on key leadership issues. Too much narrative and it becomes a drama, not a learning scenario. It is better to linger on the decision about topic, and debate the consequences at length, than rush to a decision and then find after expensive pre-work that it will not deliver the goods.

The team needs to trust each other and respect each other's contributions. Arrogance or misplaced expertise can wreck a project like this. And project planning is critical. There are complex elements to be woven together and built into the programme which therefore need tight budgeting and strong cost control.

Finally, the user needs to test everything. The team may be happy, but the fresh pair of eyes from a potential participant is priceless. Due to time constraints or tight budgets, this stage can be omitted and it is almost invariably a mistake when this happens. The team needs to know that the scenario is both gripping and effective. The use of standard TV drama techniques to build tension and suspense are very important to develop engagement, but the point is leadership learning not realistic drama. That should always be the baseline.

Lessons for others

1 To make an impact on any complex organization requires considerable investment and attention to detail. To build quality, immersive online learning requires a high-quality development team. The impact of academics and representatives of the users, alongside a professional group of interactive learning developers, made the difference between authentic and inauthentic content.

2 The decision to have an internal unit run the programme, whilst leaving day-to-day management in the hands of an external agency, was important. It meant that the agency could focus on the detail of each element of the project, and ensure that the programme would be delivered to specification and on time, as well as manage the complex mesh of partners. Meanwhile the unit was able to keep an overview of the whole programme and ensure that the interactive content, the most costly investment in development, was delivering maximum value.

3 Simulations that appear unrealistic, look amateurish, and do not have an aura of the real world, are ineffective. To build good simulations is time-consuming and expensive but can give any leadership programme an edge. The edge comes not from the quality of the technical execution, although that is important, but from the script. The model for the approach taken was TV medical drama, not other learning material. Every script had to be vetted in terms of its attention to detail and reflection of real work situations so that users would feel that the leadership programme had put its finger on tensions and problems that felt realistic. Everything had to be co-scripted. It needed professional scriptwriters working with experts to ensure rigour and authenticity. This partnership was extremely productive.

4 The virtual campus is the hub of the entire programme. It simply has to work seamlessly to create credibility for the programme as a whole. Something like this needs to be user tested constantly to make sure that it is fit for purpose. Without it, the scaffolding around the entire programme would be missing and learners would be without a home space to begin and end learning journeys. The interactive elements were not isolated from the main content. They were situated next to articles that deepened, in leadership or health delivery terms, the learning experience.

5 The entire suite of leadership programmes is deliberately located in a recognizable mirror of the organization. As much content as necessary reflects back the real world that participants know and have to engage with. This combination of actual people working in the service and actors playing recognizable roles offers an experience that reflects both reality and insider knowledge. But looking inward is not enough. New ideas and challenges to existing practice were also very important. The serious academic underpinning gives depth and credibility. Well-engineered content was essential, but not sufficient for success.

6 The voice of the learner and people working in the NHS at a service level is extremely important. The 'customer' is never forgotten, as improvement of the patient experience was a driving force in establishing the NHS Leadership Academy. The voice of the patient is woven in throughout the interactive elements. This aspect was led by one of the consortium partners: National Voices, a coalition of health and social care charities in England (National Voices, 2016).

7 This programme was never designed and would never succeed as a lonely exercise for individual students staring at a computer screen. The community, the team, the tutorial and action learning groups were all designed to reinforce the learning, and develop a strong learning community. One purpose for this was to support the learners on their journeys through the programme. But the second reason was to forge connections that would endure for an entire career. A strong and consistent network, available once the individual learner had graduated, was designed to ensure that the changes tested in the programme would lead to permanent change and consistent improvements.

8 The programme has to establish a balance between being challenging intellectually, to justify the level of qualification on the one hand, and being daunting and overly complex on the other. In some ways the simulations and the interactive elements, although

presenting difficult and challenging problems, took the participants into familiar ground and reassured them that this was a recognizable world that they could change. Sharing thousands of comments online also created the idea of the 'we' going through it together and not 'me' isolated and confused. These groups not only enhanced the learning by sharing insights but also acted as a deep well of reassurance for participants.

9 In some small way everyone was on a mission to improve leadership. The pressure to do something well, that had an outcome that would benefit all participants inside or outside the organization, drove the programme development forward. There was collective pride in the quality of what was being developed and the impact that it would have.

10 The relationship between the various partners was complex but, from the beginning, each partner knew their allocated role and this allowed productive work to be delivered from the beginning of a very tight development cycle. LEO knew what they were doing in terms of interactive resource development and managing the development of online resources, but they needed the experts from the NHS to make it all work.

11 Due to the ferocious criticism of the workings of the NHS in government reports, in particular the Francis Report (2013), there was huge impetus to succeed in this leadership development endeavour. Specific recommendations had been made about improving leadership in the NHS and this response carried an enormous burden of responsibility. The fact that it was developed under intense scrutiny improved its coherence rather than lessened it.

Conclusions

There are a number of tangible takeaways from this chapter. The contribution that realistic scenarios can make to a leadership programme is significant. It is learning by storytelling and, as the previous chapter shows, storytelling is engaging and important. But it adds that crucial dimension of reality. Here are real leadership issues that should be familiar to anyone going through the prog- amme. Solving them in a scenario reinforces the link between the learning and the world of work. It builds confidence, and demon- strates to the learners the journey they have been on. It reveals their increasing ability to understand and tackle issues in the workplace.

In spite of the complexity, the benefits make the effort worthwhile. The most important element is to ensure that the scenarios represent cases that are immediately familiar and resonant, and at the same time reflect difficult problems that have no immediate or obvious answer. The characters have to feel like familiar members of the workforce.

This use of immersive situations can work for large numbers of leadership programmes, and the length and number can be cut to fit smaller budgets. The most practical steps to take are:

- Build a team who can complete this.
- Work hard to develop credible and challenging scenarios.
- Find people who can act to play the roles. If professional actors are too expensive, then amateur dramatic companies can sometimes deliver.

Always follow through demonstrating the consequences of choices that the participants make. Limit the complexity, and limit the number of steps if budgets are tight, but do not skimp on developing the right scenarios, or asking the right questions.

Always embed the learning into the main course structure so what is being delivered is integrated into the whole. And if you are using something like the virtual campus that was used in the NHS Leadership Programme, make sure that the scenarios are part of the learning mix, and not set apart. All the elements of the programme should reinforce one another. I would encourage you to try building immersive experiences. They are very effective and they work.

References

Francis Report (2013) Executive summary, *Report of the Mid Staffordshire NHS Foundation Trust Public Inquiry*, TSO (The Stationery Office)

Gargiulo, T L, Pangarkar, A and Kirkwood, T (2008) *The Trainer's Portable Mentor*, Wiley, San Francisco, CA

Moodle (2016) Website, http://moodle.com/hq/. Moodle is an open-source learning management system that launched in Australia in 2001. It operates worldwide through a series of accredited partners, and a small central team in Perth, which is responsible for the core development of the project and licensing the partners.

NHS Leadership Programme: Interactive scenarios (Source: LEO learning private PowerPoint presentation)

National Voices (2016) Website, http://nationalvoices.org.uk

Reissner, S and Pagan, V (2013) *Storytelling in Management Practice: Dynamics and implications*, Routledge, Oxford

Smith, P (2012) *Lead with a Story: A guide to crafting business narratives that captivate, convince, and inspire*, AMACOM, a division of American Management Association, New York, NY

PART FOUR
Elements for Transformation

Action learning 09
The community develops itself

Introduction

Action learning has become a feature of many leadership development programmes. In this book, it is an element of the storytelling,
the Deakin University, and the NHS case studies. As an idea, it is
having a bit of a renaissance as it registers well with leadership
through complexity and uncertainty. It fulfils the need for leaders to
begin to work things out collectively and support each other. It is
sometimes about working in the organization, and sometimes about
working on the organization. As such it is a powerful addition to the
portfolio of activities out of which leadership programmes are built,
it requires some detailed investigation.

Action learning, as it has come to be known, was devised by a mer-
curial figure called Reg Revans. Revans was born in 1907 and died in
January 2003. He was an academic, astrophysicist (in his early career)
and latterly a writer and management consultant. His career encom-
passed a local authority education officer, director of education for
the National Coal Board, and the first Professor of Industrial
Management at the University of Manchester. His philosophy was
based on the growing recognition that adults working together as
non-experts could solve problems that eluded individual expert
attention. So far so good, but the term was never really pinned down
by Revans (Pedler, 2015) and later developments have made the term
completely familiar and rather confusing at the same time. It is
familiar because the term is in widespread use and it sounds simple.

It is confusing because it gets caught up with a whole clutch of similar terms like action research, action inquiry or appreciative inquiry, and it is sometimes very hard to tell them apart. Add the fact that the term, invented by Reg Revans in the 1970s, has been extended and developed ever since – and sometimes in a way that Revans may not have recognized – and you have a recipe for error and confusion. The outcome of this is that people proudly share their action learning programmes that are not really action learning at all, and others describe activities that are clearly close to action learning but never use the term.

In this chapter I want to resurrect what is helpful and useful about action learning, and give some practical guidelines to make it work for you. I am not going to have a semantic argument about which practice is 'purer' than any other. The explicit aim is to unwrap the concept and allow you to use it extensively in a way that makes it your own, and not force you down a rigid, ideological corridor with a checklist of dos and don'ts. But before that, it is important to share the historical context in which action learning grew and flourished and demonstrate that it is not a separate disconnected concept, but one that emerged from a rich vein of thought and experimentation after the Second World War in both Europe and the United States. And the concept continues to evolve through practitioners in many countries. If we claim that the origins are British, then we miss the extensive development in Asia, notably South Korea and China. And if we hang on to Revans too tightly we ignore the contribution that Dr Michael Marquardt from George Washington University, and his World Institute for Action Learning, has made over the last 20 years to popularize, codify and certify action learning practitioners. It is important to acknowledge that at its most fundamental level, everyone agrees what it is: small groups solving leadership or organizational problems, by asking questions and taking action, and getting better at what they do by taking action and building their capability.

1. Where does action learning come from?

To fully answer that question we have to return to the 1940s and the beginnings of applied psychology led by a remarkable German Jewish psychologist, Kurt Lewin. Lewin was a social theorist who focused on action research and social communication. He had been part of the Institute of Social Research in Frankfurt in the 1930s but was forced into exile (first to Britain and then to the United States) when Hitler came to power. Notably, he set up 'sensitivity training' at the behest of the director of the Connecticut State Interracial Commission, which was designed to make people aware of their own prejudices and become more sensitive to others. He developed these ideas in the National Training Laboratories, which he established in Bethel, Maine, in 1947 from his academic base at MIT. This research and practice had a massive impact on the direction and development of the London-based Tavistock Institute under its then director Eric Trist, and jointly they established *The Journal of Human Relations*. There are many accounts of this, but the University of Sheffield has a website dedicated to Action Inquiry and Action Research which covers the early history (see University of Sheffield, 2016).

Lewin pioneered Training Groups or T-Groups at this centre in Bethel, which focused on group development and group exploration. Meanwhile psychologists like Carl Rogers and John Rawling Rees in the United States, and Trist at the Tavistock Clinic in London, focused on helping ex-soldiers deal with post-war stress disorders. Due to the large numbers involved, this work became group based and these became known as 'Encounter Groups'. Over the next 10 to 15 years these ideas merged and splintered, but the focus on self-exploration, inquiry, and the encouragement to take action remained as a spine that linked them. At the heart of this was a new and fundamental concept of knowledge, known as an iterative process (Pedler, 2015); if you have an idea, act upon it and see what emerges. Learn from that process. This is essentially an experiential model of learning and you can trace its origins right back to the educational philosophy and ideas of the US educationalist and philosopher John Dewey. He said in his book, *Democracy and Education* (1916):

> The self is not something ready-made, but something in continuous formation through choice of action.

You could also argue that this idea of iteration from action applies equally to the development of organizations, so it is not hard to see a link between individual growth, change and organizational development. The concept of action learning links into all three of these.

Learning then is a process of discovery and iteration and is fundamentally a social process. We learn best in an environment that fosters curiosity and enquiry (Dewey, 1916: chapter 25). Dewey demands thoughtful action from experience:

> On the active hand, experience is trying – a meaning which is made explicit in the connected term experiment. On the passive, it is undergoing. When we experience something we act upon it, we do something with it; then we suffer or undergo the consequences. We do something to the thing and then it does something to us in return; such is the peculiar combination. The connection of these two phases of experience measures the fruitfulness or value of the experience. Mere activity does not constitute experience... experience as trying, involves change, but change is a meaningless transition unless it is consciously connected with the return of consequences which flow from it. (Dewey, 1916: chapter 11, paragraph 1)

Again Dewey's comments could apply to personal learning and, by extension, into the concepts around organizational development as a conscious process led by committed individuals attempting to change their environment or themselves.

There is also a strong link to the idea of 'Appreciative Inquiry'. Appreciative Inquiry emerged in the 1980s, notably in an article called 'Appreciative inquiry in organizational life', by David L Cooperrider and Suresh Srivastva, published in 1987. It is a model for organizational change based on affirming what is great about a particular organization and building on that positive potential, and is a development built out of the concept of action research.

However, it would be naive to see organization development as simply one concept. It has many branches but one solid core, which I have tried to describe above. It has evolved over 50 or 60 years and this process is described in an excellent 2005 article in the *Leadership & Organization Development Journal* by Ron Cacioppe and Mark Edwards (2005: 86–105). The article describes and comments on a number of critical landmark ideas and concepts around the theme of organizational development as they emerged over time.

These include: integral theory (Ken Wilber); spiral dynamics (Don Beck and Chris Cowan); corporate transformation (Richard Barrett), and the action enquiry model developed by William Torbert.

Torbert is still practising, and explains action inquiry in a recent video on his website. He says that every time you take an action it is also an inquiry as you do not know the outcome; and every time you ask a question (inquiry) it has an effect and an action. When you realize that they are conjoined, you can become much more powerful in the way you do that. He developed his theories whilst at Yale in the 1970s, notably in his book *Learning from Experience: Towards consciousness* (1973). The definitive volume on action inquiry was published as *Action Inquiry: The secret of timely and transforming leadership* (2004). Its origins go back specifically to the work of Kurt Lewin, which is discussed above.

2. What is action learning?

Garnett and Ecclesfield, in their recent paper 'Towards an adult learning architecture of participation' (2014), claim that:

> learning starts with the informality of social interactions [and]...
> metacognitive learning processes are best supported by social
> interactions between learners, and this is particularly true, of course,
> in adult education.

Their point is that, in a world increasingly dominated by online learning, often aimed at individuals working alone, space has to be found for social interactions and myriad discussions. In order for adults to improve effectively as learners and have the competences available to take charge of their learning destiny, they need to be exposed to social learning in as many ways as possible. The rise of action learning is partly a response to the need for getting people together to learn from each other and support each other as they begin to take action to improve their situation in the workplace.

The article pays implicit lip service to the idea of action learning. I will look at it from its original definition and exposition by Reg Revans in the 1970s, through to contemporary uses as part of larger leadership development programmes, or as a standalone process for developing leaders. Action learning is, predominantly, a structured mode of social learning. At its heart it is quite straightforward. It is predicated on Reg Revans' claim that 'there is no learning without action and no (sober and deliberate) action without learning' (Revans, 2011). It takes a midpoint stance between a completely informal process and one requiring formal or rigid structures. It is a specific and unique approach to participative adult learning, and group problem-solving and is therefore potentially an important element in any model of leadership development, particularly when much of the input is online or aimed at individual learners.

In his own words, Revans described action learning as 'sets of comrades in adversity, meeting regularly to discuss and work on each other's problems' (Revans interview, 1984). This is probably the simplest and most succinct definition possible! But there are a number of clues in that definition, which point to the heart of Revans' philosophy and approach. Firstly it is a group of 'comrades' who meet – peers who know and respect each other. These are not random groups, or forced groups, but colleagues who know each other well and freely choose to join the action learning set. They are comrades in adversity. They have a unique collection of shared problems, together with a strong motivation to improve their lot or the lot of their organization. Action learning sets do not form for one-off meetings, but become a regular meeting where they work on one of their colleagues' issues before moving on to another issue, and so on round the table. And this process holds good meeting after meeting, until the action learning process of asking good questions, and helping the person who is seeking advice, continues through the groups and on to action of some sort. And, of course, the problems have to be complex enough to sustain the interest of the group, so that they cannot be subject to simple, expert resolution.

3. The basic philosophy

There is nothing particularly complex about action learning. The model of learning is based on the idea that adult learning comprises two elements. The first is the programmed element. Revans calls this 'getting new knowledge that exists, but you were not aware of'

(Revans interview, 1984). The programme element can come from a lecture, book, structured learning materials, etc. The second element is asking questions and getting better at asking questions, that explore the unknown, and help you move forward to solve your own problem. Revans would argue that the difference between action learning and other forms of learning is simply the balance between the content delivered (P) and the questions asked in response (Q). In action learning there is much more Q than P. In more conventional learning modes, it is the other way round, ie lots of input and very few, if any, questions. The core element of action learning, however, is the action! Revans believed axiomatically that one led to the other. There was no learning without an action and no action without resulting learning (Revans, 2011: 5).

4. Why is action learning important?

Action learning has been around since the 1970s, and if you look at Google search data historically, it was being searched for quite extensively in the 1990s and the early part of this century. It then declines hugely in popularity as a search term. If you look at the Google data now, there is an uptick occurring once again. Many people are discovering its relevance in an age of uncertainty, rapid change and complexity.

I have direct experience of action learning. Under Mike Pedler's influence, the leadership programme at the BBC became one of the biggest action learning rollouts anywhere in the world at that time. The BBC ran hundreds of action learning sets and I have talked to many individuals and organizations that see the enduring value of action learning as part of knowledge sharing, management and leadership development, as well as community building. It is important, and it needs more people to know about it and feel confident to use it as a tool for individual and organizational development.

Reg Revans was born in 1907 and died in 2003. He had an extraordinarily long, and varied life. He attended the funeral of Florence Nightingale! He met Albert Einstein, and Einstein's advice to him – 'if you think you understand the problem, make sure you are not deceiving yourself' (which was quoted in his *Times* obituary) – helped him to develop his theory of problem-solving and the role of the non-expert. Revans therefore began a research process that distinguished fundamentally between knowledge and wisdom. This distinction is somewhere at the core of action learning.

He began to detest the cult of the 'expert'. He wrote a *Guardian* article in the 1980s criticizing our naive faith in experts and their power to solve all our problems, which was widely quoted but not well supported. His view, quite simply stated, was that experts suck all the air out of the room. In other words, we all defer to experts and that stops us thinking and it stops us working out our own problems. He believed that there were problems that were too difficult to be left to experts! He acknowledged that difficult problems were indeed the domain of the expert, but what later came to be known as 'wicked' problems (a term coined by Horst Rittel and others) were often poorly dealt with by experts. The problems were 'wicked' in the sense that they were complex, not necessarily bad, and had no simple straightforward answer! A wicked problem has no obvious solution. Solving a wicked problem requires wisdom as much as knowledge and, preferably, the wisdom of a diverse group who can share their insights. It is likely that no one person can solve a wicked problem. There is no template or model to follow when attacking a wicked problem, but the solution emerges from questioning and discussion. The solution is neither obvious nor simply hidden – it emerges as the group tries to clarify the issue by asking questions and challenging assumptions.

Increasingly, because of growing complexity in our world, the kinds of problems we face in organizations are more likely to be wicked as opposed to difficult! Revans also believed that when a group commits to helping to solve a wicked problem there is a more complex process going on between members of the group than if the same group were listening to an expert. Action learning builds confidence, encourages knowledge sharing, and helps build strong communities. It is also an enduring process that lasts longer than any learning programme, and becomes a tool going forward for continuing leadership development and problem-solving. Handling any problem outside the organization or the leadership of an organization (such as handing it to consultants) denies, disenfranchises and detracts from establishing an enduring process to deal with those issues. Action learning encourages proactivity and the ownership of challenges and self-help.

Revans started his career as a doctoral student in astrophysics at the University of Cambridge. He went on to become an assistant education officer in Essex. He then became Director of Education for the National Coal Board from 1945 until 1950. It was in the National Coal Board that he began to implement what later became known as action learning. Therefore, this process is well over 60 years old. Yet far from being completely mainstream, its implementation is still the exception rather than the rule. There are many reasons for this, but the process of sharing the outcomes of action learning projects does not focus on the process, and there is still some confusion in terms of what it is and what it does.

Following the National Coal Board he had a hand in establishing the University of Manchester Business School and applied – but was rejected – for the top job, largely because he wanted the curriculum of the Business School to be based on an action learning model rather than the Harvard case study model that the founding academics eventually adopted. His failure to secure the top job led to his exit from Manchester University. For the remainder of his career he was a writer, consultant and management guru. He is one of the key figures in the development of management education, certainly in the UK, and probably around the world.

In 1984 Revans recorded a videotaped interview about action learning where he tried to explain what it is and why it is important in straightforward terms (Revans interview, 1984). It is an armchair discussion about the various components of action learning, and the YouTube clip is an extract from a much longer interview that is still available to purchase from the International Foundation for Action Learning, which is a UK-based federation of practitioners and exponents of action learning.

Here are four relevant quotations:

At its simplest, [the Foundation for Action Learning] is a set of comrades in adversity.

In a changing world, it is extremely important that people should become the masters of the art of posing questions. When no one knows what is going to happen next, you must have the skills to ask questions that are likely to get you somewhere.

> The fundamental difference in action learning is that there is a small amount of P – programmed knowledge, and a large amount of Q – the ability to ask penetrating questions.

> [Action learning] is the balance between what you are instructed to do by experts and what you are finding out you need to do for yourself.

A more practical definition has been given by Mike Pedler and Christine Abbott (2013). They define what constitutes an action learning set, and basically there are four fundamental elements:

1 Each person participates voluntarily.

2 Each person must own an organization task, problem, challenge or opportunity on which they are committed to act.

3 The group is formed to help each member think through the issues, create options and above all...

4 Take action and learn from the experience of taking that action.

It seems seductively straightforward, but to get it working well requires a number of factors to align. Action learning does not work in organizations held together by fear and where there is a decided lack of honesty between colleagues, or an almost visceral unwillingness to share. The culture has to be right, or action learning has to be introduced as part of an explicit change programme where cooperation, teamwork and knowledge sharing are seen as fundamental.

The best sets are made up of diverse groups of peers drawn from across the organization, so that they can bring their different insights to bear. When one member has bigger problems, or is seen as higher status than the rest, the set will usually fail spectacularly quickly, or under the weight of its own inertia. Therefore, diversity and equality are critical.

Another key element of an action learning set is facilitation. This can be from outside the group, or a revolving responsibility of the group as a whole. The facilitator keeps the group focused, ensures that everyone has an opportunity to speak, clarifies the resulting action that emerges, and seeks the commitment of the individual to take that action. Revans never quite came down on one side or another about facilitation, and Pedler and Abbott's 2013 book aims to fill in a number of gaps whilst still offering the reader options going forward.

In an ideal set, every member has the opportunity to share a problem. When time is tight, then a few problems are dealt with, and at the next meeting the other members get their chance to pose a problem. It is often rolled out as part of a bigger learning initiative (eg a leadership development programme) where it can help cement learning, and contribute to permanent behaviour change. There have been so many examples of action learning that is it clear, from the sheer weight of evidence, that it works. And its benefits stretch beyond the problem that has been dealt with or the individual that has been helped. Some of these wider benefits include:

- It helps peers build trust amongst themselves.
- It reinforces the commonality of problems across all parts of an organization.
- It empowers groups to get on with it, and work out ways to deal with very tricky problems with little fuss and small costs.
- It teaches managers that action is the critical outcome. Thinking and talking are valueless unless they lead to some form of action.
- It develops accountability.
- It helps build or sustain knowledge share.
- It helps organizations develop explicit knowledge and create knowledge pathways throughout the organization.
- It makes leaders feel less 'alone in the world'. It offers support when leaders feel unable to cope.
- It hones questioning skills that can be used elsewhere for analysis and understanding.
- It develops mutual respect for teams. Everyone can contribute and it is everyone's contribution that is necessary to deal with the problem in hand.
- It helps alignment, and empowers leaders to take charge of their own destiny.

What is a typical action learning set?

What follows is an account of an action learning set. I used the term 'typical' but that is possibly an oversimplification of the concept of action learning. In many ways, each set has to discover its own way of productive working and its own equilibrium, but there are generic elements which can be shared.

Each action learning set has three distinct stages. All three will be discussed in some detail, but before examining that it is worth focusing on how you form groups that are more likely to be successful. There are a number of salient points:

1 The group should be drawn from the same level in the company, ie peers. They certainly don't have to know each other before the group meets, but they must see each other as of similar status with roles of equal complexity. It can be disruptive if there is one person who is perceived by the others to be at a higher or lower level than the rest of the group, as this tends to prevent the group gelling or allows the group an excuse to give more or less weight to one set of opinions, rather than to treat them equally.

2 No one should be forced into an action learning set. Volunteers work best – and it is more effective – if they come to the learning set with at least one wicked problem or nagging concern. Reluctant participants can be encouraged to try it out with the proviso that they can withdraw later if it is simply not working for them, but a group where the majority have been pressed into service is rarely productive.

3 Ideally the group should meet for a few hours so that more than one issue can be dealt with and there is no time pressure to resolve the problem. But the group has to negotiate what works for the majority. I have seen groups that choose to meet for most of a day, and groups that can only spare an hour for a meeting. Both can work well.

4 Location is important. A pleasant meeting place with light and air is far preferable to a stuffy basement room. And groups need regular breaks to stretch legs and recharge. It is usually the

facilitator's role to watch for the tell-tale signs of flagging interest and call a break.

5 Groups that know one another can easily meet online as long as cameras are switched on. If you have an online session, the meeting time is much more compressed (one hour maximum). And the facilitator has the important additional role of keeping people engaged and summing up the point the group has reached on a regular basis, in order that the actions that emerge are captured and shared.

6 It is also possible for sets to meet where most are present in one location; however, one or two members can choose to join online due to time or location issues. This requires special skills to manage, but it can be done. Again the facilitator role is critical to ensure that the online participants' voices are heard, and that they feel they are equal participants in the meeting.

7 A group should ideally commit for at least six months so that it has time to settle and evolve. Clearly, if the group is not working, or there are trust issues, it is better to jettison the group early rather than press on regardless. If successful, by six months the group should feel comfortable with each other and able to make good decisions based on free-flowing questions. If this is the case, the action learning set will continue under its own momentum.

8 Inviting each member in turn to 'host' a meeting can work well, and the rest of the set experience another part of the organization that they are not familiar with. It is also possible to rotate the individual who facilitates the set around the group, meeting by meeting.

There is some debate about the nature of facilitation, which is covered later in the chapter, and there are no hard and fast rules – Revans certainly did not make it clear what that facilitation role might be and how significant it is. Michael Marquardt, for example, has strong rules about facilitation and offers certification to become an action learning facilitator. That figure should certainly not be part of the group and plays an anchor role and ultimately 'controls' the group. In Marquardt's model (1999) the facilitator can even be the person to set the problem for the group.

The three stages of an action learning set

Stage one: getting settled and getting started

To get the set ready for work requires some effort. People arrive with their own baggage and they need to acquire focus and concentration on the matter in hand if the set is to work. It is an important role for the facilitator to bring the meeting to order and get it started. Questions such as the ones below can be helpful:

'Are we ready to start? Has anyone got any issues they want to share before we begin?

'Let's get some ground rules. Can everyone turn their phones to silent, please? Can everyone stay for the full meeting? Does anyone need to jump out at any time? If not, I can assume that you will all be here for the duration.'

'Let's begin with a quick round up since the last meeting. David, what happened when you carried out the three actions you agreed to take forward?'

'Has anyone anything else they wish to contribute?'

'What is the challenge you want to share, Mary? It is your turn now to lead off the session.'

'Can I just clarify, Mary, the challenge is...?'

Stage two: asking questions

It is always worth reminding the set that they are asking questions, not solving problems or adding their views. It can be helpful if the facilitator ensures that no one individual hogs the floor, and that the person who is answering the questions is given time to think and consider the responses, before the next question.

If that person is struggling to answer the question then the facilitator can interrupt to clarify the question or ask that person what the problem is, or perhaps engage in dialogue: 'What are you thinking, Mary?' 'Why are you struggling to answer that question?' 'What is your initial thought here?'

Sometimes the best and most illuminating questions are the ones that are most difficult to answer. Time must be allowed so that a response can be thoughtfully formulated. The person should not feel pressured into making a hurried or superficial response.

If the pressure is building, it is the facilitator's role to call time out. That single intervention can be critical in keeping the meeting on track and allowing insights to emerge for the individual and the group. Letting people think, as well as talk, is an absolutely fundamental part of the action learning process.

Stage three: moving to action

Reg Revans said that there is no learning without action (Pedler and Abbott, 2013). This is a core stage of the process, but it is sometimes hard to know the moment to shift into outcomes and actions and to define those actions clearly enough to be unambiguous. It is also important that the individuals feel accountable for their own actions. Another member of the group can be asked to hold them directly accountable, eg 'I will phone you next Monday, Mary, to see how you got on when you spoke to Bill.'

You know it is time to move to actions when:

- the questions dry up or repeat;
- the individual has no new insights;
- potential actions are piling up that have emerged from the questions;
- specific actions have been agreed – enough to get things moving and help tackle the problem.

The facilitator can help this process by suggesting or reminding the questioner of actions that have emerged, or clarifying actions, eg 'Mary, you need to get more information about this; who specifically are you going to talk to?'

Finally, the facilitator needs to summarize, or gets Mary to summarize. 'There are five clear actions here. Mary, when can you complete them? Is there anyone in the set who will help Mary achieve the actions, or hold her to account?'

It may be over-egging the pudding to have formal notes, but an account of the actions is always helpful. The key message has to be that Mary is the one who is responsible for carrying out the actions. It is not the facilitator's role to keep a note, keep track or check back. Once the meeting is finished, the accountabilities should be abundantly clear.

Facilitation

As stated previously there is no defined role for the facilitator, and to over prescribe is a mistake. In Pedler and Abbott's book *Facilitating Action Learning* (2013), they tabulate five different approaches to the task of facilitation, taken from five different accounts – some specifically on action learning facilitation and some from general facilitation roles. Three refer to the role as that of a 'set adviser', which may be more helpful as a concept than facilitator. This table is reproduced opposite and reprinted with permission (Pedler and Abbott, 2013: 68).

The authors cited are included in the references for this chapter. The key points highlight the active role of the set adviser/facilitator. They are working on the group as much as working in the group. Such small roles as 'nudging', 'encouraging', 'enabling', and 'giving feedback' are, in themselves, small interventions, but they do add up to a significant nurturing of the set. Given this significance, it is possible to understand why Michael Marquart insists on structuring, defining and credentialing the role (Marquardt, 1999). You might feel that how the role works, in practice, in your organization needs to emerge rather than be predefined. The choice is clear. What Pedler and Abbott illustrate is that having five different accounts makes it easier to select what works best in a specific circumstance or for a specific group, rather than have one fixed list that has to be adhered to. Action learning has always been messy and open, and that is part of its enduring appeal and why it works in many different ways in many different organizations.

Table 9.1 Some views on the roles of the set adviser and the group facilitator

Casey (2011)	Edmonstone (2003)	O'Hara, Bourner and Webber (2004)	Weaver and Farrell (1997)	Heron (1999)
SET ADVISERS	**SET ADVISERS**	**SET ADVISERS**	**FACILITATORS**	**FACILITATORS**
• Facilitate giving	• Reading self	• Questioning skills	• Task – the work the group do	• Planning – goal oriented
• Facilitate receiving	• Reading the set	• Active listening skills	• Process – actions and processes that help the group to get the work done	• Meaning – found in group and individual experience
• To clarify the various processes of action learning	• Sense making for the group	• Ability to give and receive feedback	• Group – understanding	• Confronting – raising consciousness about resistance
• To help others take over tasks 1, 2 and 3	• Nudging or interventions, eg action as role model, encouraging membership, ensuring the environment is good, encouraging participation, managing time, enabling learning by questions and reflections	• Understanding of group processes	• Self awareness and understanding	• Feeling – management of emotion
		• Creative problem-solving skills		• Structuring – of the learning
		• Skill of reflection		• Valuing – maintaining integrity and respect
		• Understanding the process of learning		

How can you use action learning as part of your own leadership development programme? There are a number of points to consider when you decide to move forward with action learning:

1 Make a conscious decision to include action learning in your leadership programme from the outset, and explain what that will involve. A half-hearted attempt to form groups to discuss 'something' with no structure rarely works.

2 Make some effort to define how it will take place and what the facilitator's role will be without overprescribing every element. The latter is more likely to end in failure. Action learning works best when the sets evolve into a degree of self-ownership. But they still need some structure, particularly at the beginning.

3 Take stock regularly and change the parameters, if necessary, to keep the sets on track. Sometimes a super facilitator can add value by sitting in on a number of sessions and helping share the emerging best practice.

4 Do not force incompatible groups to continue beyond the natural life of the group – this could be limited to one session only. Groups can be reformed at a later date.

5 Allow the sets some leeway in selecting members, but do not allow elites to form.

6 Integrate action learning into the leadership programme. It should not appear to be a bolt-on or an afterthought.

7 Ensure the groups focus on 'wicked problems' so that the process of working on those problems raises capability in the group and reflects positively back to the whole organization. The problems have to be meaty enough to sustain the group. Each issue should be intriguing when it is posed to the group.

8 Get feedback. Ask for feedback from the facilitators after each meeting. This should be brief but include problem solving if necessary.

9 Each wave of action learning should be introduced and evangelized by the previous groups. If it is 'sold' on tangible benefits that are shared by the beneficiaries, that will have much greater impact than any other form of introduction. The best outcome is for action learning to become part of the culture of the organization. Potential set members have to take charge once the process has been initiated.

10 Develop a cadre of action learning experts who can help other groups get started and deal with issues and problems informally. There will be enthusiasts for this way of working. Bring them into the discussion and let them 'own' the process and evangelize the methodology.

11 Do not give up too soon. The dominant culture in the organization may need to evolve to fully embed action learning. This takes time. But if there is a culture of mistrust and dishonesty among the leadership group, action learning could fail. It will encourage more honest responses but cannot work miracles in toxic leadership cultures.

Conclusions and next steps

Action learning has manifestations all over the world and has helped many organizations transform their leadership and realign their culture with great success. Large numbers of big companies (like Boeing and Microsoft), health boards and charities have all benefited from that simple principle elaborated by Reg Revans: ask astute questions of peers. This process can solve problems that elude experts or confuse individuals working on their own.

The by-product from action learning, of social learning, and increased sharing of knowledge across the organization are desirable aims in themselves for many companies. Action learning is a powerful way of pooling knowledge and encouraging leaders to respond actively to issues that emerge in this volatile and complex business environment. Using action learning builds informal processes for sharing knowledge and developing social learning. Its by-product is a stronger culture of trust, respect and sharing. Perhaps those elements are now critical for survival.

References

Cacioppe, R and Edwards, M G (2005) Seeking the holy grail of organisational development: A synthesis of integral theory, spiral dynamics, corporate transformation and action inquiry, *Leadership & Organization Development Journal*, **26** (2), pp 86–105

Casey, D (2011) David Casey on the role of the set adviser, *Action Learning in Practice*, ed M Pedler, pp 55–70, Gower, Farnham

Cooperrider, D L and Srivastva, S (1987) Appreciative inquiry in organization life, *Research in Organizational Change and Development*, **1**

Dewey, J (1916) *Democracy and Education: An introduction to the philosophy of education*, Macmillan, Basingstoke

Edmonstone, J (2003) *The Action Learner's Toolkit*, Gower, Aldershot

Garnett, F and Ecclesfield, N (2014) Towards an adult learning architecture of participation, London Knowledge Lab

Heron, J (1999) *The Complete Facilitator's Handbook*, Kogan Page, London

Marquardt, M (1999) *Action Learning*, ASTD Info-line, Alexandria, VA

O'Hara, S, Bourner, T and Webber, T (2004) The practice of self-managed action learning, *Action Learning: Research and Practice,* **1** (1), pp 29–42

Pedler, M (2015) Interview

Pedler M and Abbott C (2013) *Facilitating Action Learning: A practitioner's guide*, Open University Press, Maidenhead

Revans, R (2011) *ABC of Action Learning*, Gower, Farnham

Revans interview (1984) Action Learning: Introduction, IFAL Official, https://youtube.com/watch?v=2bJ9RXkYPSU

Torbert, W (1973) *Learning from Experience: Towards consciousness*, Columbia University Press, New York, NY

Torbert, W (2004) *Action Enquiry: The secret of timely and transforming leadership*, Berrett-Koehler, San Francisco, CA

University of Sheffield (2016) Learning and Teaching Services, https://www.sheffield.ac.uk/lets/strategy/resources/evaluate/action-inquiry

Weaver, R G and Farrell, J D (1997) *Managers as Facilitators: A practical guide to getting work done in a changing workplace*, Berrett-Koehler, San Francisco, CA

DIY leadership development   10

Ensuring leadership development when you have a very low budget

Given the size of the investment in leadership development worldwide, there is an in-built assumption in most leadership development strategies that this is expensive (Corporate Research Forum Report (Pillans), 2015) – probably the most expensive single item of L&D investment – and there is not much you can do about that. There are, however, many examples of leadership development on very low budgets where some ingenious solutions have occurred to solve the problem of how you offer a quality experience that actually works, with minimal direct investment bar the time of the participants.

There are plenty of examples in this book of high cost – but huge value – investments and this chapter adds another element to the leadership development picture. It would be remiss to omit this, but it would be naive of any reader to assume that a zero investment approach is the optimum! Like so many of the conclusions in this book: it all depends. The mix of circumstances, needs and budgets is complex, and you can select what might work, but you should only do this after some analysis. Help with that analysis of need is contained in Chapter 12.

Google's focus on fast internal solutions

In September 2011, I had an extensive conversation with Sudhir Giri (at the time, Google senior HR executive) to discuss Google's approach to leadership development. He told me that Google took a deliberate stance to pull out of the continuing development of leadership programmes and to focus, instead, on its own leadership issues. Google looked at what the strengths were, and therefore threw some light on the weaknesses of the leaders in their company. This did not happen in isolation but was part of a wider strategy around talent. This was about retaining and developing the best people working for Google, and one key factor around retention was certainly the quality of leadership inside the organization. This decision was not due to budget constraints, but an attempt to work with its community to enable tailored solutions to learning and development challenges.

Rather than guess at what good leaders did and therefore what weaker leaders did not do, Google set about analysing the mass of performance data that sat on servers all over the company. Traditionally, companies sit on appraisal records, performance notes, development conversations, and many other documents that are used once and then filed somewhere, rarely to be referred to again. Google saw this data as a potential goldmine of information. The decision to look at what this information was telling them about the quality of leadership in Google lay at the heart of what became known as Project Oxygen.

This data had to be stripped of personal references and cleaned for review. It was processed to get at the key words around performance and leadership, but most of the data gathering was based on HR staff painstakingly going through the documentation, tagging it carefully and then analysing the results. What it revealed were the clear elements that constituted good leadership across the company.

Google is a company of software engineers. Many of them, because of their technical expertise and brilliance in their role as engineers, had been promoted into leadership positions. Many were running large sections of the company and influencing the motivation and commitment of hundreds of staff, without really wanting to manage or enjoying the role that had been thrust upon them. As Google grew rapidly in the early days, many pragmatic decisions were made to create a structure and hierarchy in the organization, which meant fast promotion into leadership positions without in-depth development or much support.

The results of that data analysis are straightforward and full of insight, but amongst the obvious conclusions were some radical challenges to what had always been assumed about what staff expected of their leaders inside the company. Google discovered a number of key attributes associated with good leadership inside the company.

Good leaders tended to:

- give specific, constructive feedback which balanced negative and positive;
- have regular meetings where solutions were presented that were tailored to the strengths of the employees in the room;
- be productive and results-orientated;
- focus on what their direct reports wanted to achieve and offer help to support this;
- help staff prioritize, and try their best to remove roadblocks that stopped staff achieving their goals;
- empower rather than micromanage;
- express interest in employee success and personal well-being;
- help employees develop their careers inside the company;
- be good communicators who listened;
- encourage open dialogue, and seek out the issues and concerns of their employees;
- demonstrate a clear vision and strategy;
- involve staff in setting and evolving the vision and making progress towards it;
- have key technical skills that they could draw upon to advise and coach their team.

The 13 items gather into three clear clusters. The first is around meeting management. Staff wanted regular, constructive meetings where their views were sought and the focus was on positive resolution of issues after consulting staff on their ideas and viewpoints. The second cluster is around giving good feedback: that included praise for a job well done but also highlighted areas for development. There were also conclusions that related to the quality of the leader. They wanted leaders who listened, who could help them with technical problems, and who left them alone to do their job rather than micro-managing them. The final cluster centred around managers who showed interest in their staff and concern for their success. Staff valued managers who helped them in their careers and showed concern for their well-being and generally were interested in them as individuals and not just the work they did.

None of this reveals any unique traits that only a technology company like Google would demonstrate, and much of it is standard good leadership that thousands of companies would endorse. The big shock to Google was the fact that the technical skills of their leaders were fairly low on the priority list. Engineers who were leaders rated their own technical skills as critical for success and many leaders felt that they should be able to solve any technical problem presented by their team. This was only one aspect of good leadership though, and it was rated as helpful rather than essential.

Google then made a big decision about their leadership development strategy. The focus would be on improving the quality of the weakest 25 per cent of leaders, and let the rest carry on doing a pretty good job. Rather than highlight and extend the best, they went for maximum impact to raise the overall quality of leadership across the entire organization.

Given that most of the characteristics of good leaders were pretty generic, they focused on mentoring, coaching and supporting leaders rather than developing specific resources. When they needed resources, they pulled them from what was available internally or externally. They therefore stood their traditional approach to leadership development on its head, and over two years Google claims to have eliminated most of the poor leadership, retained more staff as a result, and generally improved staff engagement and the overall performance of the company. This was done in a systematic and low-budget way. The team focused on keeping the core issues at the forefront, and reviewing their own leadership metrics that had formed the basis of their analysis in the first place. When those same metrics began to show improvements, they knew that the process was working.

There were a number of other key initiatives at the same time that focused on the efficient use of internal resources and a do-it-yourself approach. The education team encouraged Googlers to share their skills with their peers by offering to teach those skills to others. The second initiative was designed to improve the search internally for good learning resources so that leaders could work on their team development or access resources that would help them improve as leaders. The third was an 'ask the expert' tool that put people in touch with others so that mentoring or informal support could be arranged.

The first initiative was called G2g. Everyone was invited to teach on any topic, and 200 elected to do that in the first month after the launch. Each individual was supported by members of the Education Team in Google to ensure that it was a good experience for both de-liverer and receiver, and that resulted in over 125 courses being taught on a range of topics pertinent to Google's work. In addition, a video channel called G2g was created which allowed anyone to upload a video that they made on a topic that shared a skill, or broadened expertise across the company; the emphasis was on focus in terms of topic, and short, sharp materials. To support this, some learning media studios were set up in a number of locations that could be used to make more professional looking videos. That created a standard of presentation that everyone tried to emulate.

The second initiative was called G@google. A repository of learning resources was created. Many of the resources existed in the Education Department, but were not accessible to anyone outside that team, or only in random locations across the company. Google was trawled for suitable materials and they were all relocated into one branded online repository. Each resource was tagged, and users were invited to add additional tags to any materials that they used so that a meta-tagging process could be established, generated largely by the users (not providers) of the resources. This enabled resources to be discovered easily and they were linked to key words that reflected the day-to-day reality of life in Google. The idea was to cover a range of learning topics and focus on skill and performance development.

The final component that was built was a simple 'ask the expert' tool, called gWhiz. If you wanted help in developing a specific skill then you could use the tool. Any request would reveal a list of people who were available for mentoring in that specific skill area. You could then choose one and set up some kind of process to learn from the expert. Each person's ranking on the listing relied on social tagging by staff. The more tags, the higher the ranking of the individual expert. This whole network was informal with each pair of Googlers – enquirer and expert – free to establish the parameters of their role, such as duration, communication medium, extent of support, etc.

The importance of any one of these initiatives was subsumed into the collective message that was promoted: people matter, good leadership is highly valued, there are huge opportunities to learn from your peers and you should set yourself learning targets. There was no excuse for underperformance or selfishly guarding skills. Credit was given to those staff who generously supported their colleagues and shared their expertise.

This message was reinforced by the former long-term HR director of Google, Laszlo Bock, when he talked about valuing Googler's 'learning ability' in a *Guardian* interview of 24 February 2014. He defined this in the same interview as the ability 'to process on the fly… to pull together disparate bits of information'. This is about autonomy and quick thinking and problem-solving, all of which are enhanced by the initiatives described above.

Bock's perspective was reinforced by a presentation that Eric Schmidt – Google's Chairman and erstwhile CEO – gave alongside their former SVP of products Jonathan Rosenberg. They claimed – in an HBR podcast (Schmidt and Rosenberg, 2014) – that 'the way you did a role before is less useful than the ability to think'. They also claimed that the company needed thinking generalists rather than specialists, as 'specialists tend to bring inherent bias to a problem and feel threatened by a new solution'. So the self-development strain runs deep through the Google DNA, and learning is at the core of what you need to survive. Schmidt added: 'Now we are looking at smart creatives with business acumen and curiosity' – with a passion for what Google does. As a result of this, the company developed a strategy to keep these staff members' careers on track and systems that could extend their curiosity and passion. Google realized that recruiting smart, curious people was one thing, but keeping them was a whole new process. Google had to have strategies in place to manage their people well and encourage them to develop themselves.

These processes were enabled by free access to appropriate systems and tools linked to excellent leadership. Both these elements were found to be critical. This approach also clearly reflects what Fred Garnett of the London Knowledge Lab refers to as 'an adult learning architecture of participation' (Garnett and Ecclesfield, 2014). It also endorses the McKinsey analysis of how you retain key employees in times of change (Cosack, Guthridge and Lawson, 2010). The McKinsey authors argue that retention of key employees is about much more than money, and they list six of the most efficient motivators for staff that lead to higher retention rates. These are: praise from one's manager; attention from leaders; frequent promotions; opportunities to lead projects; and opportunities to join fast track management programmes; any financial incentives. Many of these are reflected directly in the Google experiences detailed above. For Google, learning was key, as was self-development and high-quality leaders. These factors worked together and became embodied in the culture of the organization.

Other strategies

I have given a detailed analysis of Google's multilayered approach to leadership development, not because they are a role model of good practice, but because they never offer one solution but instead attempt to reinforce a vision or a strategy by multiple initiatives – some big and some small.

I have listed six separate approaches to DIY leadership below, but the general rules that have emerged throughout this book about leadership programmes also apply here. These are not single, simple solutions that will solve all your leadership development problems at a stroke, but suggestions and ideas used by other organizations that could form components of your unique approach. What you choose will depend on your deep knowledge of your own organization and what makes it tick and, essentially, what the culture of the organization will bear. Not one approach or idea mentioned is guaranteed to work in every situation and in any organization. However, everything could work. You simply have to be the judge of what might work for you and choose carefully.

These are six aspects to DIY leadership development. You do not need all six, but you probably need to combine two or three to make what you offer interesting and potentially transforming inside your organization.

1. Facilitation

An incredibly powerful way of energizing individuals and empowering leaders in an organization is to create groups to focus on ways that lead to them solving their own problems, and discussing key issues and behaviours that inform leadership on a regular basis. This discussion is facilitated and structured rather than left to the self-organization of groups. One simple example is when the director of learning and development who worked in a logistics organization decided to deal with the concerns emerging about poor leadership. He gathered specific instances that he felt needed to be tackled. He decided to raise the quality of leadership by establishing small groups of like-minded leaders who were prepared to try to work on their own problems. He helped these groups focus on a number of core issues of leadership failure that he had assembled to kick-start the discussions, and personally facilitated the groups. Initially, each group set its own rules. Members agreed norms of behaviour, length of meetings, process of outcomes, etc. Then they got on with the task of working together to solve their own problems and make decisions collectively on what could be done to improve leadership.

This short, sharp focus on improving leadership started with a small number of self-selected groups. These groups began to achieve positive results and agreed on new ways of behaving. They also wanted to continue to share mutual concerns. The result was that they acted as a leadership cohort, rather than a number of individuals operating in isolation. The word-of-mouth comments about these first groups were positive enough to encourage more groups to volunteer. This reached a point, some six months after the initiative began, when a significant number of the company's leaders were involved. The L&D director could not cope with facilitating every group himself as it was approaching a full-time job. He therefore decided to develop members of his own team as facilitators so that they would be able to work with the increasing number of groups. In doing this they would gain some deep insights into what drove leaders in that organization. This, in turn, allowed the number of circles to expand in order to cope with demand.

The number of groups multiplied around the workplace and the more mature ones became better at self-management and took on the role of facilitation themselves. Usually, by rotation, one team member became the facilitator and stood aside from the discussion. By this point, the L&D leader was able to withdraw completely from direct facilitation of groups, and had the time to audit the process as a whole, in order to ensure consistency of approach, and quality outcomes. He was also able to share insights from one group to all the rest, and help disseminate what was agreed as constituting good practice in this area, so that it would emerge and establish itself as company-wide know-how. By the end, this had developed into a significant leadership development process at practically zero budget, apart from the time invested by the managers.

This initiative was established below the waterline of the company. It attracted very little attention and continued quietly until it gained momentum and, by then, most of the kinks had been ironed out. The focus had been to raise the standards of leadership inside the organization and build consistent frameworks that would contribute to a new culture of leadership. In other words this initiative had not only changed leadership practice but also the way that problems were dealt with. This culture of self-help boosted problem-solving in many areas of the operation. If you define culture as 'how we do things around here' then this was step-by-step cultural change. And as a high ratio of L&D staff had also acquired facilitation skills, other programmes were rolled out using that model in part or in total. There was widespread support and participation and a strong sense of ownership. This gave staff a sense of not being dictated to, but being in control.

Using facilitation skills also allowed L&D staff privileged access into the real concerns of managers in the context of their work. So, in this instance, L&D's role was to help the leadership group solve their own problems with no more intervention than helping the groups work.

If you want to move forward with this, then the core skills required are:

1 Confidence to work with more senior staff and actively participate in the group. Facilitation requires strong control at times to keep the group on track, but loose participation for most of the time to let the group get on with it.

2 Being able to ask the right questions, which prompt the group into productive discussion.

3 The ability to diffuse angry exchanges and tension.

4 Knowing what to do to deal with disruptive or difficult individuals, and encourage participation.

5 Techniques for how to energize the group when the energy levels flag, and also how to know when it is time to truncate discussion when no new ground is being covered. On the other hand, knowing how to encourage continued discussion when there is much still left on the table to discuss.

6 To note conclusions and summarize what has been agreed.

7 The ability to gradually withdraw and allow the team to take charge of its own destiny and become self-managing.

The essential learning from this is 'start small' with volunteers and work out the optimum way of operating before attracting mass participation. Start as an 'experiment' and work out quickly what works and what does not work.

There has to be some sort of 'burning platform' that will bring people together. If there is no perceived problem or no sense of urgency, then this process is unlikely to gain traction. At some point, in addition, it needs validation. A note from the CEO – or an agreement in an executive meeting that this works and needs to be supported – builds or sustains momentum, and is therefore very important.

2. Mentoring

A mentor has been defined as 'a wise and loyal adviser' and that is as good a definition as any. If an organization has a strong leadership culture, then a mentoring scheme to support new leaders can be an immensely powerful way of offering support and insight without formal learning programmes (or in addition to them). Building a strong connection between senior leaders and their more junior peers can have benefits that stretch far beyond the sessions themselves. It creates a network where talent can be developed, it allows senior staff to get some direct sense of life further down the organization, and it also allows ideas and strategies to be rapidly transmitted across the employee base. A good mentor/mentee relationship lasts for a long time, far beyond the initial assignment. It also focuses on the task of leadership and shows that it is taken seriously, and that certain behaviours are expected and others frowned upon.

Too few organizations see the value of mentoring. Many key leaders simply feel that their involvement in the mentoring processes is time-consuming, and gets in the way of their own work. Even if they get involved, it is always seen as a time-limited activity. This means that when their mentoring assignment is concluded, they feel that they have fulfilled their obligation and need not be involved any longer. It is rather like doing their session of jury duty – necessary, worthy but irrelevant, and an obstruction to normal work. So mentoring is not something that can be developed quickly, in every kind of organization, under any circumstances. It needs to be nurtured and it needs to fit with the culture of the organization. Or, the organization needs to evolve to incorporate a mentoring culture where the value of mentoring is taken for granted. Having said that, utilizing the wisdom and experience of key staff can be enormously powerful as a way of unifying the culture and sharing values as well as good practice. It is almost a reworking of the age-old tradition of 'sitting next to Nellie' that became enshrined – from as early as the Middle Ages – in the concept of apprenticeship.

Mentees should see their mentors as experts. That is, someone who knows more than they do, but also someone with whom they can talk, share ideas and get advice. But that is the extent of the relationship. Mentors cannot guarantee any particular outcome or, ultimately, tell anyone what to do. They offer suggestions and ask good questions. The onus for action is on the part of the mentee. It is true, however, that during the course of this relationship some confidential information will be shared. This means that from the beginning this is a trust relationship on both sides. There is usually no disclosure of any element of the conversation unless the expressed permission of the mentee is given.

In the *Journal of Accountancy*, an article by Erik Thompson (2010) suggests that an effective mentor:

- asks challenging questions that helps mentees expand their perspective;
- is connected, in some way, to the person being mentored but does not directly line-manage them;
- challenges the mentee with penetrating insights.

Those sum up the generic characteristics of mentoring. With a focus on leadership, there are other specific benefits. A mentoring assignment:

- gives the individual the opportunity to discuss leadership issues with someone who really understands the industry, the company, and understands leadership;
- offers good advice and guidance from a perspective of knowledge and success in that organization;
- helps focus the mentee's career aspirations and suggests ways that the mentee can become more effective as an emerging leader in the company.

It is important that the mentor is neither forced into the position nor assumes the role of being a general expert on every issue. It has to be made clear that mentors do not necessarily have all the answers. What they are offering is advice and a fresh perspective. Because the rules of engagement have to be established early on it is always helpful to take some time for general discussion. To try to establish how things are going in general before plunging into detailed questions and answers. The mentor needs to get a clear view of who the person is beyond the limitations of their CV.

It is also helpful to find a neutral or even an informal location to meet. The canteen or even a coffee shop is better than the mentor's office. This guarantees more direct focus on the issues in hand. In addition, the agenda should be set by the mentee. It is their learning opportunity and therefore it is reasonable to expect that mentees should bring along issues and questions that they wish to discuss. If they have not, it is often better to rearrange the meeting with better clarity of process and outcomes.

Having said that, it is usually the mentor's role to attempt to focus the conversation and sum up what has been agreed and what specific actions have been noted. To simply begin and then abruptly end when the allotted time has expired can make the sessions frustrating for both sides. If this is impossible, and much more needs to be discussed before resolution, then agree to continue the discussion at the next session. Do not simply abandon it.

A coaching approach, where giving out the solution is avoided, is the best way forward. If you ask questions such as 'What would success look like?' or 'What are your options here?' they work much better than 'I think you should…' or 'Here's the answer…' The aim is to challenge the mentee; help them see the world differently, and encourage them to gain insight. If you do the thinking for mentees, much less will be learned. It always ends up better to help mentees come to a decision rather than telling them what to do. It may take longer, but it makes it a learning experience and the outcomes are better understood and implemented.

Occasionally, a mentor should just listen. Sometimes that is all that is needed, because mentees work it out for themselves as they go through the process of explanation. The mentor's role is to nod and show that they are paying attention, and occasionally to interject 'and so…'. Regardless of this, it is always helpful to sum up. The best way to do this is to describe what you have heard and what you believe has been agreed. Never leave a session with any ambiguity in terms of outcomes. If you are not sure that the mentee has grasped all the main issues, then send a quick, clear e-mail to reiterate the key points. This can be powerful in terms of impact. Collecting these e-mails can make a helpful record of what has been agreed over time.

It should be the mentee's job to contact the mentor to make the next appointment. It is not the mentor's role to chase up and ensure continuity. And there should always be someone in charge of the overall programme who can be referred to or who can intervene if there are problems. Mentoring can go smoothly, especially if there are common and agreed guidelines, but there has to be a backup for those times when it runs into difficulty.

As a development exercise, mentoring should be very enjoyable. It is a simple way of acquiring real insights into how the company or industry works and also how leaders fulfil their day-to-day role. It is a gift to be shown this and be given support as you move into a leadership role. But even mid-career leaders can benefit from keeping the leadership agenda open and being challenged in their leadership approach. It is like a car service. It keeps everything running smoothly and anticipates any failures that may be lurking.

Mentors should keep their own brief notes of what was agreed so that there is continuity from session to session. If mentors appear to behave as if each meeting is a complete restart and everything has to be gone over again, it does not instil confidence in the process. Finally, always agree on the duration for the meeting (an hour for example) and stick to it. A mentor's time is valuable and a mentor's commitment should be limited by design. A mentor has every right to terminate a session at the agreed time!

If you look at the issue from the perspective of the mentee there are similar, related, but not identical issues. It is important to stress to a mentee that he or she is entering an informal relationship. A mentor should do his or her best, but it is an informal relationship and mentors cannot really be expected to understand every issue. At some level, what is being offered is advice – no more, no less – and if it is not appropriate it should be rejected (politely). The more clarity that the mentee can give the mentor about what is being discussed and the kind of solution the mentee is seeking, the better for the relationship as a whole. Whatever the advice, the mentee owns the actions completely. No blame should be attributed to a mentor, and no mentor should be used as an excuse for failure or ineffectiveness.

The full benefits of having a mentor lie in the challenge and the honest relationship that can develop. A mentor can get it wrong. So ultimately the mentor gives what advice is possible and the mentee makes and owns the decisions and subsequent actions. A mentor can really help, but it is a two-way relationship. This relationship can be ruined by misunderstanding around the nature of the relationship on both sides.

The best mentors want to 'give back', are active listeners, patient, and always try to get to the nub of an issue before offering advice. They always push the final decisions and responsibility back to the mentee, and they never 'do the work' for that person. Often they have more than one mentee, and commit to this as a small part of their role in the organization.

3. Action learning and self-organized groups

The chapter on Action Learning explains in detail how to plan and organize action learning sets. As you read the book you will notice that they feature in more than one chapter as an integrated part of a leadership programme for all the reasons discussed elsewhere. They can, however, work as part of a self-managed and self-directed leadership programme and, once the culture of action learning has been established, it is possible for groups of leaders to come together to work on new problems or challenges.

In a world of radical uncertainty (see Chapter 1), the ability to work on the organization and deal with hard challenges as they arise will become more and more essential. Therefore, action learning becomes a core skill for leaders that can be enabled and disengaged as the need arises without any external help or support. Self-healing and resetting could become a standard feature of modern organizations and act as a 'just in time' adjunct to more structured learning.

It is possible to use an action learning approach as a stand-alone model of leadership development, and there are pros and cons to this.

Pros

1 A consistent and continuous way of building a strong leadership team.

2 It helps establish common standards across the organization, so staff can expect a particular leadership culture and not experience uneven leadership. It is particularly critical in smaller companies where the poor leaders cannot be avoided, and it is much harder to get away from a poor leader into a better environment. This issue is discussed in a Harvard Business Review Blog (Sher, 2014) on the consequences of poor leadership in smaller organizations. Therefore, poor leadership has a disproportionate impact on engagement, productivity and attrition.

3 It maintains attention and focus on leadership against all the other pressures that are on individuals. This means that leadership will get better across the piece, and individual 'stars' will imbue the entire organization with their ethos and values. The Harvard academic Boris Groysberg (2014) defined 'leadership ability' as the number one of the seven skills you need to thrive in the C-Suite. He based this on a survey of several dozen top senior search consultants at a top global executive-placement firm in 2010 from multiple industries and 19 different countries. To reinforce this, one consultant told Groysberg that what is being sought is 'more about leadership skills than technical ones' (Groysberg, 2014: 1).

4 Issues get dealt with quickly.

5 It builds regular opportunities for leaders to leave their day-to-day responsibilities and focus together on the more generic issues. It builds communication networks engendered by de facto action learning sets, that help establish linkages and connections that would not necessarily be present normally in an organization without such structures.

6 Action learning sets build critical leadership competences that are seen as indispensable: listening, communicating, persuading and collaborating (Goleman, 2011).

Cons

1 Much of the insight is from within the organization. There is an absence of challenge to the prevailing norms unless someone takes on the role of bringing in ideas from outside.

2 If the groups lack diversity, the members can all agree too rapidly on the wrong thing, and make poor decisions.

3 There is no audit or accountability unless the group takes it on itself.

4 Traditional power hierarchies can establish themselves quickly, so some ideas are more valuable than others, and some people are listened to more closely than others.

5 Outcomes can be invisible and less effective as a result.

Out of all the suggestions in this chapter, the concept of action learning is almost axiomatic for low-budget self-help leadership. All of the other possibilities can be made more useful and impactful by pursuing action learning intelligently. By its very nature action learning galvanizes leaders to be more acutely aware of what is wrong and how to fix it.

The factors that will tend to lead to successful action learning include: someone managing the process; clarity on the part of the members of sets about why they are there and what the purpose is. The culture of the organization has to be open, and the members have to be prepared to be honest. Some help in working out the correct challenge to discuss, and initial support in asking the right questions, can make the process more productive.

4. Access to open resources

There are an extraordinary number of open learning resources now available for any kind of learning programme including leadership. A simple definition is the one that incorporates the idea of free access of specifically licensed material for teaching, learning and research that can come in any medium, such as print, e-learning or video material.

The United Nations Educational, Scientific and Cultural Organization (UNESCO) has been championing open educational resources for a number of years. Their definition is slightly more specific:

> Open Educational Resources (OERs) are any type of educational materials that are in the public domain... The nature of these open materials means that anyone can legally and freely copy, use, adapt and re-share them. OERs range from textbooks to curricula, syllabi, lecture notes, assignments, tests, projects, audio, video and animation.
> (UNESCO, 2016)

UNESCO draws attention to a number of key networks that focus on the use of open resource in developing countries. The organization highlights the Vision for Health OER Network in Africa, where a network of health science experts agreed to openly share materials that they had developed in the field of health education and make them freely available, not only to health professionals across the continent to spur on knowledge acquisition and professional updating, but also to educators working with healthcare students to enhance their knowledge.

UNESCO also offers an open source platform to manage courses built with open resources and they established an initiative to raise standards in terms of the resources and courses that have emerged. This is called the Open Educational Quality Initiative. They have also produced *Guidelines for Open Educational Resources (OER) in Higher Education*, which is a downloadable e-book (UNESCO, 2015). It is aimed at the developing world but the general guidelines are valid across the piece and act as a *caveat emptor* for the naive learning professional wanting a quick fix. The publication points out that, 'Open Education Resources are not a magic bullet. They do not necessarily lead to a high-quality learning experience, as many other factors are also important' (UNESCO, 2015: 11–12).

In UNESCO's terms, good open resources depend on a number of other attributes. Amongst those listed are: issues about the quality of the resources and who is assuring that; the need to contextualize and personalize the resources; the ability to localize the resources for different groups; involving the users in the selection process in order to build their engagement and commitment; and adding in-house or local content to flesh out the programme and make it as relevant as possible. These points that have been emphasized hold good in all circumstances. In addition, it is important to put a comprehensive delivery structure in place and build a context that personalizes the experience and makes the selected resources relevant for any specific use.

Although this is a leading trend and almost an article of faith in educational institutions – that resources should be made shareable – and that a culture of curation rather than creation should be encouraged, there is no apparent parallel in corporate learning circles. However, companies like Google and BP have shown faith in this model and have made extensive contributions to promoting and sharing the results. As an example of this commitment, Google joined the OpenEdEx consortium two years ago to promote and extend access to open-source MOOC (Massive Open Online Courses) software. And resources that they have developed are made available with a creative commons licence. This is a licence that allows free use of the material as long as the source is acknowledged and the owners still retain copyright. Variations include restrictions on commercial usage and making any amended versions of the resources also subject to Creative Commons Licensing (Creative Commons, 2016).

And with iTunes U, Apple has built a platform that allows hundreds of educational organizations, mostly universities, to share resources and make them available to anyone who is interested as an individual learner, but also now for institutions and companies to run structured courses around those materials.

What is the scope of open resources?

It is almost impossible to exaggerate the volume of materials that are now available, as well as software and learning environments to house and distribute them. There are both open-source programmes and open education resources. The best known piece of open-source education software is Moodle, which is distributed throughout the world as a learning management system. The core software is maintained by a very small team in Australia, but the customization, installation and support of Moodle funds much larger companies all over the world. There are many apps and packages designed to work together to develop a customized and appropriate learning environment at low or no cost.

The most widely available suite of freely available education resources are those of The Khan Academy. It was set up originally as a simple video/interactive slate so that Sal Khan could help his niece with her maths over the phone. It rapidly escalated into a community of over 32 million learners in 190 countries with a million registered educators (interview with Sal Kahn at the Masie Learning 15 conference in Orlando on 1 November 2015).

The Academy covers a huge range of subject areas at all levels in maths, science, economics and finance, arts and humanities, and computing. There is not much scope for a comprehensive leadership programme but the interviews with entrepreneurs as part of the economic and finance portfolio could be valuable as part of such a programme.

The achievements of the Khan Academy have been widely documented and praised, most notably in the *WIRED* article (WIRED, 2011) and the Harvard Business Review Blog (Beard, 2014).

More obvious choices for leadership come from the huge number of TED and TEDx video lectures that are offered for free under that tag line 'ideas worth spreading' (TED). On the front page, there are nearly 300 15-minute talks posted from a huge range of topics. A search of 'leadership' nets 57 videos from extremely well-known academics and pundits, such as Linda Hill from Harvard or Simon Sinek, the management theorist. None of these constitute a structured programme of learning, but all of them could be incorporated into something larger and act as stimulus material to challenge and generate ideas.

WorldCat (www.worldcat.org) catalogues collections from more than 10,000 libraries and can help create bibliographies and lists. It tries to locate an item you wish to access in a library near where you are based or lists those libraries where the item is available. The Open Knowledge Foundation is a network of groups in over 40 countries, dedicated to sharing data, campaigning for more open resources, and promoting what they call open knowledge in the digital age.

The iTunes U initiative by Apple should be recognized as a vast repository of university level courses on free access with a delivery platform and private discussion groups for cohorts of students. It is accessed as an app on both Android and iOS tablets, and on Windows and Apple desktops. Leadership programmes are offered by over 30 providers with hundreds of courses available from specialist business schools, such as Cranfield or Ashridge. If you search, there are materials on all aspects of leadership development.

For example UNSW's course on Leadership in a Complex Environment is part of their Master of Business and Technology programme and comprises 61 short video and text segments. As part of a DIY leadership programme, this programme alone could provide rich resources for discussion and engagement.

Before you build a programme using open resources it is important that you make clear that they are not home-grown, and that you seek out contextualizing material. You should also curate the content, ie emphasize what is most relevant and why. Your own existing vendors may also be able to supply additional resources at low or no cost. But you have to ask before anything will be offered!

5. A cheap and focused portal or repository

It is possible to pull together a collection of iTunes U materials and collect them into a course and manage that as a programme of study using the iTunes U app. Assignments can also be posted if required. This is a very simple closed mechanism that can work as a building block for a larger programme or a self-contained learning programme.

There are, however, a large number of free or relatively inexpensive apps for managing this process, gathering comments and organizing discussions and debates. I would like to show how this could work by reference to two applications that are currently available and popular.

The first is SLACK (www.slack.com). It is a free application that runs as a stand-alone app on any platform and takes the form of channels and resources. The account holder has to 'enrol' the channel members, and the link supplied takes them into that specific channel. It is a simple and seamless process. You set it up by building discussion forums, distributing resources in a number of formats, and allowing interaction, communication and debate around them. It now allows synchronous video calls for up to eight attendees. That extension is named 'appear' and you access it by simply typing 'appear'. This adds a new dimension to the software. It is limited to three browsers but works well and allows users to remain in SLACK with access to all its resources whilst videoconferencing with colleagues. There are many other synchronous conference apps, which range from very expensive to relatively cheap, that allow more than eight participants and more than three browsers, if that is what is required.

So for example you can have an overall 'course' channel into which everyone is enrolled and where the key resources are kept. It would be possible to set up separate channels for course themes, perhaps 'owned' by different participants. These can be open or restricted to members. All notes, files and reports are stored on SLACK for continued use and access. SLACK allows a discrete cohort to work on a leadership development programme away from the 'mess' of their day-to-day working life and share almost every output with the group as a whole. It is attractive, simple to use, and free of charge for most applications.

The second is Docebo (ww.docebo.com). It is a cloud-based learning management system that allows you to start with small numbers of learners and scale up as you need to. It combines a resource storage and distribution system, with 'classroom' training for synchronous learning, as well as online resources. There are social forums and discussion areas and with a functionality that allows third-party applications to be bolted on. It therefore has considerable flexibility to be customized to a specific organization. As it is cloud-based it can be expanded at will. And as it is a learning management system it collects user data for the provider. For 50 active users it costs under US$2,500 a year, which is far less than most competing systems. For 350 active users the annual cost is around US$6,000 a year. This is not a sales pitch, but an illustration of how the market is evolving and how cheap and simple systems can revolutionize the establishment of frameworks to manage low-cost leadership programmes in a sophisticated way.

This kind of flexible, cloud-based model is really the future of LMS and a major enhancement to ways of delivering resources to the learner.

6. Asking questions

A leadership training provider in Brazil worked with a major bank to help energize their senior leadership and create a strong community of leaders by getting them to debate a single question per week. This was sent out to mobile phones by the CEO on a Monday, responses would come in to be commented on during the week, and a response by the CEO would be posted on the Friday. The aims were to get senior executives focusing on big complex issues for the bank to build a stronger leadership community that understood the specific challenges that each faced and to extend their leadership competences by getting them debating their role as leaders, in addition to their technical expertise in the bank.

Just one question from the CEO helped build a stronger leadership community and generated a much greater focus on leadership issues than had occurred before this initiative. Getting that group together physically was difficult due to wide geographical spread, and enrolling them on a formal programme would have been very expensive and possibly ineffectual, as little time – up until that point – had been spent on leadership issues. The message was simple. You have to get your senior staff engaged in the topic of leadership, and help them to the point of view that it is important, and that what they do as leaders makes a huge difference. The simple questions which began that journey started leadership conversations.

An Irish start-up called Elephants Don't Forget (www.elephantsdontforget.com) has turned this insight into a successful business. It writes specific questions to increase employee competence or sustain skills and knowledge. The company's modus operandi is based on the conclusions of the research of the German psychologist Hermann Ebbinghaus. He demonstrated just how much learning is forgotten without regular reinforcement. It is known as the Ebbinghaus forgetting curve. By spacing learning, retention increased and the learning process was more effective. He explained how information is lost over time and showed that concentrating learning into one single dose would inevitably cause rapid 'forgetting' and therefore had limited effect. Elephants Don't Forget reinforces the learning by asking daily questions to maintain the knowledge in the forefront of consciousness and help embed that learning into behaviour change. If the questions are not answered correctly the learner can be sent back to the relevant material to 'revise' the learning.

There is no need to use complex tools in order to ask simple questions. Sometimes generating good questions can be at the heart of learning. Indeed, action learning is based on the theory that asking questions is a powerful leadership competence, and the right questions allow deep exploration of subjects. The essence of action learning is asking good questions, not providing pat answers.

There is power in generating challenging questions and giving leaders the opportunity to debate the answers and develop new approaches as a result. It might not work as a stand-alone leadership programme, but it can add to the depth of other models and it is cheap to implement.

Conclusion

The chapter should encourage you to explore some of the DIY leadership options that are listed here. But it is not a glib, simple solution. Like all the other programmes, some thought must be given in terms of the why, what and where of the learning. This involves a complex intermeshing of perception around what is needed, resource allocation, and establishing the correct model that locks into the culture of the organization. However, this approach is more straightforward than it ever has been with low risk and even low investment thresholds for those wanting to trial different software. The possibilities are almost endless. This is perhaps an idea whose time has come!

References

Beard, A (2014) Salman Khan on the Online Learning Revolution, Life's Work Interview, Harvard Business Review Blog, https://hbr.org/2014/01/salman-khan-on-the-online-learning-revolution/

Corporate Research Forum Report (Pillans, G) (2015) *Leadership Development – is it fit for purpose?*, Corporate Research Forum, London

Cosack, S, Guthridge, M and Lawson, E (2010) Retaining employees in times of change, *McKinsey Quarterly*, August edition

Creative Commons (2016) Website, https://creativecommons.org

Garnett, F and Ecclesfield, N (2014) Towards an adult learning architecture of participation, London Knowledge Lab

Goleman, D (2011) The Must-Have Leadership Skill, Harvard Business Review Blog Network, https://hbr.org/2011/10/the-must-have-leadership-skill/

Groysberg, B (2014) The Seven Skills You Need to Thrive in the C-Suite, Harvard Business Review Blog, https://hbr.org/2014/03/the-seven-skills-you-need-to-thrive-in-the-c-suite/

Schmidt, E and Rosenberg, J (2014) How Google Manages Talent, Harvard Business Review Blog as an HBR IdeaCast, https://hbr.org/2014/09/how-google-manages-talent/

Sher, R (2014) Where There's No Margin for Toxic Leadership, Harvard Business Review Blog, 26 May 2014, https://hbr.org/2014/05/where-theres-no-margin-for-toxic-leadership/

Thompson, E (2010) How to be a better mentor, *Journal of Accountancy*, **10** (5), 42–43

UNESCO (2011; revised 2015) *Guidelines for Open Educational Resources (OER) in Higher Education*, UNESCO and Commonwealth of Learning

UNESCO (2016) Website, http://unesco.org/new/en/communication-and-information/access-to-knowledge/open-educational-resources/what-are-open-educational-resources-oers/

WIRED (2011) *How Khan Academy is Changing the Rules of Education*, http://wired.com/2011/07/ff_khan/

The shape of the future   11

The increasingly powerful role of technology

This chapter looks at some of the new technologies that could transform leadership development. Its focus is not wildly futuristic but rather it picks up on a future that is almost here and speculates on what might happen over the next few years. None of this should be ignored, but there are groundbreaking tools missing still, and much of the technology is in its infancy. It is important, however, to sketch this out and explore the area.

In a recent blog post, the learning pundit Donald Clark claimed that 'machine learning algorithms are like small Gods. Free from the tyranny of time and space, speed is no limit. They can learn faster than any of us' (Clark, 2016). He is describing a new generation of artificial intelligence tools that are programmed to learn for themselves over millions of iterations. The more they learn, the faster they learn, until their specialized knowledge can surpass human ability. In this instance, Clark is referring to the Google AI software that learned the game GO and went on to beat the world champion. But there is now a virtual doctor whose diagnosis is better than final year medical students. *WIRED Health* published an article in April 2016 entitled 'AI doctors will become "as ubiquitous as stethoscopes"'. This article (Kamen, 2016) summarizes the work of IBM's Kyu Rhee, who explains that supercomputers can process complex data far faster than any human being, and could therefore either assist doctors in diagnosis or, in theory, replace doctors in the initial diagnosis. And there is now technology that can do 'case research' faster and more efficiently than a junior lawyer. In the May edition of *Tech Insider,*

Chris Weller describes Ross as the virtual lawyer that has been purchased by a number of law firms. What Ross can do faster than any human being is sort through hundreds or thousands of pages of legal cases looking for the example that can prove or disprove a legal claim (Weller, 2016). The actual announcement on May 5, 2016 was:

> ROSS Intelligence is proud to announce that AmLaw100 law firm
> BakerHostetler has agreed to retain use of ROSS Intelligence's artificial
> intelligence legal research product, ROSS. ROSS Intelligence
> Co-Founder Andrew Arruda officially announced the partnership at
> Vanderbilt Law School's 'Watson, Esq.' conference in Nashville, Tennessee
> in April. BakerHostetler will license ROSS for use in its Bankruptcy,
> Restructuring and Creditors' Rights team. (Ross Intelligence, 2016)

What links these two announcements is IBM's supercomputer Watson. The artificial intelligence engine is now powerful enough to be harnessed for a range of high-level artificial intelligence activities, which are certainly not restricted to medical diagnosis or legal case analysis. Is this a flash in the pan, or does it point the way to something extraordinary? Have we reached a point where our learning can be dramatically enhanced by having an 'intelligent' assistant by our side to help us filter and make sense of the crushing amount of data we have to deal with in our day-to-day lives?

This chapter will explore how new technologies that are still not freely available, but a long way from simply being pipe dreams, could transform the way in which leadership development is delivered and as a huge enhancement to any provision already available. There are three critical technologies which will be explored in this chapter. The first is artificial intelligence – machine-based support for learning; the second is virtual reality software, allowing learners to enter a virtual world and feel completely immersed in its reality and therefore experience things in a way safer than the real world, but nevertheless in a completely convincing way. The third is the rise of social networking software beyond Facebook that will allow us to share knowledge and keep learning as a definitive part of the workflow. The real power, however, comes when technologies combine. Imagine, for example, putting on a virtual reality headset which, with its stereoscopic vision, creates the illusion of total immersion in a 3-D environment. Let us imagine that you do this and, when you do, you immediately enter into a room where three Thai workers, to pick a case at random, are discussing the difficulties of being managed by an American. You actually take on the role of one of those Thai workers and feel what it is like, as well as see what it is like, to be in that predicament. The conversation has not been scripted and recorded like a drama, but created by an artificial intelligence engine that knows about you and the aspects of your leadership that you need to improve, when it comes to managing a remote workforce with different cultural characteristics. The learning is emotional as well as intellectual. You could say that it is almost visceral. You leave the room with two or three key pointers about how you have to change your behaviour. Your virtual assistant will, of course, remind you to implement these changed behaviours until they become habit.

Or, in another case, you are discussing the performance of the new recruit after three months in your organization. The watch on your wrist is linked to an AI engine and is 'listening' to the conversation and prompting you: 'Be more positive', 'Mention such and such a project', 'Don't forget to say thank you', 'Have you arranged a follow-up meeting?' Finally, you open your laptop to write a briefing paper on the success of your new on-boarding programme. You do not type, you dictate. As soon as you mention your on-boarding programme, relevant data appears on the screen as a prompt. The structure of the on-boarding programme is made available alongside the initial evaluation results. You do not really need to seek out any additional resources as everything you need is provided for you, and you can just get on with the job of dictating the paper. When you have finished it, you ask the computer to send it to a shared workspace where a number of colleagues will be able to comment to improve the document. You ask your phone to now cross that item from your 'to-do' list and read out the next four items on that list in priority order.

This all sounds fanciful, but the technology to do this is already in existence – it just needs to move from trial to delivery. Within two years much of this will be familiar to anybody involved in running an organization. It may be useful to look at some of these technologies in more detail to understand the enormity of the shift that is going to occur, and the power that they have to offer across the board, but specifically in the leadership development and support realm.

Virtual reality

Everybody is familiar with flight simulators. It has been decades since the first flight simulators were invented. In fact United Airlines purchased four flight simulators at a cost of US$3 million in 1954. Now the FAA specifications for flight simulator at level D has '6 degrees of freedom, outside-world horizontal field of view of at least 150° with a distant focus display, and realistic sound alongside special motion visual effects' (FAA, 2015). It is a completely immersive 360° experience that can train pilots to a level where they can step straight into the cockpit of a real-time flight perfectly. Training hours are balanced between simulation and real-time flying, and FAA Regulations dictate the actual hours required in a plane and in a simulator.

In 2016 it is possible to purchase a device for several hundred dollars (not the millions of dollars a flight simulator costs) which resembles ski goggles. Once on your head, you enter a similar 360° virtual world which you can interact with and experience in real-time. Within five years, this notion of virtual worlds will be as commonplace a learning environment as the flight simulator is today. When the first flight simulators were produced, they must have seemed like magical devices. That is exactly the reaction that people have today when putting on VR goggles.

An Irish VR software company, Immersive VR Education (www.immersivevreducation.com), has developed a simulation of the Apollo 11 space expedition to the Moon. You can experience the full 360° sensation of space, as well as pilot the lunar module and test whether you can take off and land successfully on the surface of the Moon. It is a magical experience. This software has been designed specifically for the Oculus Rift and HTC Vive headsets, both released within weeks of each other in 2016. It is early days, but this untethered experience is compelling, realistic, and immersive. The ambition of the developer, Dave Whelan, is clear:

> We want to help inspire the next generation of space travellers, so we are offering Apollo 11 VR free to all schools and colleges worldwide. It is our sincere hope that kids all around the world get to try out Apollo 11 VR and this sets them on the path to becoming astronauts, engineers and scientists. (Whelan, 2016)

The first VR demonstrations were all game-like, but experiences such as going into deep sea, or travelling in space are compelling and unavailable in any other medium unless you are a deep-sea diver or an astronaut! But there is a strong learning component – as you are not told about this world, you actually get to discover it. This high-end experience, and the products mentioned, are relatively expensive, but entry into the world of VR is not. For less than US$10, you can buy a Google cardboard VR headset kit into which you insert your phone. The phone is the 'brain' in the device; it acts as the stereoscopic VR screen and plays out the downloaded software. And Google has made sure that there are nearly 100 VR experiences that can be downloaded to your phone and played back using the headset for no or low cost.

If we go back to the Apollo 11 simulation, it is clearly not a game. After all, the company that produced it is called Immersive VR *Education*. Their other products include a virtual reality medical training simulation, and an immersive 3-D lecture room where an avatar of the lecturer can call up 3-D objects and dynamic graphics to explain points to a group of students, actually located anywhere in the world, but who join that presenter in one big virtual room. It is a huge leap forward from traditional webinar software.

It is possible that these new technologies could be the first stage of a revolution in the way we learn. At the moment because of the complexity of producing VR software, smaller examples are faster and easier to produce. What could work really well in, for example, a five-minute segment? The answer is, clearly, learning. And given the cost of leadership development and the significant cost of failed leadership, this is a tangible possibility for the immediate future. If you imagine having a difficult conversation in a virtual world, where you appear to be in the room talking to someone else, providing the software is sophisticated enough, the experience would be more realistic, and a deeper learning experience than something recreated on the desktop in 2-D, or a written case study which simply describes the experience.

Most VR software is built on the Unity platform. It is, in essence, a game engine and therefore speeds up development, but it is also multiplatform, so you build it once, and deploy on one of 24 compatible platforms. These include mobile platforms such as phones and tablets as well as more orthodox desktop computers and VR environments. Even in that VR environment, Unity supports five different VR platforms including Oculus Rift and HTC Vive. The technology is bubbling under the surface at the moment, but it will deliver enhanced learning experiences very soon. What is holding us back now is not the technology – neither hardware nor software – but the imagination, commitment and application of the developers.

Willow DNA developed a simple model to define what learning need may be appropriate for a VR learning solution (Willow DNA, 2016). It focuses on three cognitive dimensions: risk; the need for practice; and the number of sensory elements in the learning. The higher the values in each of those dimensions, the more appropriate the VR approach could be. Some elements of leadership skill development seem to hit the 'sweet spot'. Willow's example of an appropriate area for VR is contract negotiation. This is high-risk, complex, and requires lots of practice. If you consider a more generic subject, such as negotiation skills, which is an area of core leadership competence, the relevance of a potential VR solution is clear. Willow DNA's conclusion is balanced and realistic:

> VR isn't the solution for all the performance needs in your organization, no one particular approach ever is. However, it is becoming an attainable and practical solution that can now be put into the mix when the need warrants it. (Willow DNA, 2016: 9)

This is a fair summary of the current position, and indicates that VR is now a possible consideration and not a rather strange technological fantasy. There are many real-world examples now – a recent blog post lists 20 serious, non-gaming virtual experiences that may indicate the way things will develop (Tracey, 2016).

Artificial intelligence

Machine intelligence has been a dream ever since we had computers. Alan Turing, the British code expert in the Second World War, devised his Turing test in 1950. This test was designed to identify the point at which a machine could be deemed 'intelligent'. It was a simple way to measure artificial intelligence. The nature of the Turing test is for an investigator to hold a conversation, firstly with a human being and then with a computer, asking simple questions. The machine passed the test when the investigator was not able to tell whether the conversation was with the human being or the machine. Remarkably, it is only recently that machines have the capability of passing the Turing test.

Google purchased an intelligence software company called DeepMind, run by an academic-turned-entrepreneur, Demis Hassabis. Founded in 2010, it was acquired by Google in 2014 and was their largest European acquisition at that time. They bought the company, which had no products, just ideas. This company suddenly hit the headlines in 2016 when its software programme AlphaGo beat Lee Sedol, the world's top GO player, 4–1 in a five-match challenge. Lee only won his first game in challenge match four! This is an astonishing achievement, as GO is a complex game – far more complex than chess, for example – and there are millions of permutations. AlphaGo was not programmed to play GO; it was programmed to *learn* GO, which it did over millions of iterations. It started at a very basic level, and ended by beating the world champion. AI had come of age. Fast Company estimates that AI is now a fifteen billion dollar a year industry and will grow, not diminish (van Hoof, 2016).

In the government's Final Foresight Project Report (Foresight Report, 2008), the focus is entirely on developing our mental resources rather than any other resources. This is seen as an essential task to ensure prosperity and well-being for the UK in the 21st century. Mental capital encompasses:

> a person's cognitive and emotional resources. It includes their cognitive ability, how flexible and efficient they are at learning, and their 'emotional intelligence', such as their social skills and resilience in the face of stress. It therefore conditions how well an individual is able to contribute effectively to society, and also to experience a high personal quality of life. (Foresight Report, 2008: 11)

Learning is an increasingly significant element of survival in this century. And AI technologies will be able to help the process of building cognitive and emotional intelligence. The MIT academic and computer scientist Rana el Kaliouby (2015) has demonstrated applications that can read human emotion and share that with others. She has developed software that, over millions of iterations, has managed accurately to pinpoint emotion depicted on a human face. It can distinguish, for example, between a smile and a supercilious grin, and between sadness and seriousness. The end product could be an 'emotion chip' that is added to devices to help them 'feel' and transmit those feelings to others. It is an extraordinary development, especially when coupled with virtual reality environments and learning.

The key will be to upskill the workforce to the point where automation and artificial intelligence will be life-enhancing – productivity generators working in partnership with highly skilled humans. According to a recent skills confidence survey by City & Guilds Group, 70 per cent of CEOs and senior leaders agree that automation and artificial intelligence could replace jobs in their organization in 10 years' time. However, only 53 per cent of general employees agree. This figure drops even more in the UK, where 62 per cent of the workforce is apparently not worried about the rise in automation and artificial intelligence. Censuswide conducted this research on behalf of the City & Guilds group. Across the UK, United States, India and South Africa 8,157 respondents took part. Out of that group 1,028 were CEOs or senior leaders (City & Guilds, 2016).

There is generally a startling naivety about the power of artificial intelligence. AI should be seen as a means of navigating a complex world of data saturation rather than as a threat. The Foresight Report rightly impresses the reader with the need to emphasize learning, in particular for the ageing adult population, to keep them employable and to develop their cognitive capacity:

> In the field of learning, individuals can substantially increase their employability and earnings potential by improving their skills and mental capital, and companies can benefit from helping their employees to train and retrain through their working lives. However, there is a wider social and economic case for the government to help individuals to recognize and take advantage of these benefits, supporting them in childhood and empowering them to take control of their own learning and retraining in later years, and to provide companies with stronger

incentives which take full account of the wider benefits involved.
(Foresight Report, 2008: 32–33)

Intelligent agents that sit with individuals and nudge them to greater competence have significant yet unexplored potential. It would be possible to boost the concept of learning on the job into a constant drip-feed, developmental exercise based on targeted learning, which is geared to the individual's needs and gently moves a person forward. There is a big agenda here and a key for future job security. We should ensure that software developed using artificial intelligence engines and sophisticated algorithms enhances what the individual does at work rather than displaces their role. This means recasting many jobs and reskilling many people to keep them relevant at work. There is little possibility that a top lawyer at a senior level could be replaced by artificial intelligence software. It is the newly recruited graduates responsible for undertaking legal research whose roles are vulnerable: 90 per cent of their job could be enabled much more efficiently by AI software. If there were 90 per cent fewer junior lawyers, how will that industry function, and who would be available to feed into the ranks of senior lawyers and partners? What kind of continuing professional development would be necessary for lawyers, to upskill them in order to work hand in hand with AI, and maintain the viability of their profession? These are big questions.

Google DeepMind is doing just this in healthcare – partnering with the NHS to build tools that help clinicians to faster diagnosis, so that they will be able to intervene earlier and work harder on preventive strategies. DeepMind has a partnership programme to empower clinicians by assisting them in diagnosis and helping them become more effective in their roles. This sort of partnership could be a model that is followed more generally in other specialist areas – a tool that could support company leaders to make strategic decisions by analysing data from complex sources very fast. It could also suggest strategies to deal with other leadership challenges which could pay for itself very quickly, by increasing efficiency and effectiveness, and building a more enthusiastic and committed workforce within a more responsive and productive company.

Personal digital assistant

The notion of a PDA stretches back to the early 90s when Apple CEO John Scully used the term when introducing the Apple Newton. The Newton with its touchscreen and handwriting recognition was a product that promised more than it delivered. The handwriting recognition was poor, and its ability to sync with a Mac desktop was hit-and-miss. It also ran on an entirely new operating system that bore no resemblance to Mac OS. The first task that Steve Jobs completed on his return to Apple in 1997 was to cancel the entire Newton programme and dismiss the entire Newton team. That was fairly conclusive evidence of his lack of commitment and belief in the project!

The term PDA has disappeared as there is now nothing to distinguish between that and a phone. All of the functionality in a PDA has been absorbed into the smartphone. The message pad-like Newton and its successors converged with advanced phones, notably the original Nokia 9000 Communicator. This was introduced in 1996 and became a somewhat awkward and clumsy world bestseller. In effect, the PDA became the PDA/phone, which simply became the smartphone by the beginning of the 21st century. Pre-iPhone (the original iconic smartphone) was the BlackBerry – designed to manage diaries, text and e-mail alongside phone calls. The first BlackBerry was released in January 1999 and marked the beginning of the transition which was completed in 2007 when the first iPhone was released. This was the first stage in a rapid escalation in functionality and computing power of the smartphone. These devices have grown in power and versatility to become, in the words of *The Economist* (28 February 2015), 'the supercomputer in your pocket'. We now take for granted the fact that we can take videoconference calls, listen to music, deal with e-mail and messages, and interrogate the web simultaneously, whist moving from place to place a long way from our home base.

The most obvious experience that most people have of AI is in the shape of their personal digital assistant on their phone. That is 'Siri' on an Apple device, 'Cortana' for Microsoft, 'Alexa' for Amazon, Google Assistant for Google, and 'M' for Facebook. It is a crowded field! Although Siri was ridiculed after its first release exclusively on the iPhone in 2010 as non-functioning and 'stupid', Apple continued to develop the software and it has become increasingly powerful and viable with each new release. By rolling it out onto all Apple platforms, Siri has a central role on all Apple devices, and it is clear that other tech companies' variations share a similar vision. Communicating 'naturally' with an electronic device, using voice instructions that the device can interpret and act upon, is increasingly compelling and efficient.

Without voice control, wearable devices will always have limited functionality. And if you want to access your calendar or music playlists while driving, voice control and voice instruction are essential. This is an area that is more than just an interesting add-on. The fact that Apple has enabled other developers to plug Siri into their applications (rather than leave it as an Apple-only enhancement) demonstrates not just faith in the technology but a belief in its centrality. The original developer of Siri, Dag Kittlaus, who sold his company to Apple in 2010 for US\$200 million, released a new digital virtual assistant called 'Viv' in May 2016. At the launch he claimed:

> We are going to use this technology to breathe life into the inanimate objects and devices of our life through conversation. That's kind of where we are headed with this. (Delventhal, 2016)

Kittlaus's ambition with Viv is to make it the intelligent and friendly front end to all AI systems. It is device-independent, and third-party neutral. It can work with Facebook, or Uber and any artificial intelligence system. We get a glimpse of how this might work in the future if we look at the Amazon device called 'Amazon Echo' (the new Google Home works in a similar way but is a younger technology). Amazon Echo is a small cylindrical device that has no buttons apart from an on/off button. You interact with it exclusively through voice. It sits quietly until you wake it by asking it do something: 'Alexa, can you…' It can play music, answer questions, make to-do lists, get the news and weather, and generally act as a clock or alarm clock or timer. They are all things that your smartphone can do. But this device is home based and it means that you do not have to take your phone out of your handbag or pocket. Alexa takes all its information from the Cloud and feeds it back – on demand – via its speaker system. It requires nothing more than mains power and Wi-Fi connectivity.

A similar device could eventually sit in company office space and gently prompt the user to act in a particular way, remind the person of appointments and generally enhance positive behaviours. It could act as a go-to support device, actually making appointments, setting up appropriate software and attempting to anticipate needs in the way that a traditional personal assistant might have done in the past. These possibilities are emerging rapidly, so it is not a wild assumption that such devices could have a role in helping a leader to learn every day and reinforce that learning.

When we move into the world of wearable devices such as the Apple Watch, you could argue that the viability of such sophisticated devices depends entirely on artificial intelligence engines to manage their functionality and deliver appropriate services. Again, we step into the realms of possibility rather than actuality. If you imagine someone leaving a leadership programme, and their watch gently reminds them to say thank you to the team, prompts regular catch-up meetings, or suggests making an appointment to speak to a particular person, such as a recent joiner, this could be a powerful electronic aide-memoire. A watch with its 'at a glance' functionality is far more discreet than a clunky phone which has to be dragged out and activated. Perhaps telling the time will be the least important function of such a device in the future.

For onboarding, the watch could be triggered by location sensors such as iBeacons to give information or prompt the wearer to take some action or track their course through their new, unfamiliar premises. It could even act as an in-building GPS to direct a person from one location to another or track down an individual with whom they wish to speak. In some ways, this is exporting some of the functionality of the smartphone to other dedicated or specialist devices. It is speed and convenience that are novel. What glues all this together is access to the Cloud, AI and voice control.

The rise of social networking software

As soon as you mention the words social networking, Facebook springs to mind. With almost a billion users, it is a leviathan. Although it has some business features, it is primarily designed for individuals to communicate with friends. Other developments are much more interesting from a business perspective, and are possibly transformative in the way in which we can communicate and share new knowledge and ideas at work. This is both in terms of speed and efficiency.

There are two examples of this process that exist now that could be at the start of a significant trend with far-reaching effects. The first is Slack. This is advertised as a replacement for e-mail within work teams. It allows a community to establish a channel. This channel is private and secure for its members and the only entrance is by invitation. Software allows any documents, videos or files to be shared, along with commentary that anyone can add to. It is possible to have private conversations, but the trajectory is towards adding group insights, and knowledge sharing. A Slack community is made up of a number of channels, and an individual can be a member of one channel or many channels within the community. Its architecture is such that you can see the communities on the left-hand side screen and the activity on the right. By scrolling down the screen you reveal the history of interactions within a specific channel. These are revealed in date-stamped order. This has huge advantages over e-mail, where conversations are difficult, and e-mails sent to large groups can be a nightmare of confusing unlinked responses. Slack is by no means perfect, but it does operate in the workflow and is very team-centred. If you are involved in the project, the fact that communications with the members of that project are discretely held makes it much easier to track progress, join in conversations, and generally be informed. Although newly released, its users number tens of millions already.

The second example is a piece of software released in beta during 2016 by a company called Anders Pink. The software is designed to help teams curate information and share that information amongst themselves. When you enter the software, you are prompted to set up a 'briefing' and then define who is to share that briefing. You can be very specific about what that briefing comprises. You choose keywords to define your subject matter as precisely as you want, with the ability to include some words and exclude others, and to highlight some sources and exclude others. The result is an instantly generated page of links to blogs, websites, Twitter, etc that comprehensively covers the area you wish to explore. This is updated every couple of hours. You can then highlight certain items, annotate them for colleagues, and keep them on a pinboard for later reference and retention. If you do none of those things, the items refresh over time. So it is brilliant knowledge sharing on topics that directly concern a team on a regular basis, but it also works for a single specialist search on a particular subject that is immediately useful. Any briefing that ceases to be relevant can be deleted. There is also a dashboard, which selects generic items from all of your briefings that could be of interest to the team. Finally, there is a daily e-mail that sums up the content in digest form.

In response to our information overload we tend to ignore most sources of new information data, or randomly forward information without having really looked at it. This software really helps manage the information flow and helps teams stay smart, and stay informed in a way that is very simple to use and extremely compelling. Once you have used it, it is hard to imagine working without it. It would be a perfect way for a leadership cohort to keep thinking about leadership issues beyond any learning programme, and to help in that group's self-development.

What you should take from this chapter

Much of what is discussed in this chapter is not available in any widely usable shape or form at the moment. However, the first point is that all of these areas show lots of potential for L&D, in particular for leadership development, and everybody should be interested in future developments. It is important to try to keep up with what is out there. Note a few keywords such as artificial intelligence, virtual reality or digital assistant. Get them into your vocabulary, keep an eye on those developments and look for the right opportunity to exploit the ideas and move forward.

Secondly, you should be initiating conversations with your team about some of the resources that are being produced. It is worth investigating whether there are any insights in terms of new ideas and different ways of working that these products suggest. If you have external suppliers, such as content developers, this whole area could be the subject of a very interesting discussion about how elements explored in this chapter could change the way you use resources.

Thirdly, look at areas where you could start to experiment. Start with very small tests of the models. Look at micro-development of some of those technologies. The knowledge gained could have a big impact on your future strategy. For example, your learning team could start working with Slack. There will be benefits in terms of knowledge sharing, and it can be tested thoroughly before recommending it more widely.

It is also extremely helpful to look at the future of L&D in this environment, thinking about the potential impact of these emerging technologies. Look at what you do, and think about how you could build an entirely different kind of learning operation in the light of these technologies. Then consider how you might prepare for this future in the short term.

It is really important that you do not ignore these developments because, although slightly futuristic at the moment, they will arrive, and you do not want to be taken by surprise when they do. So keep discussing their potential. However, it is also important not to over-sell the possible impact. The world will not change overnight, and everything you do now should not be discarded in favour of software and tools that do not quite work. It should be seen as important for your future strategy, but do not let it dominate your perspective or abandon your short-term goals.

References

City & Guilds Group (2016) *Skills Confidence*, survey, #skillsconfidence16

Clark, D (2016) *Plan B: The day our species lost to AI – but won*, http://donaldclarkplanb.blogspot.co.uk/2016/03/remember-this-date-12-02-2012-day-our.html

Delventhal, S (2016) Siri founder and CEO introduces new AI assistant 'Viv', *Investopedia*

The Economist (28 February 2015) The planet of the phones, *The Economist* el Kaliouby, R (2015) TEDWomen, http://blog.ted.com/a-look-at-the-tedwomen-2015-speaker-lineup/

FAA (2015) Website, https://faa.gov/about/initiatives/nsp/train_devices

Foresight Report (2008) *Mental Capital and Wellbeing: Making the most of ourselves in the 21st century*, Government Office for Science, London

Kamen, M (2016) AI doctors will become 'as ubiquitous as stethoscopes', *WIRED Health*, http://www.wired.co.uk/article/kyu-rhee-ibm-watson-ai-doctor

Ross Intelligence (2016) ROSS Intelligence announces partnership with BakerHostetler, *PR Newswire*, May 5, http://www.prnewswire.com/news-releases/ross-intelligence-announces-partnership-with-bakerhostetler-300264039.html

Tracey, R (2016) 20 Real-World Examples of Virtual Reality, E-Learning Provocateur Blog, https://ryan2point0.wordpress.com/2016/03/22/20-real-world-examples-of-virtual-reality/

van Hoof, P (2016) A Designer's Guide to the $15 Billion Artificial Intelligence Industry, http://www.fastcodesign.com/3061163/a-designers-guide-to-the-15-billion-artificial-intelligence-industry

Weller, C (2016) Law firms of the future will be filled with robot lawyers, *Tech Insider*, July

Whelan, D (2016) MEGA Update Apollo 11 VR, https://kickstarter.com/projects/1436197736/the-apollo-11-virtual-reality-experience-education/posts/1473911

Willow DNA (2016) Virtual Reality, White Paper, www.willowdna.com

PART FIVE
Lessons Learned

How to move forward   12

This book offers some deliberate, definite outcomes that are practically helpful for those involved in leadership development. Many of the books that are extremely critical of leadership development, such as Pfeffer's *Leadership BS* (Pfeffer, 2015), are strong on criticism but weak on what you need to do to put it right. One of the core purposes behind this book is to inspire those in L&D to relish the task of building effective leadership development in their organizations because it is extremely important.

Failed leadership does not just diminish the potential of organizations; it can ruin people's lives and blight their careers. In the face of criticism, I think it is important to pay attention to what works, and what is right in specific circumstances. There is no magic formula, no simple solution, but there are important indicators around the building of successful leadership development.

The purpose of this last section is to pull together a number of core conclusions that have emerged out of the research and the case studies. These are all indicators of the way that leadership development should be approached in organizations. They are not lists of what you have to do! I did not want to write a prescriptive book. There are far too many of those on bookshelves gathering dust.

Conclusions

Leadership is not an event

There is a huge temptation to make leadership development a spectacular event which is locked in time, and fades from view rapidly after it is finished. This allows you to have some sort of fanfare, big launch and an implicit message that the programme will be over soon and you can get back to the real work. For many reasons there are acute dangers with this approach. As soon as you begin to see leadership development as an inoculation which people queue up to receive – which hurts a bit, but is over soon – you create an illusion that the effort involved is timed – intense, maybe – but finishes relatively quickly. This is the opposite of building a long-term commitment to improving leadership in your organization. Without that long-term assumption, failure is almost inevitable.

Leadership development is a process. There may be more intense elements, and greater time involvement at some points, but one of the outcomes of any programme is the commitment to working from this point forward on the quality of leadership in your organization. That involves HR, a consultation process with the workforce, the senior leadership, as well as those responsible for delivering leadership development. Once you have that broad coalition of support, you have a much better chance that every element will be mutually reinforcing and you will be able to move forward.

A blend works best

Research would seem to indicate that a blended process, that combines on-line with face-to-face, delivers the optimum outcomes. This allows time to think quietly on your own, and time to engage with others. Both are important. If you want serious outcomes then there has to be a lot of interaction in groups, and interaction with line managers, alongside the broader commitment of staff. There is no quick fix; this is not a simple process and should not be seen as such.

If you have the blending, then setting up a virtual campus – or an online repository of resources – allows the programme to continue and support leaders on a needs-must basis from this point forward. The blend assures the leader that this is not simply a one-off experience but a continuous commitment to making things better.

Make sure you transfer some responsibility to the leader

If your leaders react to leadership development as someone else's problem, they will resist taking on both the responsibility and the effort to put things right. There needs to be a sense of ownership for the outcomes of any programme from both the individual and the cohort. Development programmes are far more likely to succeed if there are sanctions in place to ensure that the requirements are taken seriously, and there are consequences for non-participation.

Top leadership has to be behind this and give it time to take effect

All the most successful programmes have the total commitment of the highest levels of leadership in the organization – that commitment means more than authorizing expenditure, or attending a launch event, although these two things are useful! Commitment means active involvement and participation from the very beginning through to the logical end point. And it is important that senior leadership understand that they will start to notice changes in the organization after months, not weeks. Your role is to gather evidence that this has happened and to indicate the nature of those changes. Promising radical shifts in weeks rarely delivers. You might pick the moment when there is a lot of interest, and some activity, but the moment when changes become embedded in the culture of the organization is usually a long way further ahead.

Not stop-start but a continuous process

Every day represents a leadership challenge; every day gives leaders the chance to practise new leadership skills or simply a different way of approaching the leadership task. If the process of learning about leadership is in some way disconnected from the practice of being that leader, you will have created a very interesting intellectual forum, but you will not have engineered any kind of shift in the organization, or moved leadership much further forward.

Context matters more than models

My research indicates that it does not matter what model of leadership you select. The people who market those models want you to believe that what they offer is completely different from anyone else. The truth is that the competences are similar, and if you get people on the path towards leadership development, they will find what they need for their own purposes and move forward rapidly. The four core competences outlined by McKinsey in Chapter 1 are as good as any:

- Be supportive.
- Operate with strong results orientation.
- Seek different perspectives.
- Solve problems effectively.

Those competences are based on information from 189,000 executives worldwide. And you could argue that they cover the key areas that are required for leadership development. There are much more important areas to focus upon than the model itself. And believing that the selection of a model is the most important element of the successful leadership programme is naive and not borne out by the evidence. This mythology is brilliantly dissected by Barbara Kellerman in *The End of Leadership* (2012: 17, 255–56). As I have shown, context is very important; abstract, disconnected and theoretical models have limited enduring qualities.

Mindfulness and emotional intelligence endure

The first of the McKinsey competences is that leaders 'be supportive', but executives need support as well. There is an increasing body of research, which indicates that emotional intelligence and mindfulness development can positively impact on an executive's ability to deal with stress and cope with uncertainty. This is extremely important and underpins leadership performance as a whole. This is because it allows the leader to focus on all the other competence areas. Under negative stress, an individual cannot think straight, or perform to optimum. And that is only one aspect of the detrimental impacts this can cause, on life, family and work–life balance. One response to this is to teach leaders to be mindful and practise mindfulness. The benefits are becoming clearer and clearer as more evidence emerges of the power of mindfulness at work (Gelles, 2015).

The leadership programme in Antarctica (see Chapter 3) built in several sessions of quiet reflection and these proved to be an important component for processing the learning and the experience. Never cram a programme with content to the exclusion of time for reflection. This lesson should translate directly into the working day where reflection time is also necessary.

A recent doctoral dissertation from the University of Pennsylvania CLO Programme would support this thesis strongly. It is written by Kandi Wiens and is called *The Influence of Emotional Intelligence on the Ability of Executive Level Physician Leaders to Cope with Occupational Stress*. The thesis demonstrates the significant difference in the ability to cope with stress levels, demonstrated by those with emotional intelligence training to supplement natural levels of emotional intelligence, and those with neither the development nor the innate ability. At the very least, these topics need to be talked about and cues and tools shared.

Google, for example, has its own mindfulness training programme that over 17,000 staff have been through, which was devised by one of their long-term employees, a software engineer called Chade-Meng Tan. He later published a book on the programme he devised, and its impact within Google, called *Search Inside Yourself* (2012). The book has a foreword by the foremost proponent of emotional intelligence, Daniel Goleman, who claims:

> Meng… had the smarts to reverse engineer emotional intelligence. Meng picked it apart and put it back together again with a brilliant insight: he saw that knowing yourself lies at the core of emotional intelligence, and that the best mental app for this can be found in the mind-training method called mindfulness. (Tan, 2012: 6)

It is illogical to conceive of a leadership development initiative, which simply focuses outside the leaders on the problems they have to fix, the results they have to deliver, and the support they have to offer, without helping them understand themselves. This will help them deal with the pressures they will inevitably face. This was Meng's insight, and over 17,000 Googlers would attest to its efficacy, including most of the senior leaders in the company.

Build to an optimistic future

If you tackle leadership issues with a broad, optimistic view of how good your organization could be, and share and iterate that vision across the whole company, the value and outcome of leadership development will resonate. Instead of being for the few, it will be seen as something for the many. Focus on what will be positive rather than what is failing. An optimistic perspective galvanizes everyone. A pessimistic viewpoint depresses the entire workforce. (See Chapter 9.)

Co-creation is vital

It is obvious, that the leadership programme that develops its curriculum without any consultation whatsoever with the people on the receiving end is far less likely to succeed than a similar programme which has done its homework. There is guidance later in the chapter on how you might conduct that kind of needs analysis, but it is clear that you should, and you should take your time to make sure that it is right.

What is not so obvious is that in the resulting programme should be the indelible touch, voice and stamp of the organization. Those programmes that were co-created with representatives of the target audience have had greater impact than those programmes which did not. But co-creation is a complicated process and requires a number of elements to succeed. There are four or five ways that you can include the insights, messages and voice of your learners. The first is to feature individuals in the organization who either reflect some of the core challenges that leaders face, or have potential solutions to those challenges. The most effective way of making their voices heard is to include them as interviewees on video so that you can see them, hear them, and understand their perspective. This also creates an authentic voice at the core of the programme.

Secondly, you can ask if a group or groups of representatives from the target disciplines are willing to act as a sounding board throughout the development of the programme and then be prepared to pilot the content once it is ready for testing. This consistency can be extremely helpful. The group(s) do not have to meet all the time, but having user representatives sample the material, listen to the arguments, and ensure that the tone is right is invaluable. It is also important that the developers listen to that and not assume that they know better.

Thirdly, you should attempt to scour the organization for existing tools and techniques that are being implemented quietly by leaders. To take something that already exists – and already works – into the programme for roll-out across the organization is empowering. Critically, it also indicates that you are listening, and trying to enhance and celebrate what is great about leadership in your organization; and you are not assuming that every single leader is ineffective and has nothing much to contribute. One of the tensions in any leadership development programme is that the leader is intellectually debating about how the new content stacks up against many years of experience in existing practice. To see that it can be done better from inside can often help the process of acceptance and behaviour change. Always imposing everything from outside can be more limited in impact.

Fourthly, there can be significant help given to the small number of people on the development team, by getting members of the target group to sit with the developers and actually get involved in the process of building the programme.

Finally, it is sometimes helpful to poll potential group participants on what they think are the critical priorities, or on specific content areas where there are options going forward. This can be overdone, but keeping people informed on progress is usually helpful and can form part of the communication strategy.

The line manager can make or break a programme

I have not encountered a single leadership programme that delivered successful change in leadership practice without the active participation of the line manager. It seems obvious; however, many programmes still assume that the line manager will offer some support without actually detailing what that support should be. Many returnees from a leadership programme are slapped down by their line manager if they try to do anything differently. In those situations you can probably imagine how long the impact of the programme actually lasts. In many circumstances the line manager is the critical element that can ensure success or contribute to the failure of a leadership development programme.

Line managers who sit down with their direct report and help that individual plan what should emerge from the learning, and then help the manager implement the learning by offering support and mentorship, add greatly to the effectiveness of any learning programme, not just leadership. Robert Brinkerhoff gathered evidence of this more than 15 years ago. He claimed that active participation in the building of an action plan, and in its implementation, increased effectiveness by an average of 70 per cent over those with limited interventions. Success requires direct support (Brinkerhoff, 2002). Elements of that support can include: regular meetings to review progress; removing obstacles and supporting the leaders when they change behaviour; mentoring through the stages of the development programme; showing forthright support for the programme to everybody, not just the leader; and stretching assignments which focus on applying the learning.

Learning should be part of what you do

It is clear from research undertaken by Charles Jennings, as well as his interventions in a large number of significant companies, that learning in general is reinforced by being part of the workflow, not outside it (Arets, Heijnen and Jennings, 2015: 46). Leadership is a critical area where learning in work, and learning as work, reinforces the formal structured learning that is delivered. Jennings claims:

> Knowledge is no longer static: it's in a constant state of motion, flow rather than an item of inventory, a dynamic process of acquiring and refining knowledge that oscillates back and forth between theory and practice, working and learning. (Arets, Heijnen and Jennings, 2015: 46)

The idea that a body of knowledge imparted outside the workflow in a separate space offers sufficient substance to be implemented is increasingly naive. There is an iterative process involved as learners take the model and make it their own. This is not simply about testing what works in practice; it is about seeing work as a vital crucible for learning. There is another reason why the line manager is such a critical sounding board, who can supply some of the glue to cement the process of moving knowledge from outside to inside the organization, and from experimentation to permanent behaviour change.

Individual change occurs when the group and the organization are involved

The idea that a leader is an island, separate and self-contained, is misguided. All of the great thinkers on leadership talk about leading in context, and about followership. In a rapidly evolving environment where certainties no longer exist, a good leader has to know when to listen and learn from others. Therefore, the greatest impact on individual leadership change comes from the group. This means that senior leadership as a single process will not deliver as much as exhorting the team or group to move forward together. There are many ways to do this:

- Putting the leader into a small leadership team to work on one another's issues and challenges, such as an action learning set.

- Setting up a tutorial group where small numbers of leaders focus on the challenges of each step of a leadership programme.

- Encouraging the leader to 'work out loud' – in other words explain clearly what is being attempted with their team and ask for feedback and support as new processes are being implemented. It is possible to see changes in behaviour greatly enhanced by the immediate team around the individual making the change. If no one is clear what is happening, no one will be sure what has been achieved.

- Establishing an external support group of colleagues. Occasional meetings with friends or colleagues at a similar level in other organizations – where you talk about leadership – can be a huge resource. An individual leader can draw on the skills and insights of many, in order to work out specifically what those individuals should be doing in their respective workplaces.

How to build better leadership programmes

This section offers some suggestions about the process of building leadership programmes. They are suggestions, and some will resonate more than others. See them as a checklist and an aide-memoire, not a to-do list.

You need a context where there is a desire for change

If no one can see that there is any problem with the current leadership practice and behaviour, is almost impossible to move forward. At the very least there has to be a majority wanting change, and the change should be based on hard evidence of issues and problems.

It is a mistake to gather evidence of the need for leadership development by asking leaders or conducting tests on leaders. Any deficits in leadership are revealed by the organization itself. Just as Google, in Project Oxygen (see Chapter 10) defined leadership need by analysing data from performance reviews around the organization, there are plenty of similar ways to gather this data.

You could look at what is coming out of your performance analysis data, but it is sometimes simpler to ask staff what they like about the leadership in the organization and what they find frustrating. Clear patterns will emerge which can be tested. It is also possible to build a framework around the McKinsey competences listed elsewhere in this chapter:

- Be supportive.
- Operate with strong results orientation.
- Seek different perspectives.
- Solve problems effectively.

Each one could be turned into a question or statement to be reviewed. For example: 'I feel supported by my line manager'; 'When I encounter difficulties my line manager offers appropriate support'; 'I'm given sufficient resources to perform well'; 'My line manager helps me see the bigger picture'; 'I feel I am learning and progressing in my role'; 'My line manager helps me work out strategies for solving problems so that I can do it on my own next time.'

If you think that the Google Oxygen statements around good leadership (see Chapter 10) have some fit with your own organization, you could use them and try to find out where the trickiest issues are under each particular element. The important point is that you have some hard evidence of leadership failure (as well as leadership success) that can form the basis for building an alliance and gathering strong support for moving forward.

The whole leadership team needs to be committed

If there is agreement on this, everyone will pull together and failure will not be tolerated. In the NHS senior leaders programme, the cohort is responsible for taking the decision about who has succeeded in the programme itself (see Chapter 5). They become the arbiters of the standard and their judgement is what really counts. The cohort pull each other through the programme, and want everybody to succeed.

If you begin a programme with only lukewarm support from the leadership team which is the intended target, it is very hard to make the programme work, as everybody will walk away at the first opportunity, and no one will take responsibility, ultimately, for making it work. What this means is that the more time taken to build evidence that the need to change exists is extremely important. As is having a clear, optimistic vision of what a successful future state may look and feel like. Rushing towards a solution usually ends in tears.

Never hand over responsibility to anyone outside the organization

It is tempting, once you have recruited a supplier to deliver some or all of your leadership development, to walk away and leave it to them. This is always a mistake. You need to have a grip on the programme, be clear about what you want to emerge, and be ruthless in ensuring that this happens. The organization has the fundamental insight into what it needs, that nobody from outside can acquire quickly. If you stay on top of the programme, take all the executive decisions, and make it clear who is in charge, you have a better chance of success. Any supplier not prepared to work in this way should probably not work with you. Most suppliers are grateful for such support and close interest, not put off by it.

As we saw from the NHS programme (see Chapter 5), there were many suppliers and each had a critical role, but there was an overall steering group – together with specific development teams – for each element of the programme. They all had NHS representatives. This can be a heavy overhead, but worthwhile, because it assures alignment with business needs. You also need your internal user group to run everything past, so that they are convinced that what is emerging is fit for purpose and will work in your organization.

Only create when you cannot curate

There are so many excellent resources out there which you can access and build into any leadership programme. It is almost axiomatic now, that when we want to learn anything we turn to YouTube, Google and its variants. It is no longer strange to have a TED talk embedded into a leadership programme. It is actually stranger not to do this. It is pointless reproducing yet another way of discussing a particular topic when brilliant resources already exist. They need context, they need embedding and they need a learning flow around them, and it is much more important to spend your time creating the right kind of learning environment than duplicating content unnecessarily. We have a content fetish in learning and development, when we should have an obsession on behaviour change and outcomes. Getting to the outcome as quickly as possible, and as relevantly as possible, is the most useful strategy – not developing resources unnecessarily.

There are times when you need to develop brilliant, new resources. But for much of the time you can rely on TED talks and other stimulus material to get over key generic concepts, and therefore focus on what is unique to the situation of their leaders when it comes to development.

If the TED talk nails an issue in 15 minutes, it is better to spend your time working out the relevance of the talk to your organization, and how to build discussion around the presentation. This is far more productive.

Discussion and sharing are important

The more any leadership programme is seen as a collective responsibility, and the more the learning is shared and the challenges talked about openly, the better the glue around the cohort and the more successful the programme will be. In the BP programme, for example

(see Chapter 6), no piece of content went undiscussed, and no implementation of new leadership practice was delivered in isolation
without reference to the team and the leadership cohort as a whole.
If you can make the discussion meaningful and not simply there for
the sake of it, it is impossible to have too much.

In the Seasalt example (see Chapter 7), those who contributed
most were singled out by the chief executive to illustrate just how
important he felt their effort was. In many ways, the fact that a
number of leaders took it upon themselves to act as the voice of the
cohort became a primary indicator that the programme was working
and its message was embedding in the leadership culture.

Ten top tips to finish

1 Face up to the truth of what is really going on inside your organization. It is not about stating the culture 'This is what we do
around here', but more about what people said we do around
here. When this has been done, be brutally honest about the
impact of the leadership development programme and face up to
the reality of how it worked and then build a vision for a better,
more optimistic future.

2 Do your research thoroughly, and do not rush to a solution. Take
advice on what is required both internally and externally.

3 Ensure that everybody going through the programme has
sufficient support to get through, and sufficient pressure to make
necessary changes in behaviour.

4 Always start with what success would look like. Be clear about
what the ultimate aims are.

5 Start where your people are, use the devices they use and integrate
what you do into their existing workflow and existing practice.
Incorporating smartphones and tablets is a pretty good place to begin.

6 Don't make too many compromises to get an easy life. In particular,
never compromise on the involvement of the line manager.

7 You should brand any programme in order to sell it into the
organization. Do not assume that everyone is equally enthusiastic
about it as you are.

8 Communicate regularly on impact. Collect statements that indicate that the programme is working. This is not a comprehensive evaluation but a means of demonstrating that you are having some kind of impact. If these statements are heartfelt, and delivered on video or audio, so much the better.

9 Take a hard line on non-compliance. Most people make changes, but if you do impose discipline, the programme is almost irrelevant because the workforce will only see those elements that didn't work, rather than those that did. Non-compliance has to be unacceptable and there have to be sanctions.

10 Build your own unique programme that meets your needs. Be influenced by others, and by other programmes, but the ultimate choice is yours, and what works for you may not work for anybody else. Be confident in those choices.

My final hope is that you will deliver great leadership development that will develop great leaders, who will support great staff in a great organization!

References

Arets, J, Heijnen, V and Jennings, C (2015) *70:20:10: Towards 100% performance*, Sutler Media, Maastricht

Brinkerhoff, R O (2002) *The Success Case Method: Find out quickly what's working and what's not*, Bennett-Koehler, San Francisco, CA

Gelles, D (2015) *Mindful Work: How meditation is changing business from the inside out*, Profile Books, London

Kellerman, B (2012) *The End of Leadership*, HarperCollins Publishers, New York, NY

Pfeffer, J (2015) *Leadership BS: Fixing workplaces and careers one truth at a time*, HarperCollins, New York, NY

Tan, C-M (2012) *Search Inside Yourself: The unexpected path to achieving success, happiness (and world peace)*, HarperCollins, New York, NY

Wiens, K (2016) *The Influence of Emotional Intelligence on the Ability of Executive Level Physician Leaders to Cope with Occupational Stress*, doctoral dissertation, University of Pennsylvania CLO Programme

INDEX

Note: Page numbers in *italic* indicate figures or tables

Abbott, C 198, 199, 203, 204
Accelerate 25, 26
Act Like a Leader, Think Like a Leader 21
Action Inquiry: The secret of timely and transforming leadership 193
action learning (and) 189–208 *see also* Dewey, J *and* Revans, R
  basic philosophy of 194–95
  conclusions and next steps 207
  definition and nature of 193–94
  facilitation 204, 206–07, *205*
  origins of 190–93 *see also* Lewin, K
  reasons for importance of 195–99
  relevant quotations/ definitions 197–98
  three stages of an action learning set 202–04
    1. getting settled and started 202
    2. asking questions 202–03
    3. moving to action 203–04
  typical action learning set 200–01
Action Learning, International Foundation for 190, 197
Anderson, E G 109 *see also* National Health Service (NHS)
Antarctica (and) *see also* Foundation 2041 *and* leadership on the edge
  Antarctic Treaty (1991, 1998) 59–60
  the Drake Passage 67–68
any time any place leadership *see* BP's digital leadership development
Apple 156, 244–46, *see also* Jobs, S
  apps / app store 143
  iTunes U 227, 228
  Newton 244

Arets, J 84, 260
articles/papers (on)
  'AI doctors will become "as ubiquitous as stethoscopes"' (Kamen, 2016) 235
  'Appreciative inquiry in organizational life' (Cooperrider and Srivastva, 1987) 192
  'How to be a better mentor' (Thompson, 2010) 220
  investment in people and quality leadership (Edmans, 2011) 23–24
  'Seeking the holy grail of organisational development: A synthesis of integral theory, spiral dynamics, corporate transformation and action' (Cacioppe and Edwards, 2005) 192
  'Towards an adult learning architecture of participation' (Garnett and Ecclesfield, 2014) 193
artificial intelligence 144, 148, 167, 235–37, 240–43, 245–46, 248
  IBM supercomputer Watson 236
Auricchio, P 129, 132
Authentic Leadership Institute 70

Bad Leadership 16
Barrett, R (corporate transformation) 193
Bartlett, C A 37, 40, 38–39
Baughman, J (Harvard Business School Professor, Crotonville) 40
Beard, A 228
Beck, D (spiral dynamics) 193

Bevan, A 109 *see also* National Health
    Service (NHS)
beyond the corporate university *see*
    Crotonville (GE)
The Blended Learning Cookbook 102
Bock, L (HR Director, Google) 214
Boone, J 102
BP (British Petroleum) 174, 226,
    244–45, 264
    and Texas Oil Refinery fire 170–71
BP's digital leadership development
    (and) 129–49
    the app 142–44
    Capgemini: from virtualization to
        digitization 130–32
    the design principle: stages 139–41
        I. define 139
        II. run research groups 139
        III. design 140
        IV. develop 140
        V. deploy 141
        VI. iterate 141
    digital age learning at BP 129–30
    the digital offer – the Hub 141–42
    how it works 138–39
    individual or community 145–46
    leadership online 132–33
    measurement of outcomes 144–45
    mentoring and expert input 146
    organization of the
        programmes 135–36
    points you should take
        away 147–49
    the programmes – what they looked
        like 136–37
    the senior leaders programme 146–47
    the seven principles 133–35
Brinkerhoff, R 260
building better leadership programmes
    (and/by) 262–65
    commitment of whole leadership
        team 263
    context where there is desire for
        change 262–63 *see also*
        Google
    create only when you cannot
        curate 264
    importance of discussion and
        sharing 264–65
    keeping responsibility within
        organization 263–64

Cacioppe, R 192
Cappelli, P 39
Carlyle, T 18
Carpenter, G S 156
Cavanaugh, P (Head of
    Crotonville) 14, 35, 39, 43,
    47, 51, 54
chapter references for
    action learning 208
    any time any place leadership 149
    Crotonville (GE) 55
    DIY leadership
        development 232–33
    the future: the increasingly powerful
        role of technology 249–50
    leadership as catalyst for
        change 124–25
    the leadership context 30–32
    leadership development as
        storytelling 165–66
    leadership on the edge 81
    moving forward 266
    online learning as immersive
        experience 185–86
    rethinking executive leadership
        development:
        DeakinPrime 99
The Checklist Manifesto 139
Churchill, W 18
*Citizen You: Doing your part to
    change the world* 71
Clark, D 235
coaching 70, 84, 112, 212, 221
    groups 92–94, 97, 98
    one-on-one 101
    peer 93
Coffin, C (CEO, GE) 37
Cohen, E 41
Cooperrider, D 192
Cordiner, R (Chairman, GE) 37
core principles 5–6
    consequences of poor leadership 6
    context as critical 5
    face the truth 5
    focus on leadership, not leaders 6
    leaders' ability to help themselves 6
    leadership development as
        process 5
    start with the end in mind 5
Corporate Research Forum (CRF) *see*
    reports

Cosack, S 215
Cowan, C 193 *see also* spiral
    dynamics
Cromwell, O 18
Crotonville (GE) 14, 35–55 *see also*
    Cavanaugh, P; Jones, R; Kerr,
    S; Peters, S; Tichy, N *and*
    Welch, J
  background and introduction
    to 35–43
  as boundaryless 40
  conclusion for 54–55
  and five precepts – the GE
    beliefs 44
  Harvard case study on investment
    in 38
  learning from 50–54
  reimagining 43–50
    starting with the experience you
      want to create 47–50

Day, D 20
definitions (of)
  action learning set (Pedler and
    Abbott) 198
  blended learning (Shepherd) 102
  leadership ability
    (Groysberg) 224
  mentoring as wise and loyal
    adviser 218
  open educational resources
    (UNESCO) 225
  scaffolded social learning
    (Stodd) 152, 147
  social leadership (Stodd) 27
Delventhal, S 245
Democracy and Education 191
Dewey, J 191–92
DIY leadership development 209–33
  conclusions for 232
  and Google's focus on fast internal
    solutions 209–15 *see also*
    Google
  other strategies for 215–31
    access to open resources 225–28
    action learning and self-
      organized groups: pros and
      cons 223–25
    asking questions *and* Elephants
      Don't Forget 230–31
    see also Ebbinghaus, H

cheap and focused portal/
    repository: SLACK *and*
    Docebo 229–30
  facilitation 216–18
  mentoring 218–23
Dweck, C 89
Dyke, G (CEO, BBC) 49

Ebbinghaus, H 231
  and the forgetting curve 231
Ecclesfield, N 193, 214
Edison, T 35
Edmans, A 23–24 *see also*
    articles/papers
Edwards, M 192
Einstein, A 195
el Kaliouby, R 241–42
Elephants Don't Forget 231
The End of Alchemy 12, 21
The End of Leadership 16, 256

Facilitating Action Learning 204
facilitation 24, 159, 161, 163, 198–99,
    201, 204, 206–07, 205,
    216–18 *see also* Marquardt,
    M *and* models
Feser, C 12
Foundation 2041 58, 59–61 *see also*
    leadership on the edge *and*
    Swan, R
Francis, R (QC) 119
Francis Report 184
Friesland, B 17
Fuld, R (Lehman Brothers) 4
the future (and) 235–50 *see also*
    artificial intelligence; moving
    forward *and* technology,
  increasingly powerful role of
  considering potential impact of
    emerging technologies 249
  discussing new ideas and resources
    with your team 248–49
  keeping up with developments 248
  looking at areas for
    experimentation 249
The Future of Management 24

Gargiulo, T L 177
Garnett, F 193, 215
Gawande, A 139
Gelles, D 257

General Electric (GE) (and) 14, 23
        see also Crotonville; Jones,
        R *and* Krisnamoorthy, R
George, B 21, 22 *see also* leadership
        models
Goleman, D 224, 257
Google (and) 10, 138, 164, 209–15
    AI software 235
    analytics/Analytics 145, 148
    Assistant 244
    Bock, L 214
    British Petroleum (BP) 226
    DeepMind 241, 243
    headset 239
    HOME 245
    initiatives: G2g, G@google *and*
        gWhiz 213–14
    mindfulness training
        programme 257–58
    OpenEdEx consortium and
        MOOCs 225–26
    Project Oxygen 262–63
    Schmidt, E 214
    search data 195
    virtual reality experiences 239
Graham, C R 101
Grashow, A 88 *see also* leadership
        models
Greiner, L 41, 42
Greenleaf, R 22 *see also* leadership
        models
Grint, K 9, 20, 29, 88
    and four-fold typology of
        leadership 17–19
Groysberg, B 21, 224 *see also*
        definitions
Gurthridge, M 215

Hahn, K 57
Hamel, G 24–25
Harvey, S 107–08
Hassabis, D 241
Heifetz, R A 88 *see also* leadership
        models
Heijnen, V 84, 260
Hill, L (Harvard) 228
Hogan, K 152
Holt, L 57

Ibarra, H 21
Immelt, J (CEO) 37, 43, 54

*The Influence of Emotional Intelligence
        on the Ability of Executive
        Level Physician Leaders to
        Cope with Occupational
        Stress* (Wiens, K) 257

Jack: Straight from the gut 36
Jarche, H 27, 28, 163 *see also* models
Jenner, E 108
Jennings, C 84, 260
Jobs, S 244
Jones, R (CEO, GE) 38
The Journal of Human Relations 191
        see also Lewin, K *and* Trist, E

Kamen, M 235
Kellerman, B 16, 20, 22, 23, 256
Kerr, S 41–42, 45, 52
Khan, S 227–28
    and The Khan Academy 227, 228
King, M 12, 21
Kirkwood, T 177
Kittlaus, D (developer of Siri and
        'Viv') 245
Kotter, J (and) 22, 25–26, 27
    leadership over management 22
    top five leadership
        competences 25–26
Krisnamoorthy, R (Chief Learning
        Officer, GE) 35, 36, 43, 54

Lamprey, E 4
Lawson, E 215
Lead with a Story 177
leadership 1–6
    competency frameworks 10
    consequences of poor 6
    development process 5
    focus on 6
    four-fold typology of 17–19
    the HOW of 18
    models *see* leadership models
    nature of 1
    statements related to 9–10
    the WHAT of 18
    the WHO of 17–18
    the WHY of 17
Leadership BS 4, 253
leadership as catalyst for change 101–25
        see also National Health
        Service (NHS)

context 101–04
core lessons for 122–24
special contribution of blended
learning 121–22
leadership competences 25–26 *see also*
Kotter, J
careful listening 26
openness to new ideas 26
risk-taking 26
self-reflection 26
solicitation of opinions 26
Leadership in a Complex Environment
(UNSW course) 228
the leadership context (and) 9–32
see also leadership
changes in work 23–26
the changing climate 11–12
conclusions for 29–30
Four-Fold Typology of Leadership
(Grint) 17–19 *see also* Grint, K
importance of context 15–16
moving from individual to
organization and
culture 19–23
skills required 12–15
the social age 26–29
and leadership 28–29
three dimensions of social
leadership 27–28 *see also*
social leadership dimensions
leadership development as storytelling
(and) 151–66
introduction to/context for 151–53
key issues to consider 162–65
lessons learned 161–62
programme: curation,
interpretation, analysis and
reflection 155–58
programme structure 153–55
roles for 158–61
community manager 159
storyteller 158, 159–60, 163
workshop facilitator 159, 163
leadership on the edge: discomfort as a
learning experience
(and) 57–81, 257
chronology of the expedition 65–68
elements of the leadership
programme 70–71
elements leading to enduring change
in participants 78–81

and poem by participant (Payton
Sierra) 81
Foundation 2041 59–61
impact of action plans on the
group 76–77
the journey 63–65
leadership and the Antarctic 61–63
the participants 71–76
consultant from Singapore
(Nhan) 72–73
elementary school teacher from
the US (Persis) 74–75
engineer from UAE
(Malek) 71–72
oil and gas engineer from the UK
(Dev) 75–76
senior NHS executive from the
UK (Ghazala) 73–74
student from the US
(Morgan) 72
teacher from the UK (James) 73
'what a day looks like in the
Antarctic' 68–70
Leadership on the Hills programme
(Singh, P N and Rathore,
S S) 77
Leadership Limits and Possibilities 17
leadership models 1–2, 17–19
adaptive (Heifetz, Grashow and
Linsky) 88
authentic (George) 22
Four-Fold Typology of Leadership
(Grint) 17–19
person-based 18
position-based 18
process-based 19
results-based 18–19
servant leader (Greenleaf) 22
transformational (MacGregor
Burns) 22
The Leadership Quarterly 20
*Leadership: A very short
introduction* 17
Leading Change 26
learning
and its importance for ageing adults
(Foresight Report) 242–43
as significant element of
survival 241–42
*Learning from Experience: Towards
consciousness* 193

LEO 167–71
  as core partner in NHS Leadership
      programme 167–68
Lewin, K 191, 193
Linsky, M 88 *see also* leadership models
Lynas, K (NHS Leadership
      Academy) 104, 108

MacGregor Burns, J 22 *see also*
      leadership models
McLean, A N 37, 38–39, 40
Marquardt, M 190, 201, 204 *see also*
      models
Mayol, F 12
models
  action enquiry (Torbert) 193
  for action learning facilitator
      (Marquardt) 201
  seek, sense and share (Jarche) 27,
      28, 163
  70:20:10 model of development
      (Paine) 90
moving forward (and) 253–66
  a blended process works best 254
  build to an optimistic future 258
  building better leadership
      programmes 262–65 *see also*
      subject entry
  co-creation 258–59
  commitment of senior leaders 255
  context and core competences 256
  impact on individual change from
      group and organization 261
  leadership – not an event but a
      process 254
  learning as continuous
      process 255–56
  learning as part of
      workflow 260–61
  line manager participation 259–60
  mindfulness and emotional
      intelligence 256–58
  10 top tips 265–66
  transferring responsibility to
      leader 255

National Health Service (NHS) 101–21
      see also online learning as
      immersive experience
  Constitution for England and six
      values of the NHS 107

five-stage leadership
      programmes 103–04
Leadership Academy Award in
      Executive Healthcare
      Leadership 110
Leadership Academy
      programmes 104–08 *see also*
      Lynas, K *and* Scott-Worrall, L
  and the Francis Report/Inquiry
      (2013) 104–06, 118, 119–20
  and *Hard Truths: The journey to
      putting patients first* (DoH,
      2014) 106, 108
leadership suite of programmes
      (and) 108–20, *121 see also*
      LEO
  additional programmes 110, 112
  components of blended learning
      mix 114–18
  core modules for 112
  Edward Jenner Programme 108
  Elizabeth Garrett Anderson
      Programme 109, 110–11,
      112–13, 114–18, 120
  Mary Seacole
      Programme 108–09, 110
  Nye Bevan Programme 109–10,
      111–12, 113, 114–19, 180
  reason for selection of
      components 119–20
  structure of programmes 110–14
  virtual campus 171–73
Nelson, H 18

online learning as immersive
      experience (and/by) 167–86
  building a sense of reality,
      techniques for 175–79
  conclusions for 184–85
  context for 167–71 *see also* LEO
  the development process for 171
  impact of 179–81
  issues to note 181
  learner-produced content 174
  lessons for others 182–84
  modes for the learner 174–75
  tutor-led, collaborative
      environment and
      workshops 174–75
  the virtual campus: NHS leadership
      programmes 171–73

open source education software
        (Moodle) 172, 227
Osguthorpe, R T 101

Pagan, V 177
Paine, N 90, 138 *see also* models
Pangarkar, A 177
Pedler, M 189, 191, 198, 199, 203, 204
personal digital assistants
        (PDAs) 244–46
    Amazon Echo 245
    Google Home 245
    as 'the supercomputer in your
        pocket' (*The Economist*,
        2015) 244
Peters, S (VP for Human Resources,
        Crotonville) 43, 54
Pfeffer, J 253
    three recommendations of 4
Pillans, G 11, 12, 22, 101, 119, 209
Plan-Organize-Integrate-Measure
        (POIM) principles 38
Pressley, M 152

Rawling Rees, J 191
Reinventing Leadership 16
Reissner, S 177
reports (on)
    investment in leadership (CRF
        Report, 2015) 11–12, 14, 22,
        101, 119, 209
    *Leadership Development – is it fit
        for purpose?* (CRF, 2015) 11
    state of human capital in
        organizations (Conference
        Board/McKinsey, 2012) 13
research on
    leadership development (CRF,
        2015) 14
    leadership skills and leadership
        effectiveness (*McKinsey
        Quarterly*, 2015) 12–13
rethinking executive leadership
        development:
        DeakinPrime 83–99
    context for 83–85
    and core lessons to take
        away 96–99
    core principles for 88–89
    and differences for new
        approach 85–88

outcomes for 95–96
structure and critical success factors
        for 89–95
    1. initiation phase 90–91
    2. discovery phase 91
    3. engagement phase 91–92
    4. action phase 92–93
    5. super charge phase 93–95
Revans, R 189–90, 193–99, 201,
        203, 207
    and devised action learning 189
    quotations from interview
        with 197–98
Rhee, K (IBM) 235
Rittel, H 196 *see also* 'wicked'
        problems
Rogers, C 191
Rosenberg, J 214
Ross Intelligence (*Tech Insider
        2016*) 235–36

Schmidt, E 214
Scott, R F; Shackleton, E *and*
        Amundsen, R 66
Scott-Worrall, L (NHS Leadership
        Academy) 104–05
Scouller, J 21
Seacole, M 108–09
Search Inside Yourself 257
Seasalt Learning 152, 164, 265
'Seven strategies on how to use stories
        to increase learning and
        facilitate training' 177
Shackleton-Jones, N (BP Director of
        Online Learning) 132
Shepherd, C 102
Sher, R 223
Sinek, S 228
Smith, P 177
the social age 26–28
    predictions for (*The Economist*) 26
social leadership dimensions 27–28
    engagement 27–28
    narrative 27
    technology 28
social networking software (and) 236,
        246–48
    Anders Pink 247
    Facebook 245–47
    Slack 247
spiral dynamics (Cowan) 193

Srinivasan, R 12
Srivastva, S 192
Stodd, J 26–27, 28, 152, 157 *see also* definitions
Storytelling in Management Practice 177
Sudhir Giri 209 (Google senior HR exec) 209
surveys (on)
    ePulse (Marshall School of Business) 12
    Human Capital Trends (Deloitte, 2015) 12
    skills confidence (City & Guilds Group/Censuswide) 242
Swan, R (founder of Foundation 2041) 57, 58, 59–63, 66, 76

tables
    components of the Anderson and Bevan leadership programmes *121*
    views on the roles of the set adviser and the group facilitator *205*
Talent on Demand 39
Tan, C-M 257–58
technology, increasingly powerful role of (and) 235–50
    artificial intelligence 235–37, 240–43
    personal digital assistants (PDAs) 244–46 *see also subject entry*
    social networking software 246–48 *see also subject entry*
    virtual reality 238–40 *see also subject entry*
    what you should take from this chapter 248–49
TED (Technology, Entertainment, Design) 173
    talks 264
    TEDx video lectures 228
Thompson, E 220
The Three Levels of Leadership 21
360-degree feedback exercises 91
Tichy, N 40–41
    and work on 'teachable moments' 41

Tisch, J 71
Torbert, W 193 *see also* models
Tracey, R 240
The Trainer's Portable Mentor 177
Trist, E 191
True North: Discover your authentic leadership 21
trust 24, 29, 42, 62, 63, 73, 78, 96, 146, 153–54, 164, 181, 201, 207, 220
    building 98, 199
Turing, A 240

UNESCO 225–26
    definition of open educational resources (OERs) 225
    Guidelines for Open Educational Resources (OER) in Higher Education (2015) 226
    Open Educational Quality Initiative 226
    Vision for Health OER Network (Africa) 225–26

van Hoof, P 241
virtual reality (VR) 167, 236–40
    Immersive VR Education – simulation of Apollo 11 space expedition 238, 239
    software 236
    Willow DNA model for 240
Von Butler, H 36
VUCA – volatile, uncertain, complex, ambiguous 11, 12, 54

Wagoner, R (General Motors) 4
Weiner, J 156
Welch, J 36–42, 48–52, 54
Weller, C 236
Western, S 9
Whelan, D 238
'wicked' problems 88, 90, 93, 96, 178, 196, 200, 206
Wiens, K 257
Wilber, K (integral theory) 193
Wilson, Dr N (CEO, Legal & General, UK) 28–29

CPSIA information can be obtained
at www.ICGtesting.com
Printed in the USA
LVHW05s0403181018
593990LV00009BA/59/P